# THE TRAUMATIC BOND BETWEEN THE PSYCHOTHERAPIST AND MANAGED CARE

*Edited by* Karen Weisgerber, Ph.D.

*Contributing Editors:*
Elisa T. Bronfman, Ph.D.,
E. Catherine Loula, M.D.,
Cynthia Mitchell, Ph.D.,
and Pamela Wolf, Ph.D.

JASON ARONSON INC.
*Northvale, New Jersey*
*London*

This book was set in 11 pt. New Baskerville by Alpha Graphics of Pittsfield, NH and printed and bound by Book-mart Press, Inc. of North Bergen, NJ.

**Library of Congress Cataloging-in-Publication Data**

The traumatic bond between the psychotherapist and managed care : edited by
  Karen Weisgerber; contributing editors, Elisa Bronfman . . . [et al.].
      p.   cm.
   Includes bibliographical references and index.
   ISBN 0-7657-0180-4
   1. Managed mental health care.   2. Psychotherapists—Job stress.
3. Psychotherapists—Attitudes.   4. Psychotherapy—Philosophy.
I. Weisgerber, Karen.
   [DNLM: 1. Psychotherapy.   2. Managed Care Programs—organization &
administration.   3. Mental Health Services—organization &
administration.   WM 420 P97488 1998]
RC465.5.P79   1998
616.89' 14—DC21
DNLM/DLC
for Library of Congress                                        98-23700

Printed in the United States of America on acid-free paper. For information and catalog write to Jason Aronson Inc., 230 Livingston Street, Northvale, NJ 07647-1726, or visit our website: www.aronson.com

# Contents

# Foreword

The chief business of the American people is business.
                                                        —*Calvin Coolidge, 1925*

In 1948 when I became a psychiatrist, psychiatry's appeal as a profession was that it combined both science and humanism. Fifty years ago one attempted to understand the patient's narrative and inner life—also the novelist's task—and at the same time relate that knowledge to some kind of coherent scientific theory. At the end of the twentieth century psychiatry in the United States, in its effort to become more scientific, has lost interest in the patient's inner life, and the inner meaning of mental disorders is considered irrelevant. Consequently, psychiatry has become nearly mindless. Today I feel alienated from psychiatry and hardly recognize it as the same discipline I once embraced. This flight away from a meaningful mind may represent an aspect of American culture that is relatively intolerant of the chaos that is part of one's inner world, that welcomes easy-to-understand "practical" solutions.

As Calvin Coolidge knew in 1925, the business of America is indeed business. But in 1925 the influence of corporations did not pervade our society to the extent that it does today. The influence of huge international corporations has now infiltrated science, academia, and medicine. In the mental health professions, as in medicine, managed care companies are the handmaidens of these corporate giants. Their effect on medicine was succinctly described in an editorial by Haskell (1997) as suffering from fundamentally conflicted interests. While managed care companies profess to being committed to caring for their enrollees, they profit primarily by doing as little as possible.

What is less well known is that the primacy of financial concerns is beginning to have a corrupting influence on science as well. Lewontin (1991) documents how, in his field of genetic molecular biology, there is a pervasive conflict of interest between the disinterested pursuit of knowledge and those investigators who own patents or are officers of corporations poised to market the processes they are investigating. When corporations impinge on the professions, a conflict of interest is unavoidable.

The medical model has been applied universally by managed care to mental illness, perhaps for reasons of efficiency or because the medical model is thought to be more scientific or "objective." The medical model, however, does not recognize the psychological uniqueness of the individual, the inescapable biologic fact of individual differences, but instead creates a model of "normality," deviation from which is marked by the presence of symptoms. Lewontin (1991) comments on the medical model as follows: "A medical model of all human variation makes a medical model of normality, including social normality, and dictates that we preemptively or through subsequent corrective therapy bring into line anyone who deviates from that norm" (p. 65). The philosopher Charles Taylor (1992), describing the dehumanizing effects of such disengaged reason (of the medical model), says: "We are embodied agents, living in dialogical conditions, inhabiting time in a specifically human way, that is making sense of our lives as a story that connects the past from which we have come to our future projects. That means that if we are properly to treat a human being, we have to respect this embodied, dialogical, temporal nature" (p. 105).

Psychoanalysis was once accused by its social critics of providing a treatment whose ultimate aim was one of enabling the individual to adjust to society. I believe this criticism was justified in only one respect, in that psychoanalysts once believed in the conventional assumption that psychological maturation was linked to heterosexuality. Now managed care's use of the medical model of "normality" has led to an aim of explicitly promoting an individual's adjustment to social normality. This is outlined in the final section of this volume ("The Social and Cultural Impact," Chapters 12–14) in which the authors describe how managed care's use of the medical model supports an "objectification" of the self that in turn promotes the explicit aim of social conformity.

Social conformity assumes a model of normality that includes the control of affective experiences by means of external pharmacological agents. A symptomatic diagnosis may not differentiate the inevitable anxiety and depression that are part of ordinary life from depressive illness and anxiety disorders. A medical model treats symptoms according to an algorithmic formula that views negative, painful affects such as anxiety or depression as invariable departures from normality that require correction. A recent article in *Science* reminds us that such negative affects serve an adaptive function in our evolutionary history, and to automatically block such negative emotions by prescribing psychoactive drugs can impair useful defenses (Nesse and Berridge 1997). Treatment based on formulaic algorithms ignores the unique context in which symptoms appear. Algorithms do not investigate the meaning of the symptom to the individual, and treatment based on algorithms ignores individual differences and the variety of individual needs. This is most apparent in the preposterous idea regarding the number of outpatient treatment visits allowed by managed care—that one size fits all. If one treats a large population there will be some individuals for whom eight or ten sessions will be a good fit. But for the majority of individuals who seek outpatient psychotherapy—especially those who have experienced developmental trauma or suffered from the effects of developmental deficits—such brief treatment is travesty.

Although managed care believes its judgments are based on scientific knowledge, current advances in neurobiology indicate that the brain is unique, unlike any other organ in the body, in that in its development it does not rely on genetic information to the same extent as other organs. Instead, it relies on environmental input. This means that our brain/mind is tailor-made. Therefore mental illness cannot be categorized using the same logic that medicine uses to categorize physical disease. Symptomatic diagnoses of psychopathology, especially neurotic and characterological disorders, are arbitrary; such diagnoses are based only on agreed convention, which is subject to change due to cultural processes. *DSM-IV* is analogous to a dictionary, and we know how rapidly language can change.

Psychiatric diagnoses are not on an equal footing with medical diagnoses. The reliability of the latter depends on the fact that livers, hearts, and kidneys do not significantly vary between individuals, hence organ pathology is fairly uniform. Because our brain/mind is sculpted by environmental input, such uniformity of function between individuals cannot be assumed. I am not arguing against the use of diagnoses by mental health professionals; if nothing else, they are needed for communication between colleagues, but one should be epistemologically sophisticated to the extent that one recognizes their arbitrary nature. The scientific foundation on which managed care justifies its mental health procedures will ultimately be judged to have been built on sand.

The opening chapters (1–9) of this volume describe in detail the profound effect that managed care has had on the inner life of the therapist. The flight from meaning has turned therapist and patient away from the common humanity that formerly united them. This dehumanization of the therapeutic process is excruciatingly painful, especially for therapists trained in another tradition. But if therapists do not adapt to the ways of managed care, their financial survival may be threatened. Their helplessness may result in an inner transformation analogous to the Stockholm Syndrome, in which, through intermittent kindness and cruelty, one learns to love one's captors.

This transformation of the therapist's inner life will of course have a profound effect on the therapeutic relationship, as described in Chapters 6–9 "The Impact on Clinical Practice." Many of us believe that the efficacy of psychoanalytic psychotherapy rests in large measure on the sense of safety that is intrinsic to the psychotherapeutic relationship (Modell 1990). Traditionally, the therapeutic relationship has been a dyadic one that the patient comes to experience as a metaphoric holding environment. Over time, many patients experience a sense of safety within the relationship that they have not had earlier in their lives. With the advent of managed care, the relationship is no longer constructed intersubjectively by two autonomous participants. Rather, it is viewed as something of little significance and for obvious reasons ceases to function as a holding environment. It is no longer dyadic but triadic, with the managed care company present as a "third force" (Shapiro 1997). For some therapists *their* primary relationship is with the managed care company, not the patient.

This volume can be read from the perspective of social Darwinism: when the environment changes drastically, the individual must either adapt to the changing conditions or perish. Managed care creates its own environment and therapists will selectively adapt or choose to drop out. Training programs have chosen to adapt to the managed care environment (Chapters 10 and 11), which will have a selective influence on those who choose to become psychotherapists. Such programs will deselect those individuals who are drawn to paradox, uncertainty, and ambiguity. From this viewpoint the future looks bleak. But I think we should not underestimate the strength of the human bond that unites therapists and those they serve. There is reason to hope that the common bond of humanity that manifests itself when one makes contact with the inner life of the other will ultimately reassert itself.

*The Traumatic Bond between the Psychotherapist and Managed Care* is a thoughtful and courageous book that focuses our attention on the most serious threat to the future of psychotherapy in America.

—ARNOLD M. MODELL, M.D.

## REFERENCES

Haskell, T. L. (1997). The new aristocracy. *The New York Review of Books*, December 4.

Lewontin, R. C. (1991). *Biology as Ideology*. New York: Harper Perennial.

Modell, A. (1990). *Other Times, Other Realities*. Cambridge, MA: Harvard University Press.

Nesse, R. M., and Berridge, K. C. (1997). Psychoactive drug use in evolutionary perspective. *Science* 278: 63–65.

Shapiro, E. R. (1997). The boundaries are shifting: renegotiating the therapeutic frame. In *The Inner World in the Outer World*, pp. 7–25. New Haven, CT: Yale University Press.

Taylor, C. (1992). *The Ethics of Authenticity*. Cambridge, MA: Harvard University Press.

# Preface and Acknowledgments

This book evolved from the conversations and concerns of clinicians in the field of psychotherapy. As we began to have informal discussions about the transformation of our profession under the pressures of managed care, we noticed that it was not just our profession that was changing: we ourselves were changing. We then began to listen more closely to the conversations of those around us and noticed not only a demoralization and deprofessionalization, but a subtle yet pervasive eroding of the soul of our work.

The practice of psychotherapy, and the delivery of health care in general, has been undeniably affected by the presence of managed care. Longer-term therapies have been replaced with shorter-term, problem-focused treatments for reasons of economic urgency—employers seeking to contain the cost of insuring their employees. As a society, we are only beginning to realize the hidden costs of limiting treatment and prescribing models of intervention based on a fiscal rather than clinical assessment of needs.

As a profession evolves and changes, it is not surprising that its practitioners change as well. Yet the changes we began to notice within ourselves and our colleagues were not always so benign. The pressures to survive in the managed care environment seemed to fuel an adaptation to it, as well as a promulgation of a type of treatment and way of approaching clients that was at sharp variance with much of what we valued in clinical practice. Most troubling was that clinicians often did not notice their gradual evolution into the role as agents of managed care and the gradual shifts regarding professional ethics and values.

This volume, then, is a compilation of our observations of ourselves, our colleagues, and our profession. Its aim is to keep us aware of the myriad influences and pressures on us, and to remind us that capitulation to such pressures threatens our mission to reach our patients and be of help to them.

We wish to acknowledge the relationships that fostered the opening of our discussion and the evolution of this book. Our collaborative work as co-editors provided a constant source of support that sustained the project and our enthusiasm for it. Above and beyond this, many friends and colleagues have been of great help and encouragement to us. In particular, we wish to thank Arnold Modell, Debora Bolter, Judith Bronfman, Alex Brown, Sandy Burgess, David Dinklage, Peter Goldring, Debora Gustafson, Gerry Koocher, Elizabeth McGowan, Karen Melikian, Charlie Morgan, The Linda Pollin Institute, Jay Press, Steve Ruffins, Harry Smith, Leo Sorokin, and Lisa Strauss.

# Contributors

Ralph H. Beaumont, M.D., is a faculty member at the Oregon Psychoanalytic Society and Institute and the San Francisco Psychoanalytic Institute. He is also a clinical fellow at the Oregon Health Services University and he maintains a private practice in Portland, Oregon.

Peggy J. Bell, Ph.D., is the assistant training director of the clinical practicum program in feminist therapy at the Simmons College Counseling Center in Boston. She is also a postdoctoral fellow at Simmon College.

Ivers Bever, Ph.D., is a staff psychologist at the Brighton Allston Mental Health Center in Brighton, Massachusetts. She is a faculty member at the Psychoanalytic Institute of New England, East, and she maintains a private practice in Cambridge, Massachusetts.

Elisa T. Bronfman, Ph.D., is an instructor in psychology at Harvard Medical School and a staff psychologist in the Department of Psychiatry at Children's Hospital, Boston. She maintains a private practice at Child and Family services in Norwood, Massachusetts.

Bernard M. Edelstein, M.D., is the director of psychiatric residency training at the Beth Israel Deaconess Medical Center in Boston.

He is an associate director of the Harvard Longwood Psychiatry residency training program and an instructor in psychiatry at Harvard Medical School.

Peter Gilford, Ph.D., is an associate faculty member in psychology at National University in San Jose, California and an adjunct faculty member at the University of San Francisco. He maintains a private practice in San Francisco.

E. Catherine Loula, M.D., is an instructor at Harvard Medical School and a candidate in analytic training at the Psychoanalytic Institute of New England, East. She maintains a private practice in Brookline, Massachusetts.

Cynthia Mitchell, Ph.D., is a candidate in analytic training at the Psychoanalytic Institute of New England, East. She maintains a private practice in Cambridge, Massachusetts.

Charles Morgan, Ph.D., is a candidate in analytic training at the Psychoanalytic Institute of New England, East. He maintains a private practice in Brookline, Massachusetts.

David Pingitore, Ph.D., is a visiting scholar and National Institute of Mental Health postdoctoral fellow in the School of Public Health at the University of California, Berkeley. He maintains a private practice in Oakland, California.

Stephen Ruffins, Ph.D., is an associate professor in the Clinical Psychology Doctoral Program at Long Island University where he coordinates a concentration in Serious and Persistent Mental Illness.

Karen Weisgerber, Ph.D., is an instructor in psychology at Harvard Medical School, and a clinical supervisor at the Boston Evening Medical Center. She is also an adjunct faculty member at Boston College and a candidate in analytic training at the Psychoanalytic Institute of New England, East. She maintains a private practice in Brookline, Massachusetts.

Pamela Wolf, Ph.D., is an instructor in psychology at Harvard Medical School, and a clinical supervisor at the Boston Evening Medical Center. She is also an adjunct faculty member at Boston College, and she maintains a private practice in Brookline, Massachusetts.

# I

# The Traumatic Bond

# The Traumatic Bond between Psychotherapists and Managed Care

KAREN WEISGERBER

*Traumatic bonding* is a phrase coined by Dutton and Painter (1981) to describe the not infrequent, yet curious, phenomenon of people bonding to their abusers. The relationship that evolves is indeed a fascinating one. Over the course of the association the perpetrator holds a position of power—real or ascribed—and is perceived as controlling necessary resources. The hostage or victim believes that reliance on the perpetrator is the key to survival. From this belief a relationship evolves that has a remarkable influence on the individual in the position of hostage or victim. Profound changes occur in the individual's sense of self, affect, judgment, and reality testing.

Various events have illustrated the attachment that develops in situations of real or psychological imprisonment. Perhaps the first public account of traumatic bonding occurred in 1973, when, during a closely watched and extremely tense six-day siege of a bank in Stockholm Sweden, the relationship between the two captors and four hostages transformed in a remarkable and unexpected way. The hostages, initially fearful of and allied against their captors, grew quite fond of them. Over the course of their captivity, all four hostages became attached to, supportive of and sympathetic with their captors. At one point, when two hostages had the opportunity to run to freedom, they refused. They preferred to stay with their captors, whom they now viewed as their allies, rather than join with the police, whom they now viewed with enmity despite the fact that the police were actively attempting to free them. This paradoxical relationship between hostage and captor has since been referred to as the "Stockholm syndrome."

Closer to home, the case of Patty Hearst illustrates the seeming loyalty and cooperation that can develop in hostage situations. Again, as in the Stockholm incident, a surprising relationship grew out of a situation in which a woman was kidnapped and held against her will. During her captivity Hearst was kept blindfolded in a closet, raped, and transported between hiding places in a garbage can (Graham et al. 1994). Rather than the disdain and defiance one might anticipate under such circumstances, her response suggested that it may be the control of freedom and survival that contributes to the bond that develops between captor and hostage.

Cult phenomena, most recently evidenced in the 1997 Heaven's Gate suicides, demonstrates yet again the profound attachment that develops out of an allegiance to a persuasive leader or group that is perceived to offer some form of salvation from the difficulties of ordinary life. The vulnerability that members often have when they join a cult is the belief that they cannot thrive, perhaps not even survive, without allegiance to the group (Collins 1991). The cult, and most particularly the charismatic leader, repeatedly reinforces that belief. Members join on a seemingly voluntary basis, although a strong element of coercion is frequently present. The group becomes a lifeline. Members, therefore, voluntarily remain in the cult through adverse, sometimes dangerous and life-threatening, situations, despite repeated opportunities to gain freedom, out of the enduring bond with the leader and the group (West 1993). The suicide of the members of Heaven's Gate is only the most recent in a series of cult deaths—from Jonestown in 1978 to Waco in 1993—where members preferred death to facing life without the cult. Many Heaven's Gate members who participated in the farewell video stated that they could leave, but they desired to stay and complete the act. Yet these claims demonstrated the distortions in thinking that often evolve. They seemed to echo the hauntingly ironic sentiment of their leader, that suicide was "your only chance to survive" (Gleick 1997, p. 31).

The term *traumatic bonding* (Dutton and Painter 1981, 1993) has been used to note the paradoxical bond in spousal and child abuse, in which the victim of abuse remains connected and committed to the abuser despite the severity of the abuse and the danger inherent in the relationship. Here the 1987 case of Hedda Nussbaum, which caught the nation's eye and imagination, may be emblematic. This attractive, successful woman married Joel Steinberg, and after a pattern of spousal abuse was well in place, they adopted a child, Lisa, who soon became a target for Steinberg's batterings. The abuse culminated in a beating that left the 7-year-old hospitalized and comatose for three days, until she finally died of the internal injuries she received during the beating (Brownmiller 1989).

The bond Hedda felt with her husband was so strong that she never reported any of the spousal abuse—which ultimately resulted in her being fired from her job because she stayed home so frequently to hide her injuries. Nor did she report the continued abuse of Lisa. After the final beating, Nussbaum waited hours before finally calling for help for her unconscious daughter. At the trial, the American public saw not an attractive woman, but one with a boxed-in nose, cauliflower ear, distorted and damaged eye, legs covered with abrasions, a ruptured spleen, and broken ribs—all from the batterings of a man she claimed to love, who had beaten her daughter to death.

In all of these cases—hostage situations, cults, and domestic violence—a powerful connection develops out of the perceived need for the relationship to survive, and results in the constricted ability (or perhaps more accurately, a diminished desire) to advocate for oneself and one's freedom. Surely, then, this ultimately destructive bond must require extreme conditions in order to be forged.

However, the truth is to the contrary. Graham and colleagues (1994) argue that this phenomenon can develop under a wide range of conditions, and that actual captivity is most certainly *not* a prerequisite. Observational studies with birds, dogs, and monkeys demonstrate the resilience of traumatic bonding across species and suggest that some instinct to survive may be at play (Graham 1994). The paradox is that survival is seen as possible or desirable only through reliance on the destructive relationship. In most cases the individual has the literal freedom to leave, but exercises this freedom by staying—often in a situation that is more threatening to survival than leaving it would ever be.

## OUR FASCINATION WITH
## SELF-SUSTAINED CAPTIVITY

Concomitant with the traumatic bonding syndrome is our fascination with it. While those who are influenced by the bond seem to display little appreciation of its transformational influence, those outside the bond tend to be easily absorbed by it. During the Patty Hearst ordeal, the riveting media images of her seeming participation and willful cooperation captivated a nation. Anyone old enough to remember the situation likely has the image of a young woman dressed in dark clothing, standing feet astride, rifle in hand, participating in a robbery and providing cover for her captors, forever associated with the name Patty Hearst. Why does this image stand so strongly in our collective minds? Perhaps it represents some phenomenon we are familiar with and do not yet understand in ourselves.

The media, poised to satisfy the public's hunger, supplies such images readily. Pictures of the Heaven's Gate suicides appeared on covers of *Time, Newsweek, U.S. News and World Report,* and on the front pages of most national newspapers. The public was so eager to access the website of Heaven's Gate that the site quickly became saturated, with no direct assess possible for most users. Those who could reach it did so indirectly, through the archives of America Online, the nation's largest online provider (Brown 1997, personal communication). The American public was so involved in the story of Hedda Nussbaum that the three major networks preempted regular programming to televise the live testimony. What was it about this case, only one of thousands of child abuse and neglect, that so captivated the nation? Authors such as Brownmiller (1989) say it was the fascination of the bond between Hedda and Joel, a bond so strong that it culminated in the death of their daughter.

The ease with which we are drawn to and find ourselves absorbed by these situations is reflective of our curiosity about this powerful, yet paradoxical, attachment that directly challenges our notion of free will and the strength of individual determination. The bond, and the ease with which it can be formed, suggests that forces, perhaps not even so extreme or out of our control, may have the power to subtly captivate our loyalty and turn us into seemingly willing gatekeepers of our own bondage. One theme that seems to interest us most is the eventual struggle *against* freedom—the very fact that in all of these cases the individuals appeared determined to stay, despite the alarmingly high cost. Here the instinct for survival has run amuck, eventuating in sometimes disastrous consequences.

## TRAUMATIC BONDING: PSYCHOTHERAPISTS AND MANAGED CARE

What does all of this have to do with the relationship of psychotherapists to managed care? Here we have a situation in which therapists willingly, often eagerly, sometimes desperately, join with health care vendors or participate in capitated contracts to ensure their economic survival. The vendors would likely say that this is a voluntary relationship that the practitioners may terminate at any time, and participating therapists might well agree. These are relationships of necessity. The behemoths of the managed care industry, who are primarily concerned with the bottom line, join with the work force of therapists who are primarily concerned with the psychological and emotional welfare of their clients. Unlikely bedfellows perhaps, but partners in providing health care to millions of people nonetheless. What's the danger? Professional therapists, well trained and licensed in their craft, know what they value in therapy and how to maintain it. They are simply forming uncomfortable alliances, yet sustaining a commitment to quality treatment. Or are they? Does a transformation occur in these situations? Have these alliances subtly eroded our awareness of what we are doing, and have we become willing participants in our own captivity?

Through exploring the phenomenon of traumatic bonding, we can gain insight into the transformative power of the relationship between psychotherapists and managed care. Understanding the nature of this bond, as evidenced in the Stockholm situation, and reviewing the contributions of the psychological literature, will provide a context for our understanding. This context then gives us a useful vantage point for observing our own transformation under the influence of managed care. We then may be better able to answer two critical questions of the managed care era: Have we become bonded to our captors? If so, are we limiting our own freedom, distorting our beliefs and expectations, constricting our profession, and decreasing the quality of the treatment we offer, out of our perceived need to join with managed care in order to survive?

## A CLOSER LOOK:
## THE STOCKHOLM SYNDROME UNFOLDS

Through the lens of a single event, the forces involved in traumatic bonding may come to light. The Stockholm incident offers a useful starting point, as we have the unique benefit of interview information gathered by reporter David Lang from both captors and hostages. Using this material, Graham and colleagues (1994) have offered a thoughtful exploration of the Stockholm syndrome in the book *Loving to Survive.*

In the Stockholm siege, three women and one man were held for a period of six days by two captors. During this time, the captors openly threatened the lives of their prisoners and demonstrated intermittent kindness. The cruelty of the relationship was evidenced in the captivity itself, tying the prisoners, restraining them in a small vault, repeatedly holding them at gunpoint while threatening their lives, and using them as human shields against police bullets. The kindness took the form of such things as offering a coat for warmth, sharing food, and drying tears of the bound hostages.

Eventually, however, those things that the prisoners *perceived* as kind became more interesting. For example, while prisoners were held in tight quarters and not allowed to roam, one captor tied a length of rope around a woman's neck and allowed her to walk a bit. She reported after the incident that, at that moment, she realized how kind her captor was.

In another incident one captor told the male hostage that he would have to be shot to convince the police that the assailants were serious. The captor said he would aim for the man's leg as he stood in an open doorway, and would try not to kill him. The hostage agreed with the plan, reporting that he too felt warmly toward his captor, and walked to the open door and waited to be shot.

Finally, hoping to draw the siege to an end, the police prepared to use tear gas. The captors, discovering that this was imminent, fashioned nooses for the four hostages and themselves, stating that they feared the gas would cause permanent retardation and they did not want such a dire consequence to happen to any of them. The hostages stood for hours with nooses around their necks, awaiting the order to jump. Yet the hostages reported that this was another moment where they were convinced of their captors' kindness.

Along with the hostages' growing perception of kindness on the part of their captors, as the event continued to unfold an allegiance developed with them. Concurrently, the hostages became increasingly disdainful of the police. One hostage "practically curled her lip" (Graham et al. 1994, p. 4) at a negotiator sent in to inspect the hostages. In a phone contact set up to negotiate for freedom, a hostage stated that one of her captors "is sitting in here and he is protecting us from the police" (p. 5). Another hostage reported that "it is the police who are keeping me from my daughter" (p. 6). By this point in the ordeal, the captors were seen as kind allies, and the police were seen as cruel perpetrators of hostility and unfairness.

On the sixth day of the siege, the police used tear gas and stormed the vault. The hostages were freed unharmed and the two captors were arrested and jailed. Yet the attachments formed did not disappear once freedom was achieved. While all four hostages testified against their captors, one visited them in prison after reporting a compelling urge to do so; two of the women became engaged to the men (Graham et al. 1994).

## TRAUMATIC BONDING AND THE TRANSFORMATION OF THE SELF

What can we learn from this profound event? In reviewing the Stockholm incident and other hostage situations, precursors to the development of this bond to abusers have been identified by various authors (Dutton and Painter 1981, 1993, Fuselier 1988, Graham et al.

1994). It has been suggested that when these precursors exist, the likelihood that a traumatic bond will evolve is high. First, a power imbalance exists such that regulation of the survival needs appears to be in the control of the abuser. There is an actual or believed need to maintain the relationship bond to survive. Second, intermittent kindness and cruelty characterize the relationship; typically, the longer the length of the relationship, the greater the likelihood of an attachment. Third, ideological or physical isolation from other perspectives contrary to the abuser's further strengthens the bond. And finally, there is a perceived inability to escape from the relationship.

Graham and colleagues (1994) suggest that when these factors are present, the traumatic attachment develops across gender, age, race, culture, and species, and there is no obvious factor that renders one person more likely to develop this bond than another. "People who develop the syndrome do not do so because they have a personality defect such as a weak personality, because they were previously abused, or because they were socialized in a certain way." They conclude that "under the right conditions . . . anyone who seeks to survive will develop the Stockholm syndrome" (p. 48).

Graham and colleagues (1994) further note a progression in the relationship between the captor and hostage, that involves a gradual alteration in the person who is in the role of hostage or victim. The captor is seen as the only source of hope in a seemingly hopeless situation—forgetting, of course, that it was the captor who created the situation to begin with. Over time, this intense reliance develops into a form of relatedness. The viewpoint of the captor or abuser is gradually adopted as one's own. To manage any discrepancy between this viewpoint and one's former mind-set, cognitive adjustments are made. Distorting reality, ignoring evidence, and denying concrete consequences become the norm. Negative and harmful experiences are minimized; kind or benign ones are maximized. Conceptions of right and wrong, good and bad—a basic sense of morality—can be altered.

The pressure to adapt fuels a cognitive reshaping of affective experience as well. One's own anger and sense of danger is denied as attunement and hypervigilance to the needs and desires of the captor replace the experience of one's own affect.

The cognitive and affective distortions may be driven by the dissonance of feeling bonded to the very person who threatens one's own existence. There is a transformation from hostage to "cooperative" participant in the context of a relationship in which the captive nature has remained essentially unchanged. There are adaptive consequences to this transformation. When hostages develop views complementary to those of their captors, there is a subsequent reduction of distress and better adjustment to captivity (Auerbach et al. 1994). Further, law enforcement officers are now instructed to encourage the development of the Stockholm syndrome bond, as their research has shown that hostages attached to their captors have a better chance of survival (Kuleshnyk 1984, Turco 1987).

## PSYCHOTHERAPISTS BONDING WITH MANAGED CARE

As we consider the factors Graham and his colleagues discuss, we have a psychosocial recipe for the evolution and sustenance of a curious relationship. The common denominator is a power differential between the parties. The captor/abuser has the ascribed or actual power to regulate survival, and the prisoner/victim remains highly attuned to the obvious and subtle demands of the captor to ensure survival. In these situations the captor regulates resources and applies occasional and sometimes unpredictable abuse (such as the refusal of needed resources). The captor is the gatekeeper to resources—and sometimes to life itself. The prisoner discerns the reliance on the captor quickly. He or she naturally adopts the mind-set of the captor over time, cognitively distorts his or her own discordant perceptions, conforms to the demands, and responds intuitively to the captor so as to ensure the maintenance of the relationship. And over time, the prisoner doesn't know the difference.

Now here we have a picture of therapists in the 1990s: a group worried about survival, under the influence of the managed care companies, or pressured to form alliances to provide treatment under capitated contracts. Relationships are thus forged under the pressure to survive and to conform. The vendor controls resources and referrals, the source of sustenance for practitioners. While a kind of cruelty may be perceived in the constriction of freedom, limiting of sessions, and controlling of practice, it is the intermittent kindness, such as admission to a panel, allocation of a capitated contract, or granting of approved sessions, that often becomes the clinician's focus—for which he or she is grateful.

Has our own instinct for survival run amuck? Have we become traumatically bonded to the managed care industry? And in the process have we lost our critical thinking and the capacity to appreciate thoroughly the consequences of our actions?

Before the discussion of traumatic bonding in relation to psychotherapists and managed care is detailed, one point must be emphasized. Managed care is inexorably linked to short-term focal treatment (see, for example, Budman and Armstrong 1992). In condemning managed care many therapists have been accused of condemning brief treatment, which is in fact the treatment used by the vast majority of clinicians (Miller 1995, Stern 1993). The two are not the same.

When various short term psychotherapies were introduced in the literature, they were offered as one potential treatment option in a vast array of services. Short-term therapies were frequently described as treatments of choice for focal issues, and selection of appropriate patients was emphasized by their innovators. As Stern (1993) notes: "Brief therapy, as a legitimate field of theory and techniques, was never intended to be a universal mode of treatment. Indeed, its innovators tended to be extremely conservative about who is an appropriate candidate" (p. 168). He continues, "Most of these treatment models were developed in settings where brief therapy was but one option available to patients, so those who elected such treatment were deliberately choosing it or at least knew the limits of what they were getting" (p. 168).

The paradigmatic shift is not in using a relatively brief treatment, but in using a managed care model. In the latter, sessions are allocated by a third party a few at a time, with the frame of treatment often a mystery to both patient and therapist. No firm expectations can be held about when, and if, the clinician and patient can meet again. Aside from the ultimate cap on benefits, which the majority of patients are rarely granted, little is explicit about the treatment parameters. Thus therapist and patient set out on a venture for an unknown period of time, regulated by the third-party payer. Issues such as choice of therapist, method of treatment, and confidentiality are all compromised (Shore 1995 a,b). None of this is consonant with a model of short-term treatment. It is a treatment tailored to fit a benefit plan rather than a theoretical model of intervention.

The capitation of services, while removing the managed care company from reviewing and limiting each case, does not offer a better solution for the bind in which therapists find themselves. Here, a set fee is granted to clinics to treat a population of potential patients. Clearly, the greatest profit is realized when the fewest treatment contacts are made. Each patient is therefore pitted against a potential new patient when treatment decisions are made. It is in the financial interest of the clinician to limit services to any given patient as profit falls for each additional session or new patient treated. Once again, this is not a model of treatment per se, but a model of regulating care to ensure the greatest financial gain.

Therefore, it should be stated clearly and emphatically that brief treatment is not the problem. The enthusiastic participation of professional, well-intentioned psychotherapists in creating and advocating models of treatment that are insurance disbursement plans is. It is the realization of the traumatic bond.

## CONTRIBUTIONS FROM THE
## PSYCHOLOGICAL LITERATURE

What is it that can turn intelligent, strong-willed individuals into submissive defenders of their own psychological enslavement? While traumatic bonding itself has not been the subject of vast empirical investigation, many psychological components involved in this relationship have been investigated and theorized about independent of the hostage/captor conceptualization. The role of power and the pressure of conformity on individual behavior, the relationship that develops between subordinate and dominant persons, the cognitive adjustments one makes to lessen the internal distress of holding dissonant views, and the helplessness that one can feel—all have been studied. The threads of this research, woven together, offer familiar psychological underpinnings for the traumatic bond, and begin to elucidate some of the factors that may be involved.

## Dominance, Power, and Conformity

The frequently cited Milgram Obedience study (1963) illustrates the tremendous capacity of individuals to feel compelled to obey someone in a perceived position of power and the apparently ubiquitous nature of this effect. The research paradigm was straightforward and simple. (For the sake of brevity, only the initial obedience paradigm is reported here. For additional information, see Milgram 1974.) Subjects in the study were told they were participating in an investigation on the use of punishment in learning. They were not told, however, that the other "participant" in the study (the learner) was a confederate, not actually engaging in the learning task at all, but following a carefully crafted script. The real "subjects," then, were those who were told to administer the learning task and to give electric shocks to the supposed learner if the answers were incorrect.

When the experiment began, subjects were given a low-dose shock in order to appreciate the pain they believed they would be administering. Once the experiment was underway, the subjects were instructed by the experimenter to administer increasingly painful levels of shock with each incorrect answer. The confederates, following their scripts, missed many answers, and therefore were supposed to suffer the consequence of being administered multiple shocks by the real subject. No actual shock was administered to the confederates, of course, but the subject believed he was doing so. As the level of supposed voltage increased, the actor-confederates responded in kind, yelling and in some cases pleading for mercy.

Fully two thirds of the subjects engaged in a behavior—purportedly administering high-voltage shocks—they believed was painful and injurious to another person. The study became a controversy itself, in part because the results were so difficult to believe. In an experimental setting, where participation was voluntary and the power of the experimenter lay simply in his role as a temporary authority, subjects acted in a way they would never have believed of themselves. The actions taken by many of the individuals seemed to be at best poor judgment and at worst unconscionable. Was this truly in our nature, that we could so easily be influenced by authority to behave against our own principles? Milgram (1965) believed so, stating that "under certain circumstances, it is not so much the kind of person a man is as it is the kind of situation in which he is placed that determines his actions" (p. 75). Milgram's work corroborates in experimental form the ease with which one may be influenced, despite the type of person he or she is, by a powerful other, and that the power involved in such a situation need not be so extreme.

From another perspective and through a different methodology, social psychologists using naturalistic observations have suggested that the perceived need to conform may have a remarkably persuasive impact on an individual's behavior. A hallmark event for their observations was provided by the Bay of Pigs crisis. During this crisis, President John F. Kennedy and his advisors decided to go ahead with an invasion of Cuba that on review appeared quite ill-advised. The curiosity that arose around the incident was fueled by the fact that it appeared easily deduced from the information Kennedy and his advisors had that the invasion was likely to be unsuccessful. Yet the group decided to go ahead, with disastrous consequences. The group process evidenced in this decision making was dubbed "groupthink" (Janis 1972).

Groupthink, according to Janis, emerges in cohesive groups in which membership is highly valued and pressure exists to conform to the group's actions and point of view. The members become preoccupied with maintaining group consensus, and as a result there is censorship against dissent from the collective viewpoint. The group develops an illusion of invulnerability. It rationalizes its actions and decisions, and critical thinking is suspended. Janis speculated that in the appropriate circumstances, most people could fall into groupthink. Traumatically bonded relationships represent a situation in which conformity to the views of the captor and the development of groupthink become essential. When the mind-set of the captor is adopted and critical thinking is dissolved, distress is decreased and the chance of survival is increased—powerful motivations for such a transformation. Those involved in traumatically bonded relationships represent one singular viewpoint in which they fervently believe; disagreement is not tolerated.

Authors (e.g., Benjamin 1988, Miller 1976, Snodgrass 1985) writing from a feminist and sociological perspective offer a different vantage point for understanding the impact of dominance. These writers have explored the role of power and dominance not simply with respect to the dominated individual, but through the relationship that evolves between the power holder and the less powerful partner. This theoretical line suggests that the relationship and the subsequent actions that follow from it (such as understanding, care taking, loyalty, and adopting the affective reality of the dominant person) arise from the power differential intertwined with the regulation of needed resources.

Jean Baker Miller (1976) initially construed this differential along gender lines, suggesting that women, as the subordinate in relationships with men due to various issues of economics and societal power, develop a keen awareness of men's needs in order to survive. This awareness then develops into a sort of currency in the relationship, and the eclipsing of a woman's own beliefs and desires becomes part and parcel of maintaining the attachment. The woman conceptualizes her own needs as those of the relationship and ensures her survival by intuiting the needs of her dominant partner and meeting them.

Snodgrass (1985) argues that this intuiting is not gender based, but firmly rooted in the difference of power and regulation of resources. Through the results of her experimental studies, Snodgrass has argued that "women's sensitivity" would be more appropriately dubbed "subordinate's sensitivity." The subordinate develops a keen perception of the needs of the dominant, and then capitulates to these to enhance her own position or likelihood to survive. This transformation is not a conscious one, but one that develops out of a situation in which the power imbalance is clear. It is, it seems, a natural social tendency.

Psychoanalytic theory further suggests that there is a natural and unconscious adaptation and integration of the captor's mind-set into one's own. Analytic theorists such as Anna Freud (1966) posit that as one has been dominated and influenced by another, an identification forms with that person or institution. The individual unconsciously forms a psychic allegiance with the powerful other as one way to share the power and develop an avenue to dominate as he (or she) has been dominated. This "identification with the aggressor" is seen, for example, when children adopt the ways of their abusive parents and as adults find power and satisfaction in abusing others. In this model a person becomes what he has suffered through, and in that transformation attempts to master his powerlessness. Through such a theoretical lens the defense and promulgation of the captor's viewpoint represents the psychic adjustment to captivity, and in doing so the hostage will share in the omnipotent power of the captor.

These theories suggest that the very existence of power, coupled with the regulation of resources and the abuse that can accompany power, has the potential to transform the behavior and internal world of the person subject to that abuse.

### Cognitive and Affective Distortions

Cognitive distortions gradually occur in situations of traumatic bonding, such that one alters basic beliefs and sometimes evolves into frankly illogical and irrational thinking, despite dire consequences. The literature on cognitive dissonance offers one perspective on what appears to be a natural tendency to alter one's own beliefs in order to reduce inconsistencies between behavior and beliefs about oneself. Our curiosity about this transformation of our own thoughts is represented by the activity in this line of research—throughout the decade in which it was introduced, dissonance theory generated more research in social psychology than any other single theory (Middlebrook 1980).

Festinger (1957), in his studies of cognitive dissonance, demonstrated that when a person was in a situation that produced dissonant cognitions, he would simply and automatically adjust his thoughts in order to render them internally consistent. The rationale was that "simultaneously believing two ideas or opinions that are psychologically inconsistent arouses dissonance. Because dissonance is unpleasant, we try to reduce it by removing the inconsistency" (Middlebrook 1980, p. 19). Therefore, if the situation is not altered to become consonant with our beliefs, the thoughts can be rearranged instead.

To achieve this consonance, various rationalizations may occur: beliefs may be changed, an entire situation may be reinterpreted, or new beliefs may be developed. In the Stockholm incident, for example, to believe that one's potential killer is right by your side, drying your tears and feeding you, induces far more dissonance than believing that the police who are about to use tear gas are trying to harm you. To manage the dissonance, the situation is reinterpreted—captors are the allies and police are the enemies. With such a belief, the distress of an untenable situation is managed.

### The Perception of Powerlessness

Finally, hostages and victims who have bonded with captors often avoid advocating for freedom. Here the research on learned helplessness (Abramson et al. 1978; Seligman 1975) may offer some insight. According to this paradigm, when an action does not eventuate in a successful outcome, one can develop an attribution of noncontingency—essentially the belief that an outcome will not be influenced by one's action. This belief evolves into passivity coupled with a conviction that taking further action will be useless. In popular culture, it is perhaps best evidenced by the Winnie the Pooh character Eeyore's perpetual refrain regarding reattaching his tail: "It's going to fall off anyway." The belief that there will not be a favorable consequence is not tested beyond a few initial attempts. Eventually, as in a situation of traumatic bonding, the individual stops trying.

Many of us struggle to understand individuals appearing to act, not in their own behalf, but in accordance with the need to remain in a relationship with some influential other. How one attempts to understand the mechanisms involved depends on the theory one brings to bear, and we are aided by the related contributions of the predominant schools of psychological thought. The various components—dominance, conformity, cognitive and affective dissonance, perceived helplessness—come together in a dynamic interplay in the form of the traumatic bond. This bond dramatically illustrates, *in vivo*, the transformational quality power can have and the frighteningly pervasive nature of its influence.

## BONDING WITH MANAGED CARE

The fundamental ingredient in developing a traumatically bonded relationship is the belief that survival is at stake. This sentiment is clearly echoed by authors writing about the current state of mental health services (see for example, Browning and Browning 1996, Cummings 1995, Hoyt 1995). They argue that participating in and accommodating to managed care agreements is a matter of survival— not simply for the individual practitioner but for the profession as a whole. Throughout the remainder of this chapter, their words will be used to illustrate the current professional zeitgeist. These authors were chosen because they are vocal representatives of those who promulgate the managed care mind-set and are reflective of the wave of sentiment about the need to join with managed care—or suffer the consequences.

Cummings (1995) argues that an adoption of the values of managed care is essential for clinicians hoping to practice: "A shift in attitudes and values is difficult but *fundamental to the practitioner who survives*" and "the prediction that by the year 2000 more than 50% of current psychotherapists will be out of business . . . is rapidly moving to fulfillment" (p. 11, italics added). He argues that those who do not retrain and acquire a view of psychotherapy that is consonant with the managed care world will suffer extinction.

Such a belief has become pervasive. The professional journals of clinical and counseling psychology, psychiatry and social work have all carried articles about the extensive influence of managed care, and various publications have sprung up to help clinicians deal with the transition to a managed care frame of mind.

*How to Partner with Managed Care* (Browning and Browning 1996) is one work representative of this trend. Endorsed by the past president of the American Psychological Association, this book states that "any therapist, group of therapists, or facility that rigidly refuses to adapt its thinking, its business, and its clinical practices to the constraints of today's PPO, HMO, EAP and Managed Care 'real world' will be unable to sustain independent practice due to financial reversals, and *its story will eventually be told in the mental health practice obituary columns*" (p. 15, italics added). Cummings writes in the introduction of this book: "Many, if not most [clinicians], will suffer an identity crisis and will not survive. As you read, you are holding in your hands a survival manual that will prepare you step by step, not only to survive the new practice environment but also to prosper in it" (p. v).

The theme in literature, then, is that the practitioner who has not awakened to managed care will professionally perish. Much of this sounds like the message of the Heaven's Gate leader—that "the only way to survive" is with us.

Has this view in fact extended beyond the written word and permeated the professional community? Survey studies (see, for example, Bell, this volume) suggest that clinicians now view it necessary to enter into some alliance with managed care. Consider that most managed care panels are closed, and that when clinicians have the opportunity to join, they are often grateful. In difficult economic times, when private practice is shrinking, forming such agreements is seen as a salvation. Lost is the appreciation that these organizations are largely responsible for the shifting demographics of private outpatient psychotherapy. Rather, the captor is the liberator—and we feel lucky to have the relationship. Hospitals are merging and clinics are fighting for capitated contracts, in which the one who can limit the cost/care ratio most often wins. The relief in winning such contracts overshadows the necessary changes in practice that they are the harbinger of. The belief emerges that such difficult adjustments are necessary.

Once set, similar to the processes involved in groupthink, these beliefs are rarely challenged. With regard to the necessity for management of outpatient mental health benefits, for example, it is unclear what the economic reality is and how it has been created. Many clinicians simply believe they must join with managed care, and that while patient care may be affected, cost containment is a valid rationale for these difficult actions.

However, there has been little, if any, evidence that outpatient therapy needed to be regulated at all (Miller 1995, Stern 1993). The significant costs in mental health care are derived from inpatient and residential treatments (Miller 1995). Outpatient treatment, which serves the greatest number of patients, costs the least of all these treatments. Further, most patients in outpatient therapy self-select for brief treatment (Stern 1993); as such, practitioners have long been accustomed to seeing patients for fewer than 25 sessions (Butcher and Koss 1978). So, did these services need to be regulated? Was it possible that patients and therapists were in fact choosing cost-effective methods of treatment themselves?

Simply accepting the rationale for the limiting of benefits and joining with the managed care companies to thrive professionally is a reflection of our need to quiet the cognitive dissonance that arises from making decisions that go against our personal and professional beliefs. Becoming spokespersons for the need to provide only short-term managed care treatment solidifies our identification with the aggressor, all the while pacifying the discomfort we slowly forget.

## THE TRANSFORMATION OF PATIENT, THERAPIST, AND THERAPY

In traumatic bonding, when reliance develops out of the perceived need to survive, cognitive dissonance, compromised reality testing, and alteration of painful or anxious affects to more positive ones ensue. Does practicing psychotherapy in a managed care setting require similar adjustments?

Consider a study surveying therapists in managed care (Austad et al. 1992). Researchers investigated the modification of clinicians' practice when working in an HMO setting. Not surprisingly, the majority of respondents reported that they felt forced to use a model of brief treatment. They also reported a shift in attitudes during their time at the HMO. The respondents rated their effectiveness higher over time, but also increasingly looked forward to cancellations, had a decrease in satisfaction with their clinical load, and had a decrease in concern for their patients. They reported a decrease in satisfaction with work, decreased professional fulfillment, and burnout. Despite this, the respondents on the whole felt that they were wiser, more realistic, stronger, and had an increase in confidence and were "better people" (p. 332) as a result of working at the HMO. The authors conclude that "practicing in an HMO may set an adaption process into motion" (p. 332), a conclusion that seems obvious, considering the data, and appears representative of Festinger's cognitive dissonance experiments. The redefinition of experience and affect becomes adaptive.

A transition is set in place by working in these climates—a transition seen as both welcome and necessary by writers advocating for the profession to adjust to the real world of managed care. Cummings (1995) states: "Currently underway is the greatest resocialization of psychologists to occur since the explosion of clinical psychology in the post World War II era. *It is being stimulated by the unprecedented growth of managed care . . .*" (p. 10, italics added).

Adjusting to the managed care framework is considered part and parcel of surviving in this era. "Therapists who work in managed care are now shaping practice patterns by selecting, adapting and/or creating attitudes and interventions that are compatible with the values of managed care" (Austad and Hoyt 1992, p. 109). Successful therapists are those who "promote identification with HMO values and goals" (Hoyt 1995, p. 41). The adjustment certainly may be difficult: "The intensity and degree of adjustment is contingent upon the goodness of fit between the demand characteristics of the particular managed care environment and the theoretical model adapted by the therapist" (Austad and Hoyt 1992, p. 112). A good fit is one in which the clinician develops values consonant with managed care. A bad fit is where the clinician maintains his previously held beliefs about therapy. Dissent and practicing outside the guidelines of the HMO panel becomes coupled with the pressure of fewer referrals, being branded an inefficient provider, or possible removal from the panel.

Shifts in conceptualizations therefore become adaptive. It is difficult to work within managed care and remember that treatment could be viewed as a relationship between two persons, focused on the patient and the issues he or she brings to treatment. A relationship in which the assessment of the difficulty is primary, and the mode of treatment is chosen accordingly. A therapy to be determined by the two participants in the endeavor. To maintain this view and work within a managed care or capitation environment creates tremendous internal distress. One cannot practice with that philosophy and comfortably maintain the relationship with the liberator—the managed care company. The force of cognitive dissonance fueled by the belief in the need for the alliance will require shifts in cognition. As such, there will be a fundamental redefinition of all the factors that are central components of psychotherapy.

*Patient, Therapist, and the Therapy Relationship*

To wonder "who is the patient of psychotherapy?" may seem to be asking a ridiculous and obvious question. The patient is simply the patient, the person or persons to whom the treatment is offered, and with whom the treatment relationship is established. As for asking "with whom is the therapy relationship established?" again a similar answer might be given. The relationship is obviously between the patient and the therapist and is considered primary and sacrosanct. From our theories of therapy to the ethical guidelines that shape our professions, the relationship is considered the vehicle for change as well as the entity to be developed and protected. As for the therapist, he or she is the professional, the expert in human behavior trained to use that expertise to diagnose and treat accordingly. Despite our vast differences due to theoretical orientation and schools of training, are these basic facts not obvious?

The professional literature today suggests that the answer is a disquieting "no." The belief that "the patient is not only the individual, but the entire HMO membership" (Austad and Hoyt 1992, p. 113) permeates clinical writing and practice. Within managed care we are encouraged to think of the patient not as the individual with whom we sit, but as a set of potential patients. Any individual patient is to be thought of as a "member" of a panel and not as a single individual. The relationship the clinician forms is with the panel as a whole, and therefore any decision regarding any "member" must take this panel—unknown and unmet—into account. The management of the panel remains primary in the clinician's mind, and the "members" are juggled accordingly.

The relationship with the panel is subsumed under the relationship with the managed care agency. Clinicians are encouraged to view the relationship with the agency as similar to, and perhaps more central than, the therapist–patient relationship. The relationship with the agency must be fostered as well. For example, Hoyt (1995) states: "Our 'customers' are more and more both our patients and the large purchasers of health care that direct patients to us" (p. 41).

These relationships will likely have conflicting interests, but clinicians are encouraged to carefully consider the alliance with the managed care company whenever resolving such internal conflicts. The question arises: Among all these relationships—with the "member," the panel, and the managed care agency—with whom does the clinician foster the *primary* allegiance? The answer, arising from thoughtful clinicians in the field, is disconcerting. As an example, Browning and Browning (1996) write: "You can appeal [treatment] decisions you disagree with. Most managed health care firms have several levels of appeals. But remember this: You want to preserve your relationship with the case reviewers. If you appeal, whether you win or lose, you *lose*" (p. 241). In other words, the need to preserve the relationship with the reviewer is primary, and any treatment needs, defined by the careful clinical assessment of the patient, are secondary.

Who, then, has the therapist become? In these situations the clinician, who manages the benefit and considers any treatment options for the patient in conjunction with all other potential patients, is far more than an ally in the patient's treatment and far less than a professional exercising learned judgment. The clinician is now a benefit manager, insurance disburser, and self-preserving managed care panel member as well as treatment provider. This is a fundamental shift and one of which many patients are unaware. As tension arises between self-preservation and patient care, there is undeniably a divided loyalty, and perhaps educating patients to this would reduce the conflict, as patients would willingly enter a relationship in which they knew their care would not be the primary consideration. Pellegrino (1994), perhaps with some humor, suggests the following disclaimer: "I will serve your interests as long as they do not conflict with the cost containment and policies of our system. It is I who will make the determination of how much to spend on you depending on how I assess the benefits of treatment or the quality of life in your remaining years" (p. 10). One wonders, of course, how such an honest rendering of the conflict of interest would affect the essential trust of the treatment relationship. Yet it is this situation in which managed care therapists find themselves.

## The Practice of Psychotherapy

As the practice of psychotherapy is based on the conceptualizations of therapist, patient, and the treatment relationship, perhaps it is of little surprise that notions of what therapy is and how it should be practiced have also evolved during the managed care era. While eluding a precise definition, therapy is broadly considered to be a practice guided by technique and training to foster a change desired by the person seeking treatment. Following a period of assessment and predicated on a diagnostic formulation, treatment is carried out in conjunction with the patient by a specialist in the field of human development and psychopathology. So it was.

The alteration of therapist and patient necessitates a change in this conceptualization. Client needs, when they are assessed, are within the context of the panel of patients and balanced against the entire HMO. The primary focus is allocation of sessions, and in that context occurs the diagnosis and assessment of needs. As an example, Austad and Hoyt (1992) state: "The managed care psychotherapist must first accommodate treatment to the parameters of the benefit package" (p. 112). *First to the benefit package*—not to the patient or problem. They further suggest that practitioners decide on treatment for patients "with the paramount consideration being to use the least intensive, least expensive, least intrusive intervention" (Hoyt and Austad 1992, p. 122)—which sounds more like the guidelines for involuntary treatment than embarking on a joint therapy venture.

Treatment decisions are made with careful contemplation, not of the patient, but of the impact of the decision on the primary therapy relationship—that with the managed care agency. As noted above, treatment considerations become secondary to the preservation of this relationship. This sentiment is rampant and remarkable. It suggests that a profession alter its practice, ignore its expertise, and limit the benefits of its interventions based on the fear of loss of a relationship with the managed care company.

Typically, patients come to therapists as they go to any health professional—with the belief that they are seeing a trained individual who is, by virtue of his or her expertise, able to guide treatment to a beneficial end. However, when patients enter a treatment regulated by managed care contracts, a different process ensues. Here the expert views of the clinician are reviewed and regulated by the insurance disburser, and frequently the opinion of reviewers rather than the clinician are reflected in the choice of treatment. Browning and Browning (1996), suggest: "Except in more severe cases, it is best to see a patient referred to you by a case rep no more than once weekly. After the initial phase of treatment, it is a good idea to spread out the sessions to every two weeks, every three weeks and then once monthly. Case managers appreciate the prudent spacing of sessions. . . . It is also wise to ask the case manager if she or he has any opinion or preference about the best frequency for a given condition" (p. 253). Patients might find it frightening, therapists disheartening, and ethicists fascinating, that a master's- or doctoral-level-trained professional would defer clinical decisions to a less well-trained reviewer who has no contact with or knowledge of the patient, or, even worse, that treatment decisions would be made preemptive of contact with these reviewers simply in the interest of maintaining a favorable relationship. Treatment eventually becomes merely a commodity to be dispensed.

Matters only become worse when, due to allegiances with managed care and the primacy of cost cutting, eager therapists develop theories of treatment and intervention that fit the demand characteristics of the HMOs or capitated contracts. As with the traumatic bond, once the alliance has evolved, actions follow to keep the captor satisfied. With regard to developing therapy models, the tail wags the dog. Twenty sessions are offered by a plan, a twenty-session model is developed—which moves to twelve and then six, until some authors have advocated a single-session model (Austad and Hoyt 1992, Hoyt 1995, Talmon 1990). Without giving any parameters or data, Austad and Hoyt (1992) conclude: "The single session therapy (SST) approach was found to be helpful and sufficient for more than 50% of cases," and "The laws of supply and demand will ensure that such models thrive, for they supply a demand" (p. 115). The authors, however, don't state whose demand is being supplied. Patients have always self-selected for varying treatment lengths, and premature terminations have frequently occurred after one session, yet this was not called a "model" of treatment until there was a financial incentive to do so.

One description of this "model" (Talmon 1990) suggests: "In the initial phone conversation, you can begin with a simple question to determine whether the candidate is an SST candidate. . . . How and how soon do you anticipate the problem to be solved? How do you think therapy will help you to deal with the problem?" (p. 28). Rather than educate about the services and treatment options, the clinician is encouraged to ask what the patient knows about therapy, and use that. Thorough assessment and treatment, it seems, is to be avoided if at all possible. In the managed care era, a model of intervention simply becomes a treatment limit, with no emphasis on patient needs, pathology, or differences. And if consumers are not educated about treatment, they may well not receive it—which sets the stage for treatment elitism and favoritism.

What, then, has happened to the conceptualization of therapy? It is now a service to be offered on a sparing basis, if the therapist's relationship with the managed care company is not jeopardized by it. Assessment of treatment needs is based on greasing the wheels with managed care companies or obtaining capitated contracts. But perhaps most worrisome of all, therapists participate in this by creating and promoting "models" of treatment that are no more than limits of treatment and no less than an unethical compromise of a dual relationship.

## THE COGNITIVE ADJUSTMENTS OF TRAUMATIC BONDING

Lest these changes be unpalatable to the therapist, a solution is near at hand. Therapists by and large are a group of hard-working, dedicated individuals committed to the quality of patient care. How can such dedication be maintained when treatment is so affected? As Festinger would predict, the dissonance of practicing under these conditions will require some reshaping of our attitudes. Such cognitive reframes aid in making captivity more palatable. Time-limited therapy is now brief intermittent treatment, and problem focused is now solution focused—just as in an era of environmental consciousness the "throwaway" camera is suddenly "recyclable."

Consider the suggestion of Anthony (1993) that managed care be called "collaborative care" due to "greater consumer choice and participation in rehabilitation and treatment" (p. 794). Rather than think of ourselves and our patients as managed, we can think of ourselves as collaborators with managed care—which may well help our internal dissonance. Yet, while Anthony's effort to emphasize patients' choice can be commended, it is this type of reframe that serves to ease clinicians' discomfort with a difficult situation rather than to foster any actual change in the situation itself. The analogy of collaboration falls short when we are reminded that the ultimate regulation of resources rests solely with the vendor, and that conversely the greatest opportunity for a patient's role as collaborator occurs between the patient and therapist when each can act freely. But in traumatic bonding, to see ourselves in accordance with the perceived source of our survival minimizes distress and increases adaptation.

If the adjustment to continually taking on new patients, thereby limiting treatment to existing clients, causes distress, we can think of it as a "natural schedule of therapy" (Austad and Hoyt 1992, p. 113). As existing patients are replaced with new ones, and patients are told they will not be permitted further treatment within that calendar year, we can think: "This 'natural' schedule of therapy and access to medical charts allow the therapist to witness patients' holistic, unfolding history" (p. 113). We should not notice that the so-called natural schedule is the insurance schedule, where in January patients may reconsider treatment, despite any need for it prior to that.

As cognitive changes emerge from the pressure to become consonant with managed care, a type of doublespeak logic emerges that, within the vacuum of managed care, seems to make sense. Consider that one author warns against imposing too many sessions (rather than too few), noting that to assume "everyone must come in for 12, 15, or 25 visits, is neither realistic nor practical" (Budman and Armstrong 1992, p. 418). Another subtly implies that single-session therapy is the norm by stating: "Needing multiple sessions does not mean that there has been an SST failure" (Hoyt 1995, p. 143). These suggestions sound reasonable, yet are based on the premise that offering the least is providing the best. Finally, one author states: "It should be noted that for some people, no therapy may be the treatment of choice" (Hoyt 1995, p. 77). It is true that with psychotherapy, as with any procedure, the provision of treatment may not be indicated in all cases. However, this last comment frames the withholding of treatment as a treatment in itself. In the true nature of doublespeak, a trajectory emerges where less is more, a little may be too much, and nothing is something.

Perhaps the most worrisome consequence of these shifts in cognition is their potential to be used against patients. As noted above, some authors suggest using the patient's knowledge of therapy as the basis for defining the treatment. Taken further, this means that a patient's treatment is limited by his or her understanding of it. The goals of the therapy, the form the treatment takes, and the duration of a session will all come into question. Hoyt (1995), for example, notes that treatment "models" have emerged in which sessions are thirty, twenty, and even five minutes long. He suggests that the fifty-minute hour is a "middle-class notion" and that "persons of different socioeconomic backgrounds may not share this time perspective and may need to see valuable results quickly if subsequent sessions are to occur" (p. 79). Encased in the wrapping of cultural sensitivity, an argument evolves for offering sessions that are twenty minutes or less, simply because a client's ethnic background may not have predisposed him or her to know that more was available. If a poor urban minority patient didn't know about the latest advances in heart surgery, would we let that suffice as a rationale for not imposing our middle-class notions of intervention?

## LIMITS OF THE TRAUMATIC BOND?

Are there pockets of integrity that this bond cannot touch? If we are indeed seeing the greatest resocialization of therapists to occur in fifty years, is there a limit to the reach of this transformation? Clinical practice, which undeniably is being re-formed, is different from the educational base of the profession. Practice is a specialty built on a broad and intensive education. The educational base, which is the definitional cornerstone of a profession, need not be reshaped as therapists can later elect specialized training in any area of therapy, such as managed care. The scientific base, such as the development of diagnostic criteria, likewise should remain unaffected. And one could easily argue that the ethical base, the foundation and watchdog of clinical practice, should never be compromised. However, as with a transformation of any type, the rippling impact can be profound.

## Training

Many authors have made recommendations that graduate schools change their curriculum to adjust to the reality of managed care. "Mental health professionals have not received the graduate education, professional training, and emotional preparation necessary to fulfill the new clinical roles demanded by society. Many, if not most, will suffer an identity crisis and will not survive" (Cummings 1996, p. v). Hoyt (1995) argues that "graduate schools and professional schools generally have not yet adapted their curricula to teach the methods of assessment, time sensitive therapy and case management required by behavioral health programs . . . it can be expected that graduate and professional schools that are interested in equipping their students for the realities of contemporary practice will soon begin to emphasize the requisite skills for working under the auspices of managed care" (p. 8). Indeed, Shore (1995c) has noted that university programs themselves have begun to transform their curricula to be consonant with managed care.

Broskowski (1995) further suggests that "more emphasis should be placed on models of mental health and illness that view anxiety, depression and many forms of maladaptive behavior as episodic conditions requiring brief intervention . . ." (p. 161). Practitioners are certainly aware of the clinical characteristics and demographics for chronic anxiety and affective disorders; these are well-researched disorders with perhaps the highest validity and reliability in psychiatric diagnoses (see for example the *Diagnostic and Statistical Manual of Mental Disorders IV* [APA 1994], Goodwin and Guze 1984). The suggestion of Broskowski is that we alter our view of psychopathology, suspend knowing what we know, to match the treatment we can offer.

These suggestions are akin to advocating that those studying for a master of fine arts in literature intensively focus on the formula for romance writing rather than waste their time with the likes of

Shakespeare. After all, romance is the biggest-selling genre and the one most likely to satisfy the needs of the majority of readers. But despite the profusion of romance literature, writers do not seem to be despairing the death of their profession. They do not seem to be altering their institutions to fit the desires of multitudes of book buyers. Nor should we. Should literature graduates decide to write romance, they are free to do so—but they have the educational base to do far more, and to do it with a wealth of knowledge underneath every written word.

When we ourselves begin to advocate for altering our institutions of higher learning, and we move away from intensively teaching a historically relevant and clinically pertinent body of knowledge from which intelligent and seasoned practitioners can develop specialties, we are then advocating for our own demise. Our academic institutions simply become training grounds for the technicians of the managed care era, and the true development of a "profession" and a "specialty" is lost.

## Ethics

There is an inherent ethical compromise in acting as both therapist and insurance agent for a patient, particularly when the primary concern is to preserve the relationship with the managed care company or to limit treatment to maximize profit. Is it not feasible, given these competing interests, that therapists will make compromised decisions? The basic principle of malfeasance—to do no harm—shifts its focus from the treatment to the preservation of the bond with managed care. Out of the need to do no harm to that relationship, it is quite feasible that compromises will be made in patient care. Pellegrino (1994) writes, "Some systems control the physician's behavior through threat to her self interest by imposing financial incentives or disincentives, by linking remuneration or job security to productivity or efficiency as defined by institutional goals. All but the more virtuous will be tempted to rationalize their actions and cut corners, prematurely discharge patients, postpone expensive tests or consultations on the grounds of self protection, survival in the system, or the needs of one's family. Divided loyalty is too easily resolved in favor of the system and the organization which legitimizes self interest" (pp. 9–10), and adds that "any system of rationing provides serious conflicts of obligation for the conscientious physician" (p. 12). When threats to professional and economic survival are pitted against advocating on a patient's behalf, treatment needs are no longer paramount. The therapist, believed by the patient to be working with his or her care primary, now has another agenda.

The dual nature of these relationships, however, is rarely discussed as an ethical dilemma. For example, the American Psychological Association code of ethics expressly forbids dual relationships in which the clinician has conflicted interests in a case, yet many psychologists who are members of the APA work as double agents—simultaneously for the patient and for the insurance company (see Wolf, this volume). It seems that the relationship forged in managed care is the one ethical compromise clinicians are allowed to make.

In an effort to resolve this conflict of interest, Donovan and colleagues (1994) state that "managed mental health care practitioners must arrive at their ethical standards and professional satisfactions by assuming a public health perspective toward a panel of patients rather than developing intimacy with a few" (p. 206). In other words, our standard of ethics should be re-formed to be in accord with the adaptations necessary for practice within managed care.

Ethical principles, by their nature, are designed to be invulnerable to special interest groups. They are a code of practice and conduct, unaffected by theoretical orientation. Yet present-day developments in clinical practice that potentially pit clinicians' interests against their patients and prioritize a new managed care standard represent a serious challenge to the integrity our patients have come to expect of us and upon which the weight of the treatment relationship lies.

## THE IMPACT OF THE TRAUMATIC BOND
## WITH MANAGED CARE

Wooley (1993) has written: "Mental health providers all over the country are cashing in the expertise of a lifetime in order to survive the new regime" (p. 393). But this isn't even the scary part. While it is worrisome to see clinicians compromise themselves to survive, it is frightening to see highly motivated practitioners and researchers, concerned about the future of the field, interested in serving a wide range of patients, become eager advocates for our loss of freedom. It is frightening to see a redefinition of patient, practice, psychopathology, ethics, and ourselves promulgated to fit not a research-based or clinically determined need on the part of our patients, but a need on the part of managed care. Some of these changes may be made because of conscious efforts to adapt, but many represent the more subtle effect of bonding with forces less interested in the well-being of our patients and our profession. We change what we believe because of what we have to *not* know in order to survive. And we become glad for the opportunity to do it.

We should proceed cautiously, because we are thankful for the limited sessions given to us, like the prisoner grateful to be shot in the leg. We are increasingly courting our captors, grateful for the chance to survive, unaware of the limited length of rope tied to our necks.

## REFERENCES

Abramson, L. Y., Seligman, M. E. P., and Teasdale, J. D. (1978). Learned helplessness in humans: critique and reformulation. *Journal of Abnormal Psychology* 87:102–109.

American Psychiatric Association (1994). *Diagnostic and Statistical Manual of Mental Disorders*, 4th ed. Washington, DC: Author.

Anthony, W. A. (1993). Managed care: A misnomer? *Hospital and Community Psychiatry* 44(8):794–795.

Auerbach, S. M., Kiesler, D. J., Strentz, T., et al. (1994). Interpersonal impacts and adjustment to the stress of simulated captivity: an empirical test of the Stockholm syndrome. *Journal of Social and Clinical Psychology* 13(2):207–221.

Austad, C. S., and Hoyt, M. F. (1992). The managed care movement and the future of psychotherapy. *Psychotherapy* 29(1):109–118.

Austad, C. S., Sherman, W. O., Morgan, T., and Holstein, L. (1992). The psychotherapist and the managed care setting. *Professional Psychology: Research and Practice* 23(4):329–332.

Benjamin, J. (1988). *The Bonds of Love.* New York: Pantheon.

Broskowski, A. T. (1995). The evolution of managed care: implications for the training and careers of psychologists. *Professional Psychology: Research and Practice* 26(2):156–162.

Browning, C. H., and Browning, B. J. (1996). *How to Partner with Managed Care: A "Do-It-Yourself Kit" for Building Working Relationships and Getting Steady Referrals.* Los Alamitos, CA: Duncliffs International.

Brownmiller, S. (1989). Madly in love: the story of Hedda Nussbaum. *Ms*, April, pp. 56–64.

Budman, S. H., and Armstrong, E. (1992). Training for managed care settings: how to make it happen. *Psychotherapy* 29(3):416–421.

Butcher, J. N., and Koss, M. P. (1978). Research on brief and crisis oriented treatments. In *Handbook for Psychotherapy and Behavior Change*, ed. S. Garfield and A. E. Bergin, pp. 725–768. New York: Wiley.

Collins, J. J. (1991). The Cult Experience: An Overview of Cults, Their Traditions and Why People Join Them. Springfield, IL: Charles C Thomas.

Cummings, N. A. (1995). Impact of managed care on employment and training: A primer for survival. *Professional Psychology Research and Practice* 26(1):10–15.

——— (1996). Introduction. In *How to Partner with Managed Care: A "Do-It-Yourself Kit" for Building Working Relationships and Getting Steady Referrals*, ed. C. H. Browning and B. J. Browning, pp. v–ix. Los Alamitos, CA: Duncliffs International.

Donovan, J. M., Steinberg, S. M., and Sabin, J. E. (1994). Managed mental health care: an academic seminar. *Psychotherapy* 31(1):201–207.

Dutton, D., and Painter, S. L. (1981). Traumatic bonding: the development of emotional attachments in battered women and other relationships of intermittent abuse. *Victimology: An International Journal* 6:139–155.

——— (1993). Emotional attachments in abusive relationships: a test of traumatic bonding theory. *Violence and Victims* 8(2):105–120.

Festinger, L. A. (1957). *A Theory of Cognitive Dissonance.* Stanford, CA: Stanford University Press.

Freud, A. (1966). The Ego and the Mechanisms of Defense. Madison, CT: International Universities Press.

Fuselier, G. D. (1988). Hostage negotiation consultant: emerging role for the clinical psychologist. *Professional Psychology* 19(2):175–179.

Gleick, E. (1997). The marker we've been . . . waiting for. *Time*, April 7, pp. 28–36.

Goodwin, D. W., and Guze, S. B. (1984). *Psychiatric Diagnosis.* New York: Oxford University Press.

Graham, D. L. R., Rawlings, E. I., and Rigsby, R. K. (1994). *Loving to Survive: Sexual Terror, Men's Violence, and Women's Lives.* New York: New York University Press.

Hoyt, M. F. (1995). Brief Therapy and Managed Care: Reading for Contemporary Practice. San Francisco: Jossey-Bass.

Hoyt, M. F., and Austad, C. S. (1992). Psychotherapy in a staff model health maintenance organization: providing and assuring quality health care in the future. *Psychotherapy* 29(1):119–129.

Janis, I. (1972). *Victims of Groupthink: A Psychological Study of Foreign Policy Decisions and Fiascoes.* Boston: Houghton Mifflin.

Kuleshnyk, I. (1984). The Stockholm syndrome: toward an understanding. *Social Action and the Law* 10(2):37–42.

Middlebrook, P. N. (1980). *Social Psychology and Modern Life.* New York: Knopf.

Milgram, S. (1963). Behavioral study of obedience. *Journal of Abnormal and Social Psychology* 67(4):371–378.

———— (1965). Liberating effects of group pressure. *Journal of Personality and Social Psychology* 1(2):127–134.

———— (1974). *Obedience to Authority: An Experimental View.* New York: Harper & Row.

Miller, I. J. (1995). Managed care is harmful to outpatient mental health services: a call for accountability. (Paper available from Boulder Psychotherapists Press, 350 Broadway, Suite 210, Boulder, CO 80303.)

Miller, J. B. (1976). *Toward a New Psychology of Women.* Boston: Beacon.

Pellegrino, E. D., ed. (1994). The physician as "gatekeeper": ethics and economics at the bedside and beyond. [Adapted from: Edward Pellegrino (1994). Managed care and managed competition: some ethical reflection. *Calyx* 4(4):1–5.]

Seligman, M. (1975). *Helplessness: On Depression, Development and Death.* San Francisco: Freeman.

Shore, K. (1995a). Managed care: the convergence of industrialization and totalitarianism. *Psychologist Psychoanalyst* 15(4): 15–19.

——— (1995b). Why we need to move America beyond managed care and managed competition. *Psychologist Psychoanalyst* 15(3):12–15.

——— (1995c). The immorality of managed competition and managed care. Presented at the "Preserving Psychotherapy" conference, sponsored by the National Coalition of Mental Health Professionals and Consumers, November 4, Atlanta.

Snodgrass, S. (1985). Women's intuition: the effect of subordinate role on interpersonal sensitivity. *Journal of Personality and Social Psychology* 49:146–155.

Stern, S. (1993). Managed care, brief therapy, and therapeutic integrity. *Psychotherapy* 30(1):162–175.

Talmon, M. (1990). *Single-Session Therapy: Maximizing the Effect of the First (and often only) Therapeutic Encounter.* San Francisco: Jossey-Bass.

Turco, R. M. (1987). Psychiatric contributions to the understanding of international terrorism. *International Journal of Offender Therapy and Comparative Criminology* 31(2):153–161.

West, L. J. (1993). A psychiatric overview of cult-related phenomena. *Journal of the American Academy of Psychoanalysis* 21(1):1–19.

Wooley, S. C. (1993). Managed care and mental health: the silencing of a profession. *International Journal of Eating Disorders* 14(4): 387–401.

# II

## The Impact on the Therapist

# 2

# Managing Intrapsychic Conflict: The Therapist's Experience

E. CATHERINE LOULA

If you plant a seed in fertile soil, a plant will grow. In turn, the plant affects the ecosystem and influences what will grow in succession thereafter. Managed care has taken root and grown up in a cultural context that has favored its establishment (see, for example, Morgan and Ruffins, Gilford, and Pingitore, this volume). It has now become a part of that same cultural context and, along with other factors, significantly influences how we practice as psychotherapists.

To examine the many ways that managed care affects the therapist, one could consider changes in the kinds of patients therapists work with. One could look at changes in the environment in which the various tasks of psychotherapy take place. One could examine the therapists' satisfaction in effecting their tasks. One could even analyze rates of illness and disability in therapists and infer the etiology of work-related disturbances. Instead, this chapter will focus on what might be happening inside the mind of the therapist. There can be no doubt that the pressure exerted by managed care on the field of mental health treatment has an impact on therapists, some of which occurs outside their awareness. Using the particular lens of psychodynamic theory, this chapter examines the unconscious adaptations therapists make to the often conflictual situations in which they find themselves as well as some of the consequences of these adaptations.

A significant bias of the dynamic models is that emotional pain is to be understood, rather than simply banished, for example, by "thought-stopping" or medication. In medical school the young doctor learns that as a species we would not have survived without pain. Pain keeps us from using an injured limb until it heals. Pain brings us to the physician for an appendectomy that can save our lives. The absence of pain leads a man with diabetic neuropathy to cause serious damage to hands and limbs through burns from the stove or blisters on his feet. Like physical pain, emotional suffering exists for a reason; it marks something being wrong. The something that is wrong can be internal (as in a conflict between competing wishes), external (as in a difficult work environment brought about by shifting economic tides), or, most commonly, a combination of both.

Frequently, psychic defenses will intervene and act to diminish emotional pain and conflict. Psychic defenses provide relief for psychic pain just as ibuprofen and aspirin provide relief for physical pain. However, when a patient seeks to continually avoid pain, such as one with a chronic headache who refuses to see a physician and instead escalates his ibuprofen use, the consequences can be deleterious. The headache may be the marker of a slow-growing tumor; if caught early, it could be curable. Similarly, psychic defenses can mask insidious, deep-lying pain and have deleterious consequences. So, rather than seeing the task as making the pain disappear, the psychodynamic bias would focus on the discovery and analysis of what might be wrong. Then the individual can decide whether he or she wants change, what change he or she wants, and what psychic, cognitive, and behavioral costs might follow. In the case of the psychotherapist, a lack of awareness of his or her personal use of defenses, for the purpose of minimizing psychic pain in the clinical situation, can potentially lead to an impairment in the ability to provide the kind of help the patient needs.

In the decades leading up to the 1970s, many therapies were influenced by psychodynamic concepts (Kovel 1976). By the 1990s it can fairly be said that behavioral management techniques and psychopharmacology have usurped the place formerly held by psychodynamic psychotherapy. Although the field is still in its infancy, daunting advances in the neurosciences have rightly contributed to the increased value of the psychopharmacologist. Yet a troubling consequence has been the biologization of psychopathology as well. In its most extreme form, biological psychiatry can lead to reducing the individual to his neuronal system. This often leads to the fantasy that human nature need not be understood because there is a mechanistic solution to what is now seen as a mechanistic problem: too few or too many molecules of a neurotransmitter binding with this or that receptor.

As a result of fiscal screws tightening and managed care reviewers watching each patient's length of treatment, the pressure has increased to find rapid cures for symptoms. The unique biography of the patient is lost and a biological algorithm plays the central role in the treatment. The idea that a cure for major depression is ten outpatient sessions or five hospital days feels seductive not only to the case managers, but also to the one suffering from the symptoms. Who would want to suffer one extra day of depression? Why not just take fluoxetine (Prozac) or nortriptyline, or use a rubber band on the wrist as a thought-stopping reminder?

The wish for quick fixes, though understandable, can have a significant impact on the way the therapist views his or her task. Is the task to fix or to understand? How does the therapist help—through understanding or by reducing the most manifest behavioral symptoms? Through which method does the longest-lasting benefit ensue? The short-term treatment cures of which managed care proponents are so proud are in fact analogous to transference cures (see Beaumont, this volume). Recent evidence suggests that longer, open-ended treatments are of more lasting benefit to patients suffering from mental illnesses (*Consumer Reports* 1995, Lott 1997). Seligman (1995) notes that in the *Consumer Reports* study individuals did better in long-term treatments than short; when length of therapy and choice of therapist were limited by insurance or managed care, the outcome was worse. Despite fiscal pressures, these studies suggest it is imperative that dynamically based open-ended therapy remain a part of the field's armamentarium.

Most therapists who trained in long-term dynamic psychotherapeutic approaches would say that they continue to do this type of psychotherapy because this approach is useful and sometimes essential to the clinical situation. However, if therapists experience massive conflict between their training and the approaches fostered by the current environment, what will the outcome be? In his book, *The Wisdom of the Ego* (1995), Vaillant asserts that conflicts that engage the use of unconscious defense mechanisms arise from multiple sources. They can originate from our desires (or drives), from the commands of our conscience (our ego ideals, cultural taboos, or superego), from our interactions with people, and from the impact of other aspects of reality. Vaillant believes that the realities of the environment have an effect on who we are, and engage the need for psychic defenses. Writing more than forty-five years earlier, Erik Erikson was among the first to emphasize the extent to which our environment, our social milieu, has an impact on the meaning and value we attribute to things. In *Childhood and Society* he noted that the self is always defined within a social reality: an "individual['s] way of mastering experience . . . is a successful variant of a group identity and is in accord with its space-time and life plan" (1950, p. 235).

If a therapist becomes surrounded solely by a biological language, a focus on the external, an emphasis on symptoms, and a valuation of managing the patient rather than finding the balance between medications and empathic understanding, his identity as a dynamic therapist will likely become compromised. The desire to continue to be a therapist who specializes in the productions of the mind and the mind's effect on personality, cognition, and behavior in an environment that doesn't support that view will lead to conflict. Psychic defenses intervene to diminish the therapist's discomfort. By definition, these defenses act beyond the awareness of the individual. As such, they can change the way the therapist thinks about therapeutic work without that change being consciously noted. The employment of defenses can lead to situations in which the therapist believes he is acting in a dynamically informed, therapeutic way, without that being the case.

In health care delivery, third-party payers and managed care contracts have changed the milieu in which treatment takes place; as a result, the reality of the practice environment has changed. The therapist is frequently placed in a position in which his or her dynamic knowledge of the patient would lead in one direction of treatment, yet the culture and context increase the pressure for another form of treatment. In any such situation, defensive maneuvers will intervene when a conflict arises between internal beliefs and the expectations of the social milieu. While these defenses help the therapist feel less conflicted about the situations in which he or she works, they may at the same time compromise the therapeutic endeavor. As evidence begins to accumulate that open-ended and long-term psychotherapeutic treatments are benefiting patients, it becomes important to inquire whether the environment is making it increasingly difficult to maintain such a therapeutic stance.

A professional is an individual who has advanced study in a specialized field. Not only competent in the technical aspect of his field, he or she must also be able to make thoughtful recommendations based on the knowledge gained by advanced study and experience. When the professional loses authorization to make decisions about when to employ a treatment or a technique, he or she becomes a technician. A surgeon not only knows *how* to perform an appendectomy, he or she has the responsibility to think through the clinical situation and give a recommendation as to the conditions under which surgery is indicated. To perform surgery only when told to and to decline only when told not to relegates the surgeon to being an expert in a technique, not a professional. If the surgeon continues to be regarded by the patient and society as one authorized to act professionally, despite having tacitly accepted the limitations of being a technician, he or she is no longer acting responsibly. This change may occur slowly and insidiously. These shifts can take place outside the awareness of the individual and society when the changes are themselves solutions to conflictual situations.

Mental health professionals of all disciplines study and acquire knowledge. Some of this highly specialized knowledge overlaps various disciplines (nurses, psychologists, social workers, psychiatrists can all be therapists); however, separate professional roles create specific areas of expertise. With knowledge and expertise a professional is given a role and task that in turn requires responsible use of that knowledge and expertise. For example, such expertise is essential when first engaging a patient in treatment. As a therapist, to understand unconscious process and conflict is to be responsible for taking a patient's ambivalence about engaging in treatment into consideration. If the patient feels hostile to treatment, we must assess the reason. For example, the patient may be defending against fear, or feeling injured by the need for treatment. After this assessment, the task becomes finding a way to work with that ambivalence in order to allow the patient the best opportunity for help. Treatment decisions are of necessity informed and influenced by our knowledge, our formulation of the patient as a whole person, in whom the symptom functions as a sign.

## THE DEFENSES

In the remainder of this chapter, a number of defenses will be illustrated through brief clinical vignettes garnered from the experiences of therapists working in a variety of settings. These settings have been heavily influenced by managed care policies and practices. As one would expect, treatment decisions were affected by practices within the managed care environment. More significantly, however, the way the treater experienced and fulfilled his or her professional role was significantly affected, and often out of the immediate awareness of the clinician.

### Disavowal of Knowledge: Is the Professional Still a Professional?

In response to conflicts brought about by current economic pressures and managed care's intrusion into the therapeutic relationship, one common defense on the part of the therapist can be to disavow his knowledge. This leads to a compromise of the need for acting with responsibility. For example, due to third-party payer and HMO contracts, one acute inpatient unit received approximately 30 percent of its referrals from a single outpatient clinic. Numerous patients referred for hospitalization came with recommendations from their outpatient psychiatrists for electroconvulsive therapy (ECT), the end of the treatment trajectory within a biological paradigm—the main paradigm used by this clinic. One patient, Mr. A., who suffered from a narcissistic character, was causing too much trouble fighting with his high-achieving wife and daughters. He was referred for ECT even though he evinced no symptoms of major depression (with the exception of a chronic dysphoria), no symptoms of mania or psychosis—conditions for which ECT is indicated. Another patient, Ms. B., a passive-aggressive 20-year-old woman with the demeanor of an adolescent, lived with and was cared for by her older brother. She was referred for ECT after threatening to kill herself in her therapist's office. Once on the inpatient unit her affect appeared bright. She felt excited about a new procedure and her mood was not depressed. Yet she received ECT nonetheless. Because of limitations and incentives related to time and money (such as, for example, those that go with capitated contracts), there was little acknowledgment of transference or countertransference, no acknowledgment of the need to bring an individual's character into treatment. To do this would have required that more time be invested in the work. In this particular setting, only cognitive-behavioral and biological interventions were used because they are routinized and short courses of treatment.

In the above examples, the patients were suffering from character problems. They were frustrating the treaters, who had expectations of quicker fixes, and the situations were rife with countertransference hate. Both patients had become difficult to treat. ECT can become a quick, albeit perverse, sublimation of aggressive impulses on the part of the therapists who made the referral. The psychiatrist on the inpatient unit might have argued that ECT was not indicated and would not be administered, but in doing so she may have angered the referring clinic. This might have seriously risked the financial solvency of the unit. In addition, to speak against the ECT posed a risk to her job, as it would be easier for the medical director to replace one psychiatrist than to find another lucrative referral source. In a similar case one psychiatrist actually said, "The patient wants it. The outpatient psychiatrist wants it. There aren't any absolute contraindications. It won't help any, but *who am I to stop it?*" Implicit in this statement is a change in the psychiatrist's belief about her role in treatment. It is the difference between doing what she is told and acting on an independent clinical decision.

Here, this psychiatrist's difficulty arose from the conflict between the external reality and her ego ideal. According to her training (her ego ideal), it was inappropriate to perform an unnecessary procedure. Among other risks, ECT carries with it the risks associated with general anesthesia and seizures. In taking the course, "Who am I to stop this?" she loses her judgment about when to perform a procedure and when not to. The absence of contraindications combined with pressure from a referral source is not equivalent to an indication. The therapist, however, treats it as such. Consciously or unconsciously, the psychiatrist has rejected acting on the knowledge and expertise of her training, but is, rather, acting in the role of technician. She is *doing what is asked to be done.* The solution to the conflict is to eliminate the conscience, the superego, and ego ideal, and go with the demands of external reality. This path is less consciously conflictual. The psychiatrist does not need to think and ask, "Is this the right thing to do?" She simply does what she is told to do. This may preserve the relationship with the important outpatient clinic, and may preserve her job. In the process, however, she disavows her professional knowledge to avoid the conflict between her internal beliefs and pressure from the environment. The disavowal creates room to circumvent prohibitions against doing procedures she feels are unnecessary. By taking this course, ultimately, and without being aware of it, she actively participates in the trend toward deprofessionalization.

Mr. C., another patient, had made several suicide attempts over the course of the past several decades. He and his inpatient therapist soon realized that in his current life circumstances he was involved in the repetition of early relational experiences. Mr. C. wished to pursue a treatment that would allow him to understand these repetitions in greater depth so as to free himself of their grip. The inpatient psychiatrist referred him to a long-term treatment center that could focus on the dynamic issues. Since his managed care company covered only acute inpatient treatment, Mr. C. knew that he would have to pay privately for the treatment if he chose to pursue it, which he did. When Mr. C.'s spouse demanded that the HMO reimburse for the treatment, the HMO complained to the clinical director of the inpatient service, who then reprimanded the primary inpatient therapist for making the referral. The clinical director explained that no one could really know which treatment was best for any patient. She instructed the therapist not to give recommendations to patients unless the recommendations were within what the HMO provides. In other words, even if the patient could afford private treatment, it should not be recommended unless the HMO covered it. The reality of the managed care company's wish to avoid conflict with its patients led to an intrusion into the private arrangements of a patient and therapist. When asked how to respond when a patient seeks aftercare recommendations, the clinical director said it would be best to try something like telling the patient, "We suggest you deal with the issues that have come up for you during this hospitalization."

In the case of Mr. C., the clinical director, a psychologist and analyst, was not unfamiliar with unconscious process and the repetition compulsion. Her suggestion to tell patients they "somehow deal" with their issues contradicted her understanding of human nature and the nature of her role as a therapist. To tell patients simply that they should "deal" with their "issues" is to assume that they know *how* and *where* to deal with them. These assumptions contradicted the dictum that the repetition compulsion is a *compulsion*. The clinical director's mission to avoid losing a managed care contract (the external reality) conflicted with her knowledge and understanding of her professional role (her ego and her ego ideal). Her resolution to this conflict was the repression or disavowal of professional knowledge and of the awareness of her role requirements. One does not need to spend years in training, becoming a psychologist, psychiatrist, or social worker to tell patients that they need to "deal" with their "issues."

## Identification with the Aggressor:
## If You Can't Beat Them, Join Them

Disavowal or repression can be used to buttress the deeper and more primitive defense mechanism of identification with the aggressor. Its origins are similar to those of traumatic bonding (see Weisgerber, this volume). The managed care company, with its power to deny the therapist her needed economic security or survival by rescinding a contract, becomes the object of identification. The experience can fully resonate with the life-sustaining, loved and feared parents of childhood. As children do with their parents, "If you can't beat 'em, join 'em!"

In the case of Mr. C., the clinical director believed it was important that recommendations for treatment be withheld when they were for treatment the managed care company did not cover. She identified with the company she wanted to please. From the company's perspective, it was preferable that patients not hear anything that could bring them into conflict with their managed care insurance. The therapist too came to believe that the best solution was avoiding a situation of conflict between patient and insurance company because her unit's financial solvency was dependent on the contract with this company. In the case of identifying with the aggressor, the therapist took on the beliefs, goals, and standards of the company that funds her livelihood. In this identification, the ego ideal shifted without the awareness of the therapist.

### Dissociation: One Clinician with Two Funds of Knowledge?

In the case of Mr. C., another defensive strategy may be at work. When an individual can hold two contradictory beliefs, it is worth asking if there is a disconnection of associations that would otherwise lead the individual to notice the contradictions. This is the use of the defense of dissociation. Although popular in clinical writings on trauma, dissociation has also been described in lay terms. George Orwell (1949), in his book *1984*, describes a phenomenon he named "doublethink" that is relevant to the example above.

> Doublethink means the power of holding two contradictory beliefs in one's mind simultaneously, and accepting both of them. The [person] knows in which direction his memories must be altered; he therefore knows that he is playing tricks with reality; but by the exercise of doublethink he also satisfies himself that reality is not violated. The process has to be conscious, or it would not be carried out with sufficient precision, but it also has to be unconscious, or it would bring with it a feeling of falsity. [pp. 176–177]

Orwell speaks of doublethink as both a conscious and unconscious process. In the example under discussion there may be unconscious, preconscious, and conscious elements. The clinical director may rationalize that she keeps her two professional roles separate (private analyst versus salaried clinical director on inpatient unit) and to this extent she is conscious of what she does. She may not be aware that her analytic knowledge ought to have implications concerning the treatment recommendations she gives to patients, regardless of whether the patients are in the hospital or see her privately. To withhold comfortably certain treatment recommendations because the HMO doesn't provide that service, even when the individual can pay privately, is to actualize a disconnection between knowledge the psychiatrist values highly in one clinical situation and devalues in another.

### Rationalization: Is the Individual a Consumer or a Patient?

Another defensive maneuver involves the rationalization of changes in our use of language in mental health. Rationalization is "the procedure whereby the subject attempts to present an explanation that is either logically consistent or ethically acceptable for attitudes, actions, ideas, feelings, etc., whose true motives are not perceived" (Laplanche and Pontalis 1973, p. 375). In psychotherapy the term *consumer* came into fashionable use after the term *client*, which itself supplanted the term *patient*. Perhaps these linguistic changes were in response to the excesses of some who pathologized much of their patients' experience, and were attempts to create greater respect for the person. Yet alternative motives might also be at work. In the case of Ms. D., a 15-year-old Hispanic girl who arrived in the emergency room with her mother, we can see an example of this use of linguistic change. Until the previous day, mother and daughter had what was described as a very close and loving relationship. The daughter respected her mother and had always been eager to please her. The daughter said that she could not live without her mother's love. Apparently, on the previous day, the mother found the daughter with a wallet that did not belong to her. The daughter claimed she found it and intended to return it. The mother believed the daughter had stolen it. She hit her, repeatedly told her that she no longer loved her, and that she was no daughter of hers. The daughter took an overdose and came to the emergency room with the mother. After medical clearance, and separate discussions with the mother and daughter, several things became clear. The mother continued to reject the daughter. The daughter continued to say she needed her mother's love to live. Yet the daughter didn't want hospitalization and stated that she would not kill herself. The family had no insurance and the department of mental health refused to pay for admission. If the daughter was committed against her will, the hospital would have to pay the cost of the admission. As the admission would fill the last bed, patients from capitated contracts would have to be sent elsewhere at the hospital's expense. The clinician felt that since Ms. D., as a "consumer," said she didn't want hospitalization, he would let her go home.

In this particular complicated, enmeshed, mother–daughter relationship, simply trusting that the daughter would not overdose because she says that she would not has certain dangers. The clinician was under the pressure of fiscal realities to make a certain decision, that is, not to hospitalize her. In our current culture, referring to patients as "consumers" confers on them the autonomy to make decisions on their own. A consumer *decides* whether or not to use mental health services. What has not been said about this linguistic change is that the term *consumer* does not allow for unconscious motivations for declining to use mental health services. This girl may have feared even greater reprisal from her mother if she was hospitalized. Or she may have felt that if she were to tell the truth about a wish to kill herself, she would be prevented from following through. To take at face value what she says is to deny the capacity to formulate the case. In this situation, at the time of release from the emergency room, nothing apparent had changed in the constellation of circumstances that had led to the daughter's overdose. The mother was bent on punishment; the daughter insisted she could live only with her mother's love. She remained vulnerable to impulsive, suicidal acting-out. That she had no insurance and that the unit had only one vacancy led to a rationalized decision in which the girl's words were used to justify a convenient decision. Referring to her as a consumer was an intellectual manipulation that enabled the clinician to ignore the conflicts, defenses, and relational constellations that made up this girl's life in order to effect a decision most convenient for him and least costly for the hospital. Is she really a consumer, or is she a patient?

## Isolation of Affect, Distancing, and Intellectualization: Is the Treater Still a Therapist?

It is commonly felt that empathy, the placing of oneself, even momentarily, in the other's shoes, is a necessary but not sufficient condition for the therapeutic process. Standing in another's shoes is a guide for interventions that can further the therapeutic goal. Empathy allows the therapist to know whether the verbal intervention will reach the patient or fall, so to speak, on deaf ears. Isolation of affect, distancing, and intellectualization may all be defensive maneuvers that are necessary at times for the therapist's psychic survival in the therapeutic encounter; yet they also at times impair the therapist's capacity to be empathic and function effectively. I will draw on my own past experience here to illustrate the unwitting use and consequences of these defenses.

> After changing employment from a treatment unit that did very little managed care work to a short-term locked inpatient unit whose patient population was predominantly served by managed care, I noticed changes within myself. In the first facility, the difficult work seemed possible because the therapist was encouraged and supported by the milieu in making an empathic connection with the "person in the patient" (Havens 1993). However, in the second facility, in the environment of a high turnover of very ill patients who were barely changed at discharge, an inherent pressure to avoid empathic connection developed. Immediately after the transition to the new unit, I spent one and a half hours or longer with each new patient, trying to get a thorough understanding of the dynamics and finding a connection with him or her. This helped greatly in the work. I noticed, though, that others treated the patients in a different way. After I spent some time with Mr. E., a depressed man, I realized that I was having a difficult time trying to understand his internal experience. Unlike some who feel relief that someone can listen to what they have to say, he felt relief in someone's presence but could not articulate what he was thinking and feeling. All that was clear was that he met the cri-

teria for major depression. It was somehow difficult to get hold
of his unique experience. After trying to understand what he
was experiencing, I suggested that he try, over the next twenty-
four hours, to put his experience into words. The next day he
said he realized that he felt something he had never felt before, that his "soul" had been "stolen." He went on to recount
that he shared this in the previous day's hospital group only to
be corrected by the leader: "Now I wouldn't put it that way,
another way to think of it is . . . things haven't gone your way
lately." The leader may have been trying to restructure his cognitions, but the consequence was that she distanced herself and
others in the group from the profundity of this man's statement.
Her rewording conveyed less affect than the words that Mr. E.
himself had chosen and in her rewording the uniqueness of his
experience was lost.

I soon realized why Mr. E. had been corrected. Over time,
I found myself deeply saddened as I left at the end of the day. I
now recognize I was identifying with the hopelessness and helplessness of the patients, unable to provide for them in any meaningful way in four to six days. Before being aware of the changes,
I began shutting down; each person became another "admission." I, too, began looking only on the surface. I saw the symptoms and the medication choices. The goal became how to help
with the external symptoms and how to facilitate discharge. In
retrospect, I realize I had changed. I avoided too much of a connection, and went home at the end of the day less distressed. This
change in myself most likely left the patients feeling more alone
and less understood. When I noticed what had been happening,
it seemed disturbing that I could shut off and treat human interactions in a relatively impersonal way. While I didn't say to a
patient, "I wouldn't put it like that," I also did not pursue an understanding of the internal experience of the individual. In retrospect, I distanced myself from patients' experiences. I used an
intellectual manipulation, simplifying the individual into a uni-
dimensional being, in order to help with the distancing. I could
fulfill my role as psychiatrist without feeling very much about
what I was doing—essentially, an isolation of my own affect.

In summary, these defenses against empathic contact (isolation of affect, distancing, and intellectualization) intervene to allow the preservation of the therapist and to save the therapist from psychic distress. As psychotherapy becomes more and more difficult to provide, utilization of defensive maneuvers becomes commonplace. Creating and using dynamic formulations becomes increasingly impossible as there are fewer and fewer internal data about each patient. Rather than trying to stay with the individual's experience, managerial solutions to the patient's problems pop into mind. The question left to be answered is: After closing off in such a way, is the treater still a therapist?

Defenses, by definition, are employed beyond the awareness of the individual. For the therapist in the clinical situation, the involuntary use of defenses preserves the equilibrium. In these examples, therapists needed to defend against conflicts brought about by milieu demands that oppose internalized therapeutic standards. The solutions worked for the individual situations. The new equilibrium, however, is bought at a price: the capacity to function therapeutically. The tree that grew in fertile soil, managed care, effected change in the ecosystem. The therapist who no longer gives professional recommendations, because of the managed care company's expectations, will stop thinking about what those recommendations might have been. The therapist who repeatedly calls a patient a "consumer" in order to make a less complicated decision will forget over time that the patient has an internal world. He or she will forget that it is useful to pay attention to this internal world and will forget how to engage it in treatment. The psychiatrist who provides ECT simply because it is requested gives up his or her professional role. In all of these examples, and in practice as it is now unfolding, when the therapist changes what he says or does in response to environmental pressures, a profound change also begins happening internally. The lesson to be learned is that, for most of us, the preservation of one's beliefs in a particular kind of treatment becomes the victim of a greater need: to live within a social milieu, to look for calm seas, and never to rock the boat.

## REFERENCES

*Consumer Reports.* (1995). Mental health: Does therapy help? November, pp. 734–739.

Erikson, E. H. (1950). *Childhood and Society.* New York: Norton, 1963.

Havens, L. (1993). *Coming to Life.* Cambridge, MA: Harvard University Press.

Kovel, J. (1976). *A Complete Guide to Therapy.* New York: Pantheon.

Laplanche, J., and Pontalis, J. B. (1973). *The Language of Psychoanalysis.* New York: Norton.

Lott, D. A. (1997). Making the case for long term psychodynamic psychotherapy. *Psychiatric Times,* September, pp. 14, 78.

Orwell, G. (1949). *1984.* New York: New American Library.

Seligman, M. E. (1995). The effectiveness of psychotherapy: the *Consumer Reports* study. *American Psychologist* 50:965–974.

Vaillant, G. E., (1995). *The Wisdom of the Ego.* Cambridge MA: Harvard University Press.

**3**

---

# The Refusal to Feel

CYNTHIA MITCHELL

"Vehicle: Insecurity"

The way the voice always, always gives it away, even when you
    weren't aware yourself you felt it,
the tightness in the middle range, the hollow hoarseness lower
    toward the heart that chips, abrades,
shoves against the hindpart of the throat, then takes the throat,
    then takes the voice as well,
as though you'd lost possession of the throat and then the voice
    or what it is that wills the voice
to carry thoughtlessly the thought through tone and word, and
    then the thoughts themselves are lost
and the mind that thought the thoughts begins to lose itself, de-
    spairing of itself and of its voice,
this infected voice that infects itself with its despair, this voice of
    terror that won't stop,
that lays the trap of doubt, this pit of doubt, this voiceless throat
    that swallows us in doubt.

—C. K. Williams, 1987

In a clinical conference, a therapist presented her work with a 36-year-old single woman, the mother of five children, aged 7 to 19. The woman, diagnosed with a major mental illness and posttraumatic stress disorder, had worked with the therapist in weekly sessions for seven years. During this period she had been hospitalized several times for depression. After hearing the summary of the treatment and the patient's progress in managing her suicidal wishes, the consultant responded abruptly, as if he had been listening to a foreign language. Operating from a managed care perspective, he spoke, with disdain and disbelief. He said, "You mean you think the treatment is about the relationship?"

The therapist lost her voice. She said, "Yes," but then she—usually an outspoken member of the staff—said nothing. It was as if the careful weaving of seven years of work had been undone in one sentence. Later, in supervision, she spoke of feeling erased and negated, and concluded: "I don't belong here. I need a new job." In the case conference she had suppressed her feelings and been unable to speak because she felt there was no one who would hear or understand what she had to say. Her very language and way of articulating experience was no longer valued. Her experience affected her patient. The therapist, losing her voice, felt dislocated, as if she weren't in her right place. Her patient felt the change. As the therapist withdrew, closing herself off, the patient began to feel "lost." In her effort to get her therapist back in familiar contact with her, the patient began talking about her wishes to die. Thus the change in the therapist's experience had a profound impact on her patient.

By questioning the importance of the therapeutic relationship, the consultant had challenged this therapist's beliefs about therapeutic change. In response, the therapist felt alienated and helpless. She did not look for another job. She began a process of rationalizing, of believing it is possible to be separate, to work in the managed care environment and to hold different, private views. She resolved to take managed care cases and to continue to be present, empathic, and curious with her patients. Months later she realized that she was now surrounded by the language of managed care and that this language had influenced her.

Despite her resolve to remain flexible and to continue to work according to her own standards and values, she noticed that her work had been subtly changed by the managed care environment in which she practiced. In the treatment of an 8-year-old boy who disclosed sexual abuse by a neighbor, the same clinician found herself focusing on the end of treatment rather than on the process, as she had been accustomed to doing. She said: "I was working in a 'fast as you can get them through' manner. I felt I had to go for the facts, so I spent less time on the boy's feelings than I would have." In the past, and left to her own devices, she might have thought more about the relationship that might develop and be of use to her patient, and more about the feelings her questions might have stirred in the boy and how he would be able to bear them. For this clinician, the shift from an emphasis on the therapy relationship and treatment process toward an emphasis on "treatment goals" occurred so gradually that she was shocked to see the way her own actions and values had been transformed.

This example illustrates several changes that have occurred as psychotherapists have been affected by and responded to managed care. These changes include the different values placed on the therapeutic relationship, on the sense of time, and on the view of the therapist-self, as well as the therapist's decision to suppress or limit her own feelings in order to proceed in the new environment. This chapter will address some of these changes in more detail, drawing on comments from other psychotherapists that illustrate their reactions and the methods used to manage, assimilate, and defend against the changes in the mental health environment.

Managed care, while not a theoretical model for therapy, involves an understanding of the nature of reality and the nature of change that differs from that held by many psychotherapists, particularly those practicing within humanistic or psychodynamic models. The following comments from one psychotherapist portray this difference vividly: "My work involves creativity—it's organic, elliptical, poetic. It is based on the interior, on the imagination, on terror, anxiety, control, and mastery and on the usefulness of language to create something more useful. Managed care isn't asking *how* we work with the terror of another human being; managed care is asking for outcome measures." While clinicians operating from a psychodynamic perspective may assume that change occurs internally, in the view of managed care change is visible and can be quantified in external behaviors and observable goals. This is a crucial difference regarding the nature of change.

Another important difference involves the understanding of time. The managed care model views therapy as happening at a different frequency, duration, and intensity than do psychodynamic models of therapy. As one clinician commented: "They want us to do it faster and furthermore they want to know why we need the sessions we have requested. My pride was hurt because I thought I was a pretty good, responsible clinician and I thought if I said [to a managed care reviewer] a patient needed something, I should be taken seriously."

The experiences of individual psychotherapists in response to the managed care environment are varied and complex. Some clinicians wonder how it is possible to do good and helpful work, work that is not assaultive, depriving, abandoning, or repeating the pain of the person's life. Other therapists feel pressured by limited sessions to learn very quickly about the patient's experience, what gets repeated and replayed, what it is that feels not in control or not free. And then these therapists wonder how it is possible to offer a new experience to their patients. (It is likely that similar concerns have often worried therapists and that the demands of managed care bring these questions to the surface once again.) Other therapists have adopted short-term skills and value those skills. Still others feel seduced to comply with managed care, because compliance is promoted as the only way to keep one's practice. Perhaps this link to economic survival, whether real or imagined, is one reason therapists report changes within themselves that they did not intend. One such unintended change occurs as clinicians get lulled into speaking a new language, and then find they have gradually accepted restrictions that once incensed them.

## THE LOSS OF LANGUAGE

My original language is psychodynamic. For me this is a language of meaning, one that expands what it is possible to think, to understand, and to feel. This language is not something I learned primarily in graduate school. It is a language I learned internally, a part of myself that I then studied when I found it in the world. It is a language that speaks of affect and has the ability to evoke affect. Recently, I was struck by a colleague's comment: "Nobody talks about affect anymore." How has this happened? And what has happened? A significant loss is involved in changing one's clinical language. In my view, affective experience is essential to psychotherapeutic work, central to the patient's experience and to the therapist's experience of the patient. The psychotherapist's capacity to feel and to help patients identify feelings and articulate experiences is diminished by losses in the language and by the shaping of a new discourse. Certain words and associated meanings have been dropped from the clinical language. It has become rare, for instance, to hear clinicians speak of "attachment," "deprivation," or "loss."

Rather than a connection between the language spoken in clinical meetings and affective experience, there is a disconnection. Words that emphasize the meaning and history of relationships both intrapsychically and externally are used less frequently. The word *structure* is frequently heard, where once *connection* and *relationship* were useful words. The language of dynamics, systems, and personal experience has been eclipsed by the pressure to translate emotional experience and internal experience into behaviors. Clinical attention is focused less on the experience of depression and more toward the behaviors and symptoms—for example, the hours slept or not slept— as if it were important to "prove" depression. Thus there has been a shift in language, one that translates internal experience into behaviors or actions. When the focus is on action alone, the integration of intention and action and the integration of subjective perception and behavior are lost.

Language now focuses on economics as well as on symptoms. Patients' needs are quickly translated into dollars, and then, over time, clinicians begin to speak a language of dollars. To justify continuing with individual treatment, for example, therapists write, "Weekly psychotherapy [i.e., less costly] will prevent psychiatric hospitalization [i.e., expensive]." That is, weekly psychotherapy needs to be justified and the argument is economic. It will save insurers money because it will prevent future admissions. The emphasis is now less frequently on helping patients find language for expressing their internal experience and more often on connecting them with resources in the external world. As one therapist explained: "The language of therapy is being lost. The language of business is being superimposed on the language of therapy. It's not just learning a different language, the language of our work is being lost. You can't use words like 'countertransference.' Even 'transference' is . . . liberal."

In an autobiographical work entitled, *Lost in Translation*, Eva Hoffman (1989) describes the way words in English, her new and second language, could not evoke her past experience or history the way words in her native Polish could. She writes: "The words I learn now don't stand for things in the same unquestioned way they did in my native tongue. 'River' in Polish was a vital sound, energized with the essence of riverhood, of my rivers, of my being immersed in rivers. 'River' in English. . . . has no accumulated meaning for me, and it does not give off the radiating haze of connotation. It does not evoke" (p. 106).

Hoffman's experience is similar to the experience of clinicians trying to adopt and work in a language not their own. Using a set of words neither able to evoke familiar affects nor intrinsic to the sense of meaning the clinician holds creates a sense of unreality or numbness. . . . "it does not give off the radiating haze of connotation." If clinicians cannot use their authentic voices, they do not have as great an access to their feelings. And, in a circular way, if clinicians feel separated from their feelings, it is difficult to speak with authentic voices or to help their patients find their own voices. It seems likely then that clinicians, by not speaking in authentic voices, model for their patients a language of dissociation, denial, and suppression. Or are they still able to speak a language of affect with their patients? It appears that managed care has affected not only what clinicians say about their work but what they actually do.

## THE SHAPING OF DISCOURSE

Old languages are being lost and a new discourse is being shaped. Where there was once a mix of languages and perspectives—cognitive, behavioral, dynamic, humanistic, gestalt—now there is a single way to look at a case—the way that will conform to and satisfy the needs of insurance providers. When therapists have only one language, they lose opportunities to be enriched by the views, perspectives, and theories of others. Jean Baker Miller (1976) writes that people tend to internalize dominant beliefs alongside their own concepts and that tension between the two sets of concepts is almost inevitable. However, keeping more than one language in a hidden or secretive way creates more than tension. It creates a kind of dissociative phenomenon, like splitting, which is a perversion of the therapist and of the therapy itself.

Miller (1976) states: "If a large part of your fate depends on accommodating to and pleasing the dominants, you concentrate on them" (p. 11). She further states, "It is not surprising then that a subordinate group resorts to disguised and indirect ways of acting and reacting" (p. 10). Therapists reported such disguised and indirect styles of reacting. They described speaking different languages in different contexts—speaking one language for insurance case managers, another for staff meetings, and a third with patients. In this way, by working in parallel languages, clinicians preserve their particular clinical language while adapting to the language preferred by insurance providers. Unfortunately, the effort to keep more than one language is often unsuccessful, and much of the former language of therapy is being lost. The two languages do not translate easily from one to the other, and there is a level of deception. As Renik (1992) explains, speaking of fetishism, "A final judgment between two contradictory ideas is never made: at times one holds sway, and at times the other, with equal power" (p. 549).

Weingarten (1994) considers the notion of authentic voice and wonders whether one could come to know and share oneself "without the crucial condition that you are felt well listened to and supported by others" (p. 10). She continues: "The shift from the idea of authentic voice to the idea that voice depends on who listens to it has been central to me. It has turned my attention away from voice itself to the contexts in which voice is produced. It has made me deeply interested in conditions that are related to voice" (p. 10).

Some insurance providers support, encourage, and shape a mono-discursive view. Where once we heard different theories and the languages of these theories, now one language of goals and symptoms is predominant in mental health settings. Weingarten (1994) writes, "In any culture, some ideas and values become dominant, forcing alternative ideas and values to the margins, or underground" (p. 16). She explains that people whose feelings conflict with the dominant ones may feel awkward expressing themselves and may be silent for fear that what they say will be dismissed or denigrated. In staff meetings therapists notice or hear themselves apologizing for presenting a theoretical position, aware that theory is not welcome in the current climate. The therapists' need for a receptive context in which to speak and the therapists' need for acknowledgment and regard are critical. Moreover, therapists experience conflicts over speaking a particular way in order to fit a particular context.

The loss of language and loss of voice are significant for both patient and therapist for they lead to a sense of marginalization and invalidation. As the following example illustrates, dissociation is one reaction clinicians have when they expect that their view of the treatment will be disregarded: "I zone out on what the patient is really saying and refuse to be in his shoes [and feel his experience] because I get so mad at him because he's going to get me in a conflict with my supervisor [over the need for treatment and frequency of sessions], and then I feel helpless and don't even want to do this job." This clinician would rather not hear and feel what the patient is saying. She finds it impossible to be with only her patient. Instead, thoughts about how she will have to defend herself and her clinical decisions to her supervisor fill her mind. She feels pulled between two forces—the desire to help her patient and the desire to avoid conflict with her supervisor. She feels uncertain about where her energy should be spent. Without a receptive context in which to talk about this conflict, the therapist is more likely to withdraw her attention and empathy from her patients and from herself. She wants to close up and quit, rather than feel the conflict and helplessness her situation engenders.

Clinicians are also instructed to speak to managed care reviewers in the language the reviewers want to hear. For instance, a clinic director advised his staff about their interactions with the case reviewers at a particular HMO. He told them: "Don't talk trauma when you talk to that HMO. They don't want to hear about trauma, they want to hear the patient is out of catastrophic care and needing fewer sessions." In another example, the representative from an HMO met with a group of clinicians, potential providers for that HMO, and questioned them in a group setting. Clinicians who respond in the language of the HMO were rewarded with a copy of *DSM-IV*. In this way language is shaped and individual views are suppressed. According to Weingarten (1994), "Ideas become dominant not just because some words are used more often than others, but because we use words to generate meanings among ourselves, and these meanings become part of our social world" (p. 22).

Health maintenance organizations and insurers are generating meanings, and through their power to fund or deny access to services they are altering how the culture views mental health care. Describing the contributions of Benjamin Whorf, Chase (1956) writes "that the structure of the language one habitually uses influences the manner in which one understands his environment. . . . Speakers of different languages see the Cosmos differently, evaluate it differently, sometimes not by much, sometimes widely" (p. x). Under the influence of managed care, clinicians are asked to write treatment plans differently in order to conform with policies of insurance companies. Initially, changes in how to write notes and how to adopt a symptom-oriented formulation seemed easy to do—perhaps annoying but not harmful. Later, therapists reported "waking up" to see that their thinking had shifted and to recognize the ways they had participated in making the change. While the new treatment plans may be clearer, more organized and consistent, they require the clinician to stop writing formulations that locate the problem in the patient's history, in the patient's conflicts, or as a reaction to recent loss. Some therapists feel they are in the awkward position of writing against their own theories. One can imagine the clinician writing in one language while thinking and experiencing his or her work in another, or, more troubling, that the clinician is experiencing a dissociation or dislocation from his or her own theory and context. Furthermore, after a number of case conferences in which a clinician is criticized for using words no longer acceptable or in fashion, that clinician may stop thinking in those terms, even privately.

This phenomenon did not originate with managed care. Years ago, clinicians stopped using the word *supportive* to obtain approval from Medicaid, because Medicaid did not fund supportive therapy. Yet this alteration was minimal; it did not challenge or undermine the theories on which psychotherapeutic work is based. It is noteworthy that there have been other times when psychotherapists felt stifled by outside factors. At one time therapists felt unable to dissent or to speak their true feelings in hospitals or psychoanalytic institutes because they believed that, by speaking out, they would jeopardize their source of patient referrals. In mental health, as in many other areas, there is a history of an identified "outside" that suppresses the "inside." One might wonder what it is about managed care that made therapists vulnerable or that led them, to some degree, to abandon long-held ways of thinking and speaking about their work.

It is possible for some therapists to be optimistic, positive, and bilingual—that is, to speak the new language along with their original language. Yet many therapists who are resilient people, accustomed to making accommodations all the time, find it difficult to make the change or even to become bilingual. Perhaps it is because the heart of the work for many clinicians is the emotional richness of the process, and this richness of experience is being moved aside or neglected.

## THE THERAPIST'S AFFECT

Changes in language and losses of language are linked to the therapist's experience of affect—to the avoidance of feeling and to experiences of withdrawal, dissociation, polarization, and anger in response to the demands of managed care. One clinician describes the polarization that can occur: "I feel defensive, in a deadlock, that's the way managed care companies want it—there's not a negotiation, the sides have split apart. You get into a polarized position, or you try to participate by refusing to feel." In this model of polarization, working with managed care insurers becomes an adversarial process. Clinicians who adopt this view see themselves as victims pitted against managed care, the oppressor. Clinicians also perpetuate the polarization, in part because they lack a model that respects and values their need to retain their own voices while participating in the managed care environment.

In response to a sense of frustration and helplessness, another clinician stated: "We have to be insanely optimistic. It's insanely optimistic to think you can do anything therapeutic under these time constraints. Everybody works from the heart here, but everyone is angry because nobody has the time." Unable to do what is required by one's individual professional standards, clinicians are left feeling frustrated, helpless, and angry. Another clinician points to the parallel experience of denial by patients and clinicians under managed care. He stated: "I can't feel my feelings, because my job involves telling my patients not to feel theirs. I am supporting the patient's denial, saying directly or indirectly, 'Don't say that, don't feel that.'" There is a tension repeated in many of the clinicians' comments between closing down affect and opening it up.

Many clinicians resolve to focus on the work with the patient in the room and not on the bureaucracy of the hospital or clinic or insurer. This may work to manage a sense of helplessness, but these clinicians then avoid clinical team discussions and lose the support they once received from other clinicians. The clinicians become isolated, and they do not get involved in making policy changes that might alleviate the pressures they experience. Other therapists who once viewed themselves as talented human beings now view themselves as quantified parts of a financial plan. They experience simultaneously both despair and the wish to continue to practice and to be useful to their patients.

The perceived lack of validation for the therapist and his or her way of working can lead to the minimization of feelings on the part of the therapist, as portrayed in the following example. A clinician working on an inpatient unit for children was worried about a 7-year-old patient. Pressured by limited hours in her day and by the number of new admissions, the clinician was aware that she had been neglecting this particular child. The clinician shared her concerns with the unit director, who said: "We've all neglected that child; the school said she always looked neglected. She's the kind of kid who makes people feel they neglect her." There was no discussion of the clinician's feelings. The problem was attributed to the child. This appears to be a new way of pathologizing the patient, similiar to the way some therapists disown their difficulties making progress with a patient by saying "the patient is borderline." In this case example, the problem of limited resources and limited time was shifted back to the patient. At the same time, the problem that existed in the relationship between patient and therapist was externalized to the patient so that the staff was "not responsible." The predicament of how or why the staff was contributing to the child's sense of being neglected, or even why the child might need to feel neglected, was left unexamined. It was as if someone had said, "Don't worry about neglecting her, don't worry about your relationship, don't feel anything about it." The lack of recognition of her feelings and concerns encouraged the clinician to put away her feelings, her worries, and her curiosity.

In various ways, therapists may shut off their feelings, attribute them to someone else, or fail to hear them in their patients. Refusing to understand and recognize one's own feelings can lead to therapist enactments and can lead therapists to stop noticing areas of difficulty. Not identifying and acknowledging one's own feelings can feed the therapist's blindness. For example, a particular patient makes a therapist furious; however because there are only five more allotted sessions, the therapist may not stop to reflect on how his feelings or rage are informing the treatment. The therapist's feelings are an important tool or indicator. To keep oneself out of the process, to lose contact with one's feelings, is a great loss to the patient.

The difficulties in identifying and using emotional experience exist not only for therapists; they also significantly affect patients. When therapists do not have time for their own feelings, the impact on their patients is profound. A therapist spoke in a hospital meeting: "I can't remember the last time I said, 'This kid's making me really sad. . . .' I find it awful, I work with very bright kids in their twenties, very ill, and I don't talk about the way it affects me. . . . I don't feel my own emotional responses and then I don't use them. I am working not to get involved instead of trying to learn how to get involved, as I would if the length of stay here was more open-ended." Something is lost. Other staff concur and emphasize the need to control affect (their own and their patients') so the patients can leave the hospital rather than address the depth of the problem. Again the emphasis is on closing down feelings rather than opening them, as the following statement illustrates: "The focus is on the control of kids. It's a soldering, instead of a healing, it burns off, it stops there, but the cause of the problem is not addressed." Instead, clinicians feel pressured to move on to the next case, and, in a parallel process, solder off their own feelings. They don't address them and sometimes they don't even identify them.

In other instances therapists may quickly name the patient's affective experience, and may then foreclose the patient's experience of feelings. This can happen when the therapist, uncomfortable with the patient's feelings, "gives words too soon." In these instances the therapist frames or labels the patient's experience before the patient has the opportunity to feel and identify the feelings. For example, a therapist quickly responds to a patient's painful memory, saying, "You're feeling sad," making the comment perhaps ten minutes before the patient would have realized it on his own. In subtle ways the therapist has shifted into a different gear and cannot follow his or her own intuition about a patient. As a result, instead of expanding, opening, and learning more about the patient's memory and current experience, the therapist's comment forecloses the possibility of a new experience and a new feeling for the patient. When there is a blocking or avoiding of the therapist's affect, it limits the patient's awareness of his or her emotional response. If the therapist is avoiding his or her own affect, his or her capacity to listen and be receptive to the affect of the patient is diminished. The space created between patient and therapist and what is permitted, accepted, or invited into that space is changed and constricted.

In the face of a new culture and new language, it is not surprising that, a number of therapists report struggles with authenticity. Clinicians are losing contact with their work and with their feelings, and they are beginning to take on the dominant view, the view of insurance providers, which frequently regards psychotherapists as inconsequential and interchangeable (or perhaps as necessary to see the patients, but at the same time potentially threatening to the economic bottom line). Other clinicians are hypervigilant about their work and worried about their own integrity. They doubt whether as therapists they are doing anything helpful. These doubts are painful. As some clinicians state, there is no time for them to have doubts. As described above, individual therapists have different ways of managing their uncertainty and discomfort.

## THE THERAPEUTIC RELATIONSHIP

The treatment relationship is now influenced by the development of a new relationship—the relationship with the insurance company. As one clinician commented, "The importance of the relationship with the patient has been eclipsed by the importance of the relationship with the managed care company. You are supposed to be using your self with the patient, but now you are using your self, your charm, charisma, intelligence, and interpretative skills to get one more day of inpatient coverage." There is pressure to court managed care companies, to get on panels, and to get referrals. Once the therapist has the referrals, there is pressure to further court managed care groups to get more referrals. One strategy is to complete the therapy in fewer than the number of sessions authorized. Some companies review each clinician's record each year. It has become a business of counting and outcomes.

The relationship with the insurer can also be used by clinicians in ways that are not therapeutic. One clinician recognized that his discomfort with a particular patient led him to use the insurance-recommended limit on sessions as a reason to end a patient's treatment. The clinician then found himself in the position of deciding who is expendable and who is not, weighing one patient's needs against another's. Thus patients are managed against one another, as therapists decide whom to "go to bat for" with the insurance company and whether a request for more sessions will jeopardize the therapist's standing with the insurance company and his or her source of future referrals.

Some therapists find themselves withdrawing from the therapeutic relationship in response to insurance providers who approve monthly sessions. A psychologist, given six sessions to treat a patient over a six-month period, noticed that he, the therapist, was emotionally leaving the treatment. He was creating distance in the relationship, and found himself talking about a referral to group and about a medication consult, not because these referrals were warranted, but because the therapist felt unable to help the patient himself in six monthly meetings. He wanted to "fill the patient" with other things to assuage his guilt that he could not do more. When presented with limited sessions or sessions at monthly intervals, therapists move away from focusing attention on the relationship in the room and move toward "outside" programs, such as Alcoholics Anonymous, Overeaters Anonymous, or parenting groups. A pattern emerges in which therapists find it hard to make the necessary commitment to the patient, then withdraw and use distance to cope with the changes. Then, therapists' feelings about their level of commitment evolve to guilt about the distance, to difficulty feeling effective in dealing with insurers and the patient, and finally to a sense of helplessness.

Scarf (1996) points to the confusion of relationships in which therapists find themselves. She asks whether it is possible to know "whom the clinician is actually working for—the patient? The HMO? The fee-for-service insurer? The employer-owned group insurance plan?" (p. 38). These questions point to the struggles with autonomy and helplessness that clinicians are confronting. Do they feel able to make their own choices in the room with the patient or do they feel constrained? Do they see themselves as victims of the managed care policies? If so, do they try to "trick" their oppressors? Is managed care "the devil we know"? How have we become trapped in one premise—that we can survive only through our association with managed care providers?

Treatment outcomes are emphasized without acknowledging that it is the relationship between therapist and patient that promotes the desired outcomes. This devalues the therapist and makes the particular therapist expendable. He or she may feel the relationship is jeopardized, interfered with, or undermined by a variety of factors. The therapist doesn't know how long the insurer will approve the treatment. Should he or she get close to the patient when treatment may have to stop in the middle of the process? Directly or indirectly, therapists are also communicating to their patients about our new policies and new language. For example, when I fill out an insurance form with my patient, a 16-year-old girl with a two-year history of bulimia, she reads what I have written and says: "You're hamming up my problems." Therapists also introduce information (so many sessions left, etc.) that they do not control, and that has an impact on them, on their therapeutic stance, and on their sense of self, such that both therapist and patient are being affected by the external facts of managed care insurance.

How do the new demands of the clinical environment interfere with the therapist's feelings, with being able to experience them and use them? What happens when clinicians feel expendable, hopeless, and disillusioned because the therapy relationship is no longer viewed as central? The importance of the treatment relationship is not just for the patients. The relationship is crucial for psychotherapists as well. It is the way they get involved, the way they work.

## WHO ABSORBS THE COST OF CARING?

Therapists make independent choices within the mental health systems in which they work. But this has costs. Therapists may feel they are going out on a limb for a particular patient, and the hospital's response to "too much caring" is that there's something wrong with them. As one clinician explained, "To do the job the way you feel comfortable means doing longer hours, getting to know the child, and getting connected." That is, clinicians who view the relationship as the vehicle through which change occurs choose to take time to develop the relationship. They do this on their own time and without reimbursement. She continues, "This is not expected anymore, so you can't report true hours or a patient's true mental status. Then, because you don't, there is a discrepancy—the paper trail 'proves' something different from what is actually happening." That is, the gains made for a particular patient were not made in the amount of time noted in the record and were not made in the time allotted by the managed care insurer. The gains required additional time supplied by clinicians beyond job requirements and at their own expense. Yet, on paper and in the medical record, managed care seems to have worked efficiently.

Who absorbs the cost of care? Of caring? Individual clinicians do, and this is one reason clinicians in hospital and mental health settings are under considerable stress. One unit director says to his social work staff, "You are all burning out because you are insisting on doing your job like you used to do your job." One staff member writes very long notes, preserving herself, her language, and her perspective in that way, though it makes the rest of her job more stressful. She is told to write shorter notes, while another staff member is told to stop coming in on her day off.

## THE TRAUMA OF THE THERAPIST

Managed care has introduced a language and an understanding of the nature of change that differs from that of many psychotherapists. The language, which values external, quantifiable goals, does not acknowledge psychodynamic views of the therapeutic relationship, of time, or of the therapists' experiences of self and affect. The reaction of some therapists can be understood using a trauma model. Changes in language have led to changes in value and meaning. In response, these therapists describe loss of feeling, numbing, dissociation, decreased sense of self-worth, and loss of voice. Therapists note a gradual shift to managed care models for treatment, a shift that has altered their former ways of thinking. These therapists struggle to retain an authentic voice and to secure their therapist-self. To do this they need to be able to listen to their own feelings and to use them. However, for some, feelings are blocked or suppressed.

The loss of language and voice has serious repercussions for patients. When a therapist "zones out" or feels helpless, the patient reacts. He may get louder to draw the therapist back. He may feel more hopeless and regress. Will the therapist, struggling with his or her own reactions to the changing environment, recognize the changes in the patient? Will the therapist be able to protect and preserve the therapeutic space for patient and therapist? The therapist needs a context and a responsive space in which to work so that he or she can provide an attentive, responsive, listening space in which the patient can work. When the therapist is not able to experience his or her own feelings, the patient's ability to know and express feelings is limited. The defensive responses of numbing, minimizing, denying, or refusing to feel, while protective of the therapist, undermine the process of therapy for the patient. These patterns inadvertently provide for patients a model of not feeling, of limiting the expression of feelings, and of denying one's authentic voice.

## REFERENCES

Chase, S. (1956). Foreword. In *Language, Thought, and Reality: Selected Writings of Benjamin Lee Whorf,* ed. J. B. Carroll, p. x. Boston: MIT Press, 1995.
Hoffman, E. (1989). *Lost In Translation.* New York: Penguin.
Miller, J. B. (1976). *Toward A New Psychology of Women.* Boston: Beacon.
Renik, O. (1992). Use of the analyst as a fetish. *Psychoanalytic Quarterly* 61:542–563.
Scarf, M. (1996). Keeping secrets. *New York Times Magazine,* June 16, pp. 38–41.
Weingarten, K. (1994). *The Mother's Voice: Strengthening Intimacy in Families.* New York: Harcourt Brace.
Williams, C. K. (1987). *Flesh and Blood.* New York: Farrar, Straus, and Giroux.

# 4

# The Crowded Imagination

CYNTHIA MITCHELL AND IVERS BEVER

As we began to explore how managed care has altered our clinical work, we considered two broad perspectives on psychotherapy. One involves imagination, psychic reality, intuition, contemplation, and a sense of time that is infinite. This is an internal-exploratory view, which draws on language and the introspective exploration of emotion and behavior. The other perspective is an external-observational view. It considers diagnosis, symptoms, concrete behaviors, and a sense of time that is finite. From the observational view, therapy focuses on changing target behaviors, often with little verbal mediation and minimal exploration of the meanings of experience. While in our own training as psychotherapists we studied both, it seemed as if the observational perspective rested upon the introspective. It was from an understanding of the patient's psychic reality that the symptoms and diagnosis made sense. The two perspectives were not in opposition, nor did one replace the other. Instead they were complementary, with varying emphases on the internal and external aspects depending on the patient's psychopathology and the individual theoretical inclinations of therapists.

In practice today, the external-observational perspective threatens to replace the internal-exploratory view. While the two work together to help individual patients, it is the external view that is promoted and requested by managed care insurers. This view is accompanied by time limits, which shorten, tighten, or make impossible the use of imagination and the sustained reflection of the first view. The assumptions that underlie treatment are called into question, yet the mental health world is changing with such speed that there is barely time to examine the questions.

Mental health professionals whose training emphasized introspection now confront significant changes in their practice when working with patients who have managed care insurance. Some of these changes are discussed in other chapters of this book. Therapists who believe that part of successful therapy involves the exploration of behavior and experience using language and reflection are an unusual match for managed care. The managed care model discourages contemplation, favoring quick action and symptomatic relief. The therapist thus loses the opportunity for relaxed interior reflection that was once an integral aspect of psychotherapeutic work. In this chapter we will reflect on the psychotherapist's mind and imagination as they are crowded, hurried, and frightened by managed care.

By *imagination* we refer to the way the mind opens and the way the mind is able to think—with freedom or the readiness to move into new space, to create, to see things in different ways, to go with another person, and to imagine how it is to be that person. This freedom to wonder and to imagine is essential to contemplative psychotherapy. In contrast, when our thinking and ways of working—both naturally and the way we were trained—are impinged upon and cramped by the guidelines of managed care, the freedom to wonder is lost. In reaction, the mind becomes guarded, cautious, and constricted.

For example, a therapist meeting a new patient, a chronically suicidal man for whom medications have not been helpful, whose insurance allots one visit per month, might wonder whether she will have room in her schedule and *in her mind* to see this man so infrequently and to hold so much. Given monthly meetings, will therapist and patient be able to make a space that will feel both safe and helpful? In her imagination the therapist is feeling her way, figuring out how close and how far away to be in order to help the patient feel he will have room to move (literally, emotionally, and in his imagination) even if he remains very depressed. In this process the therapist learns about the patient's losses, his early deprivation and neglect, and his wishes for revenge. She wonders whether they will have time to explore the collection of facts and emotions and what happens to them if they are not explored. Her imagination, once open and free, now begins to feel distracted by her questions, by what she wants to do, what she feels she cannot do, and by the feeling that she does not have enough space and enough time. She is relying more on deliberate analysis and less on exploratory thought and imagination.

## THE CROWDED MIND

It is typical of managed care work for a therapist to meet a patient who will be seen for a limited number of sessions. This experience is different from that of beginning psychotherapy when the agreement between patient and therapist is open-ended. To adjust to changes in time and frequency of treatment, psychotherapists have to organize their minds differently—perhaps like a computer, with different directories, where short-term, managed care cases go into a specific directory in the mind. Possibly, when a therapist knows he or she will see a patient only five times, the image of the patient does not get imprinted on the therapist's mind in the same way as it does when an open-ended relationship is anticipated. There is a tendency to feel less involved with patients who are seen less often, although the therapist may also feel more anxious because of the lack of contact. As a therapist's caseload increases beyond a given point, the experience of attachment and relationship is altered. There may be less investment in each particular patient. In the managed care view the cost-effective goal is the termination of treatment. In this model, can one also be working to create a relationship with the patient?

Meeting with a patient less frequently does not relieve the psychotherapist of the impact of knowing and working with another person. The psychotherapist bears the responsibility of listening and of assessing safety. He or she may feel left to hold the person's history and affects over long periods between sessions. Although patients may be seen less often, psychotherapists must still manage, within themselves, the complexity of the clinical responsibility for individual lives. Collected facts and the affects associated with them fill the psychotherapist's mind. How do clinicians do their work when their minds are crowded—by numbers? By knowledge of a person or people obtained quickly, without elaboration and without context? By facts that are not integrated because of limited time? Or by affects—one's own and one's patients'? It is not only a question of the available space, but how the space is filled—whether one holds an integrated evolving experience or separate, disparate pieces.

An increase in the overall number of cases seen places particular burdens on the psychotherapist's mind. In our discussions with colleagues, a number of concerns were raised. As one therapist explains, "When, in accordance with various insurance plans, I began to see more patients for fewer sessions and at greater intervals of time (every two weeks, every month, every six weeks), I noticed this affected my work and my memory. I began to experience a loss of space—the space inside me. I felt cramped and as if I had no room to hold another person in my imagination." Thus a psychotherapist accustomed to attending to and remembering the emotions and experience of his or her patients may feel overloaded. Often there is not enough space in the therapist's mind for the patients, their names, their difficulties, their histories, and, along with that, the guidelines of various insurance companies regarding the direction and amount of psychotherapy each patient will receive. The therapist explains further, "This felt like a crowding of the amount of internal room I need to do my work or even to live my life in a comfortable way." With their minds filled by the expectations and voices of insurers and hospital administrators, colleagues report that they cannot always remember an individual patient's particular qualities. As one clinician notes, "I needed to see, physically in my office, a particular patient before I could recall that patient's history and that patient as a whole being." Others shared the experience of expecting to meet one person in the waiting room and finding someone else—a confusion, an overload, a juggling, and a loss of the calm, predictable schedule and the intimacy essential to psychotherapy.

## FEAR AND TIME

The fear that therapists experience is rarely spoken of, but fear is a salient factor affecting clinicians who feel hurried, crowded, and frustrated. When clinicians do not necessarily have time to make a good working alliance with a patient, fear is heightened. Clinicians feel frightened for their patients and for themselves. They experience the fear of not having done a good job, the fear of abandoning the patient, and the fear of leaving the patient vulnerable to further difficulties. In reaction to the experience of anxiety and fear, everyone is hurried—the patient, the therapist, the relationship. As a colleague stated: "Managed care is creating a population of terrified therapists." What does it mean to be frustrated and frightened? One clinician explained, "When I'm frightened I *do* things—I use much more action."

Some anxieties lead therapists to discuss their own feelings about managed care in ways that deviate from their accustomed practice. For example, a clinician discussed with a patient his written request for additional sessions from the patient's insurer. At the same time, he spoke to the patient about his own concerns regarding privacy and confidentiality. This anxiety did not belong to the patient. It represented the therapist's confusion about his relationship to the managed care company and his relationship to his patient. A therapist's anxiety is often registered by the patient. That anxiety can lead to action or disclosure, or to increased emphasis on external behavior rather than on the underlying process or experience.

Over time, the managed care model becomes the frame for the therapist's imagination. When therapists see four new patients a week and are allotted eight sessions for each, it is hard to take each new patient into the imagination, into the therapist's mind. As one clinician stated: "I don't give the patient as much space, I jump in." The imagination is taxed by the pressure to come to premature closure or premature finding, to say, "This is it," very quickly diagnosing a specific problem that requires certain treatment. Other therapists mention the tendency to give up on the patient when insurance runs out. Still others report that they become bossy, directive, and active in response to treatment limits, or they try to say everything quickly.

Therapy is no longer a search; it is not an open process but a narrowing down. Again the factor of time is apparent. The process of finding and being found takes contemplation; imagination and creativity cannot be hurried.

What is enough time? Can it be known in advance? As a colleague, expressing her dilemma on meeting a new patient, states: "I am struck by the urgency of the issues and the limited time available to work on them. You have to teach patients how to be in therapy before you can do the therapy. With HMOs, you don't have time to teach them. You don't always have time to create a mutually safe environment. You [the therapist] are reluctant to try because you know it takes time." The perceived lack of adequate time leads psychotherapists to feel limited and not as willing to invest themselves.

## REACTING TO INSURANCE COMPANY DEMANDS

Therapists are finding themselves in the uncomfortable position of considering the needs of the insurer before the needs of the patient. They report that they begin to weigh the insurer's need to limit sessions as well as the patient's need for continued psychotherapy. This effort to balance insurance considerations along with patient needs can inhibit and distort one's actions as a therapist. Remarking on a similar feeling of inhibition, a colleague said: "It is so defeating, never to feel the freedom to do the work because there is always another insurance limit you are up against. Furthermore, there is pressure from the institutions (hospitals, community mental health clinics) to please the insurer, to adhere to their limits, not to ask for anything that is not absolutely necessary." Clinicians find themselves moving away from the patient's perspective and thinking about what is "right" according to the standards of the insurance company.

Adopting the perspective of the insurance company, clinicians are susceptible to feeling that, if they request more sessions, they are doing something they should not be doing. As the rules and guidelines of managed care become internalized, clinicians find themselves valuing—or overvaluing—the judgment of the managed care reviewer. Then they want to demonstrate to the committee of insurance case managers that therapy is progressing, even when the standards that measure that progression are not those of the therapists. Furthermore, clinicians can feel judged by an imposed, external model that differs with each insurance. Professional self-esteem becomes connected to insurance approval rather than to work accomplished with patients. The psychotherapist's mind is crowded by the guidelines and regulations of insurers, by complex emotions including resentment toward insurance companies, and by wishes for autonomy and time. In some instances the guidelines of insurance companies begin to take priority over the patients' emotional responses. Perhaps some therapists begin to feel that the responsibility for the treatment lies with the insurer, rather than with the therapist. Yet ultimately it is the therapist who is responsible, even though the insurance company may dictate treatment. This creates a serious dilemma, with ethical and personal implications.

In the case of the depressed man described earlier, the therapist's imagination and experience of space was inhibited by infrequent meetings and by limits to the number of sessions each year. The following example illustrates a different set of dilemmas that may occur when the therapist's imagination feels crowded. The therapist, describing a 28-year-old man who left his wife several weeks before the birth of their second child, said:

> He believes that all marriages get boring, that fathers leave after a few years as his father did. He sees his life as a role he will play, not as something individual and particular to him which he has chosen or feels to be true. I envision this patient learning to make room for himself, to have the space to figure things out, and to be able to accept ambivalence. In a sense I want to give him a place where he can wonder and imagine different possibilities for himself. We have a limited number of meetings and, instead of creating space in which to wonder, I find myself giving him different words, my own words instead of his, and more ways of looking at his situation and experience. In this way he is robbed of the experience of discovering for himself. I have turned to a greater reliance on action. Most likely, according to managed care reviewers, I am constructing this patient's problems and the solutions according to the wrong criteria, the "criteria" of the internal perspective. I wonder then what it is possible to make accessible for people within the managed care guidelines and whether this pa-

tient and I are doing anything that makes for any kind of change. I wonder if, by focusing on specific symptoms, I am contributing to a fragmented sense of experience. Am I reducing a complex experience to a story? And am I helping him replace one story with another? How will he learn about himself?

This therapist, attempting to balance her view of how psychotherapy might proceed with the symptom orientation of managed care, begins to doubt her ability to help the patient. Other clinicians report feeling similarly inhibited by the anticipated responses of the managed care reviewer.

## TIME AND ACTION

While use of the imagination may be threatened and circumscribed by the pressures and presence of the managed care model, not all psychotherapists respond with hopelessness or helplessness. Clinicians present a spectrum of responses to feeling hurried, anxious, or prone to action. Working with the depressed man in the above example, some clinicians would have requested more time and additional meetings from the patient's insurer; others would not. Many therapists are clever, devious, resourceful, and angry, and they are able to use these qualities to obtain needed services for their patients within the managed care systems. Recognizing and discussing the organization and parameters of psychotherapy with managed care insurers allows some clinicians to be effective and prevents them from feeling they are victims of the system.

The uncomfortable experience of tighter limits or "crowding" challenges clinicians to be creative. Despite constraints, many clinicians find ways to provide the services their patients require. One colleague commented that she likes to give managed care patients some piece of knowledge about themselves so they have something to think about, something to know, because there is not enough time for the patient to have a new experience in the therapy. Is this therapist providing transitional objects in hope that the patient will continue the work of psychotherapy after their meetings end? Perhaps she feels some guilt that she cannot give the patient more time and more of what she considers to be good treatment. In this instance guilt and a sense of responsibility may lead her to be creative in finding ways to be useful to her patients.

Another clinician notes:

> It has been important for me not to narrow my thinking about a person to accommodate the limits of managed care, but I have had to force myself to think about what would work. Not, "Given only managed care resources, what would work?" but beyond the limits of managed care, what would be best? I have had to strike a new balance, creating a whole new space in my mind, accommodating to managed care, and also considering how I might think . . . how I would have in the past. . . . I have thought about my obligation to my patients—to use myself to enable them to use more of themselves. This is very different from recommending self-help books, books on divorce, homework, though these approaches are not mutually exclusive. I have found myself using different tools, tasks, and wondering what kinds of compromise I am making.

Many therapists experience a tension between contemplative listening and doing, fixing, and acting. They work toward a balance, which involves integrating aspects of the introspective and observational perspectives described at the beginning of this chapter. Reacting to the influence of the observational, external perspective, therapists may feel impatient, may wish to fix things, or may wish to interrupt the flow of thoughts and process of the patient to offer advice. There may be a tendency to think the therapist should fix the problem rather than provide perspective and the freedom for the patient to solve the problem. This is not to imply that being more active precludes reflection or contemplation. There are different mixes of action, instruction, listening, and intention in each psychotherapy and with each patient.

Therapists work now under a model of cost control and symptom control, but not a model of exploration, of life, of depth. A parallel process occurs: as psychotherapists begin to think within the structure of managed care, patients do as well. As one clinician reports:

Patients have lost the idea that they internalize what happens in the therapy. Instead, on leaving my office, they say, "What should I do?" "What should I think?" "Is there homework?" This is the medical model, where they are accustomed to a doctor who says, "Take this pill three times a day, jump in a puddle, and you'll turn into Snow White." There are therapists who believe change begins externally and the mind will follow. If they can change behavior they've done the job. For instance, my colleague does not want to get into anyone's heart or soul or muse about anything, he wants to see progress, he's an agent of change.

Clinicians may feel hurried by the patient's experience of time. A colleague states: "Patients are operating on an assumption anyway. Fix this arm, I broke it. Fix this nose, it's crooked. The underlying assumption is speed. When I tell them they have twenty sessions a year for a problem, some of them think that's a lot."

## THE IMPORTANCE OF INFORMING THE PATIENT

Patients who come to psychotherapy with a prescribed number of sessions often believe that the number of visits allotted equals psychotherapy. Many patients are used to thinking if it's not covered, it's not necessary, as if the insurance company knew them and could evaluate their needs. Few patients have the idea that their insurance pays money *toward* psychotherapy. If therapists also begin to assume that insurance coverage equals therapeutic coverage, patients may not realize that they can *choose* to engage in the process of therapy, a process that will involve time and expense, and one that can significantly change their lives.

As patients and therapists begin to think within the confines of managed care, their sense of space and time narrows, and they may inhibit some of their former ways of thinking. One result is that therapists may forget to speak honestly to patients about psychotherapy, its cost, its benefits, the limits and extent of insurance coverage, and the absence of any guarantee that psychotherapy will lead to the desired result or change. Therapists may feel discouraged, helpless, and without power. In an uncomfortable alliance with the managed care companies, some therapists stop thinking or feeling and accept the structure and rules from outside. Managed care companies ask clinicians to believe that what the insurer offers is sufficient, adequate, and good. Many therapists feel pressure to make patients want, be satisfied, and be happy with "this" amount.

Why is it so difficult for therapists to speak freely? If it is important to have a dialogue with patients, why doesn't it happen more? As one clinician asks, "Why is it so hard to become effectively indignant on behalf of our patients or on behalf of what we believe we know?" Again, fear plays a part. Pressures to keep clinics and agencies open may contribute to the constriction and blunted imagination for some clinicians. More significant than the possibility of jeopardizing one's own standing with a managed care company is the notion (myth or fact) that one therapist's indignation can put an entire clinic's contract with that managed care company under scrutiny. Therapists may stay quiet, believing they are protecting their colleagues' jobs or their commitment to the patients they work with.

Therapists need to clarify the differences between their perspectives on psychotherapy and the managed care model for themselves and their patients. The therapist might say, "The concerns you are presenting might be more than we can deal with here. . . ." It may be essential for therapists and patients working with managed care to acknowledge *together* what can and cannot be dealt with in the sessions allotted. It is impossible to expect patients to want a treatment they do not know about or understand. As is done in medicine, psychotherapists need to educate patients regarding treatment options. Otherwise, patients are encouraged to believe that insurance coverage equals therapeutic coverage. It is possible that they also want to believe it. Managed care colludes with the patient's ambivalence, and it magnifies the therapist's ambivalence as well. Therapists confront questions about loyalty and ethical considerations that can frustrate or hurry the therapist's mind. If therapists do not educate their patients about psychotherapy, the confusion between the managed care model of therapy and other forms of psychotherapy is perpetuated.

## WHAT IS LOST

When the mind becomes crowded and therapists find themselves working less with the imagination, many of the specific experiences they have grown to value in exploratory psychotherapy are lost. Instead of evolving an open-ended search and feeling a confidence in not knowing, the therapist becomes an expert imparting specific knowledge. The crowded imagination does not allow for the natural anxiety, uncertainty, and confusion of psychotherapy. There is a loss of creativity, a loss of the opportunity to develop a unique, individual language and experience with one patient at a time. The collaboration of therapist and patient from inside the patient's experience is relinquished to an observational, outside position in relation to the patient. In addition, there is a loss of autonomy. As a colleague states, "The work under managed care is qualitatively different in terms of my experience of myself, of the work, of the dynamic between me and my patient. I'm working for someone else. There is an authority that has control. The motivation to buy into this hierarchical model is fairly compelling if I care about and want to work with my patient."

Embedded in the discussion of psychotherapists and managed care is the philosophical dilemma over whether one can work according to someone else's values. Additionally, there is a potential alteration in the understanding of human nature and human change. Despite these profound challenges to clinicians' experience of autonomy and to their beliefs in how psychological change optimally occurs, it is possible for some therapists over time to regain their sense of their work and the power of the imagination. Perhaps this represents a process of integration and development in relation to managed care. Regardless of how individual therapists have adapted to managed care, it is apparent that the nature of clinical work as we have known it has been altered.

## CONCLUSION

The image of the crowded imagination is a metaphor for many of the confusing experiences facing psychotherapists working with managed care. Clinical minds are crowded by numbers of patients, by emotions—the patients' and their own—by knowledge of patients that has little context, and by pressures from managed care guidelines and managed care reviewers. In addition, "time" under managed care is externally regulated, which contributes to the sense of crowding. Therapists feel hurried and frustrated. These feelings are further exacerbated by the fear of not doing a good job, of abandoning vulnerable patients, or of being constrained in one's ability to provide adequate treatment. Ideally, as therapists interact with managed care, they will increasingly find ways to regain a complementary balance between the internal-exploratory and the external-observational perspectives.

# 5

# Changes in Therapeutic Process Integrity

PEGGY J. BELL

As the American health care system undergoes a revolutionary transformation, psychotherapy is at a watershed. Some writers have described this situation as a crossroad (Austad 1992). Others are issuing warnings that psychology is under attack by health care businesses motivated by profit alone (Fox 1995, Welch 1995), and the growing crisis is amounting to a national nightmare (Karon 1995). Few meaningful analyses of the impact of these marketplace changes on psychotherapy have been conducted. Although several long-term outcome studies are reported to be underway (e.g., by the National Institute of Mental Health as well as managed care corporations), most of the current literature is long on opinion and short on data.

The nature of mental health care, and in particular psychotherapeutic practice, will be fundamentally changed by the new health care environment (see, for example, Austad 1992, Brown 1994). The various benefit structures and allowances, the requirement of providing what was once confidential patient information to case reviewers, and the mandatory involvement of the case reviewer in treatment planning—all affect the parameters of the psychotherapeutic process

(Blum 1992). In this way the essential nature of the therapeutic relationship is altered. Even so, the principal goal of the professional practice of psychotherapy is to assure the high quality delivery and continuous improvement of care. The implications of managed care become profound when business management considerations threaten the provision of high quality care, which appears to be the case, according to Thompson and colleagues (1991). In their research on practitioners' experience with managed care, they found that therapists do perceive and plan treatment differently according to whether patients pay for services via managed care insurance or are nonmanaged care patients. Their results also indicated that the great majority of the study's participants felt that managed care had lowered the quality of care in the community. The providers noted that they had too few sessions to work with and treatment was therefore more superficial. They also believed that treatment options were limited. This study opens the door to vital and troubling questions: What will these fundamental changes be, and who will they benefit? The need to answer these questions with empirical data is overdue. This chapter reviews a study recently conducted by this author to collect data on the impact of managed care on therapeutic process integrity.

## GATHERING DATA ON THE
## EFFECTS OF MANAGED CARE

One critical issue concerning the predominance of the managed care brand of brief therapy conducted today is that most practitioners have been trained in a more traditional model of psychotherapy. This model was primarily long-term (Nahmias 1992). In the past, clinicians were independent professionals. Usually based in their own offices, these providers were free to work according to their own inclinations and were accountable only to their patients for the treatment they provided and the fees they charged. Open-ended models of treatment were well suited to this context. The theories of the therapeutic process, goals of treatment, and methods of intervention were all influenced by the existing economic and cultural context. Therefore, brevity of treatment, cost-effectiveness, and conservation of resources were not primary considerations in treatment. In the managed care era, the overwhelming need for cost containment as American businesses began to spend 10 percent or more of their operating budgets on health care has created the current context and the impetus for the rapid development of managed care corporations (Cummings 1986, Hymowitz and Pollock 1995). Such a contextual shift undoubtedly impacts the practice of psychotherapy, as the process, goals, and methods of intervention are all affected.

The purpose of this study was to collect data on what is actually occurring in therapists' offices as a result of cost-driven changes in the marketplace. More particularly, it was designed to garner data on whether practitioners are treating patients differently based on whether the patient's care is paid by a managed care plan or through nonmanaged means. The questionnaire was sent to one thousand Massachusetts psychologists. The practitioners chosen for the study were in private practice at least ten hours per week and depended on managed care reimbursement for at least 20 percent of their private practice income. The questionnaire consisted of open-ended and multiple choice questions designed to gather information on how managed care is practiced and to assess the therapeutic integrity of such practice in comparison with nonmanaged care treatments.

Stern (1993) identified five factors that are critical to the integrity of any therapeutic process regardless of context. Therapeutic integrity is described by Stern as the establishment and maintenance by a competent therapist of the conditions necessary for successful therapeutic work. In identifying the necessary or optimal conditions for therapeutic change, Stern argues that those conditions most threatened by managed care are not therapist skills or qualities such as empathy, neutrality, and authenticity. Instead, they are "'meta-level' conditions that define the relational context or therapeutic frame" (p. 165). The five "meta-level" factors are openness, mutuality, safety, resistance, and termination. The first three represent the relational frame of a mutually derived therapeutic process. Resistance is described as the natural reluctance of patients to change problematic behavior patterns. The factor termination represents the concept that termination should be up to the patient or determined collaboratively between patient and therapist.

The study results demonstrated that the stakes are high for both patients and psychotherapists in the managed care environment. In this sample there is a statistically significant difference in the way practitioners are practicing as well as the way they are managing the integrity of the therapeutic process according to payment method. Further, the responses indicate that there is much less involvement by the practitioner in attending to therapeutic integrity with managed care patients.

Therapist concerns that emerged from the data were changes in theoretical framework, professional and personal dissatisfaction, the erosion of therapeutic integrity, and effects on theory and ethics. A discussion of these themes is presented below, followed by an examination of the interface of the data with Stern's five factors of therapeutic integrity.

## PRACTITIONERS' CONCERNS

The majority of responses to the study's questionnaire indicate that professionals are concerned about many issues with their managed care patients, including conflicts of interest between payors and patients, risking good standing with payors if the limits of patient benefits are explained to patients, adopting less than optimal treatment plans, modifying mandated treatment plans without notification to the insurance company, and focusing on symptom reduction to remain in good standing with payors. The level of concern for non-managed care patients with regard to these issues is significantly less. This not only presents the therapist with the ethical conflict of needing to weigh the interests of managed care companies with those of patients, but also creates a situation in which the method of payment affects the type of therapy a patient receives, and the client's best interest is pitted against the therapist's ability to make a living.

## CHANGES IN THEORETICAL FRAMEWORK

Perhaps most important, the data indicate that the increasing prevalence of managed care and insurance review has changed the theoretical framework of psychotherapy. Many of the responses expressed psychotherapists' doubts about the theory and practice of therapy, noting that they feel forced to use methods they know are not effective for all patients. Many respondents questioned the viability of the profession in a market dominated by managed care. Among the comments: "Insurance mandates destroy the theoretical underpinnings of psychotherapy." "The managed care concept of change is different from my training and beliefs." "The relationship is perverted as one worries about one's profile." "People think they are getting treatment in ten hours: this is ridiculous and impossible." "I feel disempowered: treatment is not guided by the relationship and client dynamics, but by managed care treatment plan guidelines." "There is less depth in the therapeutic relationship: treatment is more didactic, confrontive, and directive." "I would not recommend this profession to anyone."

Responses also provide evidence of a divergence from traditional psychotherapy theories that are based largely on the primary importance of the therapeutic relationship. For instance, responses to questions regarding termination indicate that with managed care patients, 62.10 percent of therapists are terminating treatment unilaterally in accordance with managed care mandates rather than allowing patients to determine when termination will take place or determining the timing of termination mutually between therapist and patient.

Any change in theoretical framework may generate resistance from therapists. Not only did practitioners feel "harassed" and "a lack of autonomy," but many stated that their very identities as therapists are being challenged along with their theoretical training. They point out that the efficacy of such treatment has not been established. Respondents reported feeling that their training, knowledge, and the intricacy of clinical thinking are being devalued in a process that is focused on symptom reduction rather than clinical need. Responses included: "I have anxieties and doubt about how the intrusion of third parties affects clients." "Working with managed care makes me feel like I am doing piecemeal work in a sweatshop." "Brief treatment is not universally acceptable." "I question what this profession is becoming." Overall, respondents felt that both content and context of therapy with managed care clients has been altered, which raises the question of what terminology accurately describes the work that therapists are doing with these patients, that is, should this type of work be called psychotherapy, or is it really psychoeducation or skills training?

## PROFESSIONAL AND PERSONAL DISSATISFACTION

Other response themes provide an expression of professional and personal dissatisfaction, even despair. The few positive themes included the demystifying of the profession through a more directive and psychoeducational approach of brief therapy and making practitioners more accountable to payors and patients: "Managed care has made my colleagues get serious and specific about what they are doing." A few respondents mentioned that the necessity to self-advocate for benefits helps to "empower" patients and "engenders less fostering of dependence." Other comments included: "I have had to accept a lower fee, but I have learned new skills." "I have increased referrals and increased income." "Patients must recognize that they must pay something, and providers need to charge what patients can afford."

The majority of themes, however, included concern over an eroding of the attitude of the public to psychotherapy, the overall limitations on patients imposed by their finances, and the decline of private practice viability.

In addition to statements regarding the destruction of the theoretical underpinnings of psychotherapy, many respondents noted the shift of therapeutic focus to symptom reduction and advocacy: "There is a narrow focus on symptom reduction," and "The focus shifts to advocacy from treatment: much treatment time is spent on explaining coverage or strategizing for more coverage." Many themes concern the inexperience and failings of case managers: "HMO clinical liaisons are inexperienced to the detriment of the client/counselor relationship"; "There is an increase in arbitrary criteria for one patient over another in getting evaluations approved." Practitioners described feeling conflicted by having to balance the needs of patients with those of insurance companies. Many describe the methods they have developed to advocate for patient benefits as "fudging": "I have learned to fudge treatment plans that get approved"; "I have learned to be good at a model of treatment I know rarely works." Practitioners state that as reimbursement declines and paperwork increases, time for research and reviewing literature decreases. As psychotherapists begin to be concerned about their status on provider panels, they indicate that they are less invested in clients.

Many themes dealt with the personal impact of managed care, such as disempowerment, depression, anxiety, and concerns about livelihood. Some respondents are considering leaving the field. Responses included: "I am looking for an alternative career"; "I am depressed by comprehensive adverse effects on my livelihood"; "Managed care has increased my practice as I have joined panels, but at too high a cost personally and professionally"; "It has devastated my income base"; "Decreased work satisfaction"; and "I have gone through various stages of grieving."

Another theme focused on the negative impact of managed care on clients. Themes include the lack of awareness of the compromise in treatment, the preferential or arbitrary review process, the lack of patient confidentiality, and the expectation for medication. For example, "Patients do not always understand the compromise in treatment"; "Clients feel that their confidentiality is compromised"; and "Clients no longer expect anything but medication."

## RESPONSES TO QUESTIONS
## REGARDING THERAPEUTIC INTEGRITY

In essence, the themes in these data give support to the literature that predicts that the effect of managed care is to corrupt the professional practice of psychotherapy. Of particular importance to this study is the literature concerning Stern's (1993) five factors of therapeutic integrity (openness, mutuality, safety, resistance, and termination).

The emphasis in managed care to formulate treatment plans rapidly and initiate interventions by the first or second session interferes with the therapist's ability to maintain an open and mutual process that allows a relationship to develop between patient and therapist. Furthermore, a therapist who does not maintain openness and mutuality throughout the therapeutic process can miss obscured or affective components of a patient's concerns (Shulman 1988). When practitioners were asked if they were concerned that the treatment plan dictated by a third party was not the optimal treatment for the client, 82 percent indicated that they were sometimes or always concerned with managed care patients. For nonmanaged care patients, 88 percent were never concerned.

Safety within the formal framework of the relationship includes the therapist's reliability and trustworthiness; the therapist's abstinence from personal gratifications that would interfere with the therapeutic task; and the provision of a controlled, protected setting for therapeutic work (Stern 1993). These elements are compromised by third-party intrusions into the therapeutic relationship as well as when practitioners struggle to balance personal interests with client and corporate interests. Also problematic is the concern of many psychotherapists that they feel a conflict of interest between their own financial interests and those of their patients. Respondents have clearly indicated that these intrusions do occur and that negative effects are experienced by clients and by themselves. When practitioners were asked if they were concerned about a conflict of interest between client treatment needs and meeting utilization expectations, 91.5 percent said they were always or sometimes concerned for managed care patients. For nonmanaged care patients, 72.5 percent indicated that they were never concerned.

The self-discovery and change process is not one that can easily be pushed onto a patient. Only the patient can determine when he or she is willing or able to change. Without attending to the resistance to change and learning why a new skill may present complex challenges to a patient, the possibility for significant, lasting change remains tenuous. Practitioners were asked if they were concerned that they needed to focus on symptom reduction to remain in good standing with a third-party payor. Eighty-seven percent of practitioners were always or sometimes concerned for managed care patients. A large majority, 78 percent, stated that they were never concerned for their nonmanaged care patients.

Therapist- or third-party-initiated terminations obviously violate the theoretical assumption that the patient, alone or mutually with the therapist, needs to make the decision to terminate (Barron and Sands 1996). Clients may feel abandoned by therapists and taken advantage of by insurance companies (Barron and Sands 1996). Although financial resources have always had an influence on therapy, under the managed care system this influence is made more direct by the involvement of the reviewer and the review process. This external representation of loss can become the focus of therapy, thus avoiding the patient's conflicts about separation, autonomy, and other developmental conflicts. The necessary processing for both patient and therapist of these important issues is impeded. The presence of managed care often merges different phases of treatment by generating anxiety over the entire treatment process. More to the point, when unplanned termination is a constant threat, the therapist and client must work under a cloud of uncertainty (Barron and Sands 1996).

## EFFECTS ON THEORY AND ETHICS

The growth of managed care in third-party reimbursement has outpaced the ability to develop a theoretical understanding of the structure and meaning of managed care in psychotherapy. Yet theory and the ethical base upon which it stands is the foundation of all effective psychotherapy regardless of payment method. Ethical treatment is conducted by an appropriately trained therapist, practicing within his or her level of expertise and within an identified theoretical orientation that informs the therapeutic frame, technique, and conceptualization (Saakvitne and Abrahamson 1996). Further, the ethical practice of psychotherapy also includes the commitment "to do good"—to do our best to help patients—and "to do no harm"—to practice with patients' interests paramount, and not to interact in such a way as to serve our own needs over those of a patient. Even so, the results of this study demonstrate that some practitioners are experiencing the pressure to act ineffectively and unethically.

According to the overriding spirit if not the specific letter of the American Psychological Association Ethics Code, any treatment differences that arise between patients should be based primarily on patient need (Keith-Spiegel and Koocher 1985). The patient is primary, not his method of payment. In the past, with both nonmanaged care and indemnity insurance patients, practitioners were freer to focus on the patient's needs and worked around the limits of the insurance company.

Within the managed care system, obstacles to treatment can be increased as the system communicates to the patient the societal and institutional devaluation of mental health services, and of mental health itself. Instead of communicating a belief that one's mental health is as central as one's physical health, a primary focus on symptom reduction diminishes the importance of one's emotional experience. By imposing itself on the therapeutic relationship and limiting sessions and treatment options, the system perpetuates the cultural denial and stigmatization of patients, which in turn impedes their progress toward their goals (Saakvitne and Abrahamson 1996). The intrusion of insurance review invites passivity and regression in the patient, who, frustrated in the attempts to seek treatment, may become a docile recipient of decisions made by others. This process clearly contradicts the therapeutic goals of psychotherapy.

The practice of two types of treatment based on payment method and performed without the patient's awareness is clearly unethical. At the very least, the responses of this study's participants indicate that new aspects of the therapeutic context should be the subject of an ongoing discussion of the therapeutic relationship and the therapeutic process. The managed care review process needs to be approached in the same way as other events in therapy, that is, it needs to be noticed, named, examined in its relational context, and understood in terms of present, historical, interpersonal, and intrapsychic meaning. For example, the patient who is willing to concede power to the therapist to advocate for benefits with a utilization reviewer might plan with the therapist what information is relevant and to discuss personally with the reviewer what the process entails and what the patient can expect (Saakvitne and Abrahamson 1996).

## BRIEF THERAPY

Brief treatment modalities by themselves do not impede the therapeutic relationship or negatively affect the integrity of the patient's treatment process. Although these modalities are less focused on the relationship between therapist and patient as an integral part of the therapeutic process, the relationship retains a significant role. For instance, Beck and Weishaar (1989) describe the roles of cognitive therapy as correcting faulty information processing and helping patients modify assumptions that maintain maladaptive behaviors and emotions. Cognitive and behavioral techniques are "used to challenge dysfunctional beliefs and to promote more realistic adaptive thinking" (p. 299). Initially, cognitive therapy focuses on symptom relief, including problem behaviors and distortions in logic, but its ultimate goal is to remove systematic biases in thinking. Beck and Weishaar describe the therapeutic relationship as collaborative: the "therapist functions as a guide who helps the patient understand how beliefs and attitudes influence affect and behavior. The therapist is also a catalyst who promotes corrective experiences that lead to cognitive change and skills acquisition" (p. 299).

Further, a number of outcome studies have demonstrated its efficacy, especially in the treatment of depression (Beck and Weishaar 1989). In terms of managed care and brief therapy one might ask: Was this empirical support for positive outcome of cognitive therapy conducted within a managed care environment? How many sessions were Aaron Beck and his team of researchers allotted to guide patients toward cognitive shifts and corrective emotional experiences? Did they know when the time limit would be exhausted? How many hours did these treaters spend on the telephone and filling out paperwork in order to receive reimbursement? Were these treaters told that their patients' treatment was not "medically necessary"? Perhaps more to the point: Did these treaters have to make a treatment choice between symptom relief and attending to the process factors that contribute to corrective emotional experiences to the detriment of a patient's long-term mental health? Were they mandated to do so?

Essentially, brief therapies themselves are not harmful to patients. Rather, it is the context of managed care, whether the treatment is psychodynamic, cognitive, or behavioral, that impedes the course of treatment. In this context treatment plans may be mandated as well as being nontheoretically based and without evidence of efficacy. Termination is controlled by a third party. We must ask ourselves, as therapists, as patients, and as human beings: Do we want treatment methods, in lieu of psychological theory, to be created by corporations? Any such theory or method will be tied both to profit objectives and to marketing and will be influenced accordingly. This is not good news for patient care and does not suit the field of psychotherapy. For practitioners to think that a business would not operate according to a profit motive is either extremely naive or disingenuous. Practitioners in managed care work within a frame that clearly states "a penny saved is a penny earned." Therapists capitulate to this frame due to pressure for economic and professional survival. In so doing they survive, but they lose the attachment to providing the highest level of care as the struggle with managed care limitations becomes constant and fruitless.

Although these data do not indicate the precise meaning of the difference between the treatment of nonmanaged and managed care patients, the responses indicate that practitioners are less involved with managed care patients. Thus the integrity of the therapeutic process is damaged. Practitioners indicated that they attend less to the establishment and maintenance of the conditions necessary for therapeutic work with managed care patients than with nonmanaged care patients. In the opinion of clinicians participating in this study, the patient is negatively impacted by the increased prevalence of managed care, and the integrity of the therapeutic process is negatively affected as well. Managed care treatment guidelines corrupt the theoretical framework of psychotherapy and the therapeutic relationship. Practitioners have raised doubts about the integrity as well as the viability of psychotherapy as a reflection of what is happening in their treatment of patients, not as a matter of opinion or as a reaction against change.

## ADVOCACY AND ACCOMMODATION

Any efforts to advocate for psychotherapy or to accommodate to managed care must take the ethical, practical, and theoretical concerns expressed by this study's participants into consideration. Insurers clearly need to be informed that the way they are implementing their policies is undermining the integrity of the therapeutic process, and therapists need to acknowledge that their practice colludes with this. As this study's data show, some practitioners are finding ways to subvert managed care systems by "fudging" or not reporting changes in treatment plans. One can assume that at some level efficacy will be undermined. Therapists are not practicing as they would without managed care and managed care is not getting the treatment that they are mandating. Insurers are paying for compromised treatment, and one would expect a high rate of recidivism. A patient returning to therapy after having experienced ineffective treatment may present more complications than during the initial treatment, costing insurance payors more money and generating less profit. This lack of long-term cost effectiveness may act as a major force of change in the managed care system as it is now being administered.

It might be possible for a managed care company to use the results of this study to conclude that the therapists in this sample should not be invited to participate on panels if they feel that their work is compromised and feel personally devalued. This writer believes that conclusion to be shortsighted. The skills and knowledge of an experienced therapist are developed over many years of practice and reflection. Managed care companies need these qualities in their clinicians and administrators if they are to evolve in ways that allow the companies to survive both legislation and lawsuits. There can be a sharing of knowledge through established vehicles such as training and supervision. Clinicians can be invited to learn the theory and methods of brief therapy as implemented by managed care and, as a result, perhaps make these practitioners better able to work with the system. Concomitantly, clinicians can be included in the development and research of new theory, methods, and outcomes of brief therapy that do not have as many harmful implications for practitioners and patients alike. This process can also begin in the training of students and beginning therapists.

Therapists who practice under the current managed care system need to be clear with themselves and their patients that this treatment is not psychotherapy, based on theory and supported by research. To highlight the words of one respondent previously quoted: "People think they are getting treatment in ten hours; this is ridiculous and impossible." Many questions remain to be investigated. Perhaps most important are: What kind of treatment are managed care patients receiving, and what are the implications of this for how we define ourselves as psychotherapists?

# REFERENCES

Austad, C. (1992). Symposium: psychotherapists in independent practice and in managed health care settings: a comparison. *Psychotherapy in Private Practice* 10:1–6.

Barron, J., and Sands, H., eds. (1996). *Impact of Managed Care on Psychodynamic Treatment.* Madison, CT: International Universities Press.

Beck, A., and Weishaar, M. (1989). Cognitive therapy. In *Current Psychotherapies*, ed. R. Corsini and D. Wedding, pp.285–320. Itasca, IL: F. E. Peacock.

Blum, S. (1992). Ethical issues in managed mental health. In *Managed Mental Health Services*, ed. S. Feldman, pp. 245–265. Springfield, IL: Charles C Thomas.

Brown, F. (1994). Resisting the pull of the health insurance tarbaby: an organizational model for surviving managed care. *Clinical Social Work Journal* 22(1):59–71.

Cummings, N. (1986). The dismantling of our health system. *American Psychologist*, 41(4):426–431.

Fox, R. (1995). The rape of psychotherapy. *Professional Psychology: Research and Practice* 26(2):147–155.

Hymowitz, C., and Pollock, E. (1995). Cost-cutting firms monitor couch time as therapists fret. *The Wall Street Journal*, July 13, p. 1.

Karon, B. (1995). Provision of psychotherapy under managed health care: a growing crisis and national nightmare. *Professional Psychology: Research and Practice* 26(1):5–9.

Keith-Spiegel, P., and Koocher, G. (1985). *Ethics in Psychology.* New York: McGraw-Hill.

Nahmias, V. (1992). Training for a managed care setting. *Psychotherapy in Private Practice* 11(2):15–19.

Saakvitne, K., and Abrahamson, D. (1996). The impact of managed care on the therapeutic relationship. In *Impact of Managed Care on Psychodynamic Treatment*, ed. J. Barron and H. Sands, pp. 27–72. Madison, CT: International Universities Press.

Shulman, M. (1988). Cost containment in clinical psychology: critique of Biodyne and the HMOs. *Professional Psychology: Research and Practice* 19:298–307.

Stern, S. (1993). Managed care, brief therapy, and therapeutic integrity. *Psychotherapy* 30(1):162–175.

Thompson, J., Smith, J., Burns, B., and Berg, R. (1991). How mental health providers see managed care. *Journal of Mental Health Administration* 18(3):284–291.

Welch, B. (1995). Health care reform: from crisis to siege. *Practitioner Focus* 8(1):6.

# III

The Impact on
Clinical Practice

# 6

## *"Private" Practice: An Oxymoron in the Age of Managed Care*

PAMELA WOLF

$M$any psychotherapists in private practice affiliate with managed care plans in order to protect their livelihood. Often such alliances are motivated by therapists' anxiety and worry about not having enough work. They feel they have to join forces with managed care in order to sustain their careers, often thinking they have no other choice. Thus the partnership with managed care is a marriage of necessity.

The observations in this chapter are drawn from my experiences and discussions with some of my colleagues in private practice. Many of them report that financial concerns, as well as the desire not to be left out of an opportunity to enhance their livelihood combine so that they feel they cannot *not* join managed care. There is a strong current that many feel they can no longer resist; while they say they would rather not succumb, they are compelled to do so. Reminiscent of the concept of traumatic bonding, therapists bond with these forces to survive, and eventually come to take on the values and beliefs of the dominant culture whose views were previously at odds with their own.

Curiously, the marriage between private practice and managed care somehow changes therapists and the nature of the therapeutic work they do. Many of them describe not feeling free to think, act, know, and speak the same way they did or the same way they do with their nonmanaged care patients. This self-perceived gagging or inhibition leaves the therapist feeling bound and constricted. Other therapists experience dissociated splits between their thoughts and actions. They feel unable to act in accord with their thoughts, values, and beliefs. While many of the detrimental effects of managed care on clinical practice have been widely described, little has been written about the effect on therapists of not feeling free to think, act, or speak in accord with their beliefs (see Bell, this volume, for a further discussion). Even less is known about how this constriction influences their clinical work.

One of the essential characteristics of managed care plans is that they endow the insurance companies with the exclusive power to grant or rescind sessions at any time. This gives the insurance companies a great deal of power over the practitioner. The limitation on the therapist's freedom emerges as a by-product of the provider's working within nonclinically derived guidelines established by the insurance companies. My colleagues report that they experience such splits and inhibitions less frequently in their work with patients who are not in managed care plans. It is the adjustment to working with managed care that leads to an altered experience in the therapist.

## CONSTRICTION OF FREEDOM
## ALTERS THERAPISTS' THINKING AND WORK

Having to adhere to someone else's guidelines derived outside of the clinical context restricts the freedom of therapists (Morriem 1988). According to Haas and Cummings (1991), "although managed care can take several forms, its common ingredient is restriction on freedom or intrusion into the formerly private contractual world of provider and consumer" (p. 45). While individual providers might not agree with the guidelines established by the managed care executives, the perceived need to collaborate with managed care requires that they must adhere to their policies. Some authors (Beauchamp and

Childress 1988) have gone so far as to suggest that therapists who decide to work with managed care plans must concur with their treatment philosophies. Since complete agreement is impossible in every situation, the providers typically have to reconcile their different opinions with what they have to do. Over time, having to continually accommodate to these conflicting thoughts and behaviors may well cause therapists to change the way in which they think and work.

Consider the following example. Through his affiliation with a panel that referred its patients directly to him, a colleague of mine, Dr. B., saw managed care patients for psychotherapy in his private office. Part of Dr. B.'s agreement with the panel involved his seeing patients only while their coverage was in effect, that is, not working out some other self-pay arrangement to continue treatments after patients' insurance ran out. It was as if the managed care plan had "ownership" of its patients; after one of its patients used his benefits once, the managed care plan had the right to be involved in deciding where the patient went and whom he saw from that point forth.

After treating a patient, "Charlie," for just a few sessions, Dr. B. became convinced that Charlie needed longer-term therapy, so Dr. B. requested permission to make a referral to another provider outside the panel who would be able to see him on a more open-ended basis. The administrator in charge of case dispositions reprimanded Dr. B severely, reminding him that this was not the first time he had not been able to stick to the managed care plan's "term limits" that restrict clinical contacts to the length of time the patient's coverage is in effect. The fact that Dr. B. had worked well on a short-term basis with the previous fifteen cases referred to him was not noted. Although the administrator reluctantly agreed to make the referral, Dr. B. was certain that she intended to report his "transgression." He was also concerned that she might recommend that he be dropped from the managed care panel due to his inability to live in accord with the plan's cost-cutting policies. He worried that his fear might prevent him from making a similar recommendation for the next patient who needed more or a different type of treatment.

After this experience, Dr. B. became concerned that he would not feel as free to speak his mind and advocate for the next patient needing something other than what the managed care plan typically offered. Dr. B. felt that he might stop allowing himself to *think* ongoing treatment should be contemplated or undertaken, given the difficulty of implementing it. He worried that he might stop considering what he previously felt was the best treatment option.

## COMPROMISED CLINICAL CARE

Private practitioners work with managed care in several different ways. They may (1) treat patients in their offices, as Dr. B. did, through an affiliation with a hospital clinic having capitated contracts; (2) work part-time at an agency having multiple managed care contracts; or (3) participate in a group practice that has secured contracts with a variety of managed care panels or arranged to provide capitated services. Regardless of the particular arrangement, all therapists doing managed care work agree to certain general terms set by the contracts. These terms are written generally to apply in the majority of cases, and do not tend to encourage taking into account the needs of the individual. For instance, most managed care plans have session limits for particular problems. Locations in which patients are to be treated are also specified. Treatment plans are spelled out for particular disorders or presenting problems, and may differ from those the individual provider would establish were he or she working independently. In addition to deciding when a patient's treatment must end, managed care plans often control to whom they will refer patients should they need further or adjunctive treatment. Hence, the method of practice, length of treatment, location of meetings, interventions, and referrals are all frequently regulated.

In practice this often amounts to establishing different kinds of treatment frames with patients based on the funding source. For instance, the therapist who agrees to do brief or intermittent treatment with every client who has managed care insurance is altering the frame in a particular way by ceasing to make individual treatment decisions grounded in clinical judgment. In some cases brief treatment is not what will best serve the patient, and therapists practicing it exclusively with managed care patients will experience an internal conflict about doing something in practice that opposes their beliefs and values about what will be most helpful to the patient. They may feel they have fallen short and are failing their patients.

In my work with patients having managed care insurance, I have often found myself undertaking treatments more behaviorally or superficially oriented than the ones I conduct with my other patients. Having to document demonstrable change on paper after a few sessions—and having only a few sessions in which to treat a patient—necessarily alters the nature of the treatment. My focus in these cases is more on resolving symptoms than trying to understand deeper, underlying conflicts. As my focus changes, the goals change too. In one case, against my better judgment, I ignored current stressors, family problems, and work difficulties, deciding that a few sessions could not begin to address them, and structured a treatment primarily around providing symptomatic relief of a sleep disturbance. While offering information on sleep hygiene, establishing a bedtime routine, and developing a protocol for insomnia recurrences aided the patient initially, when it came to understanding what might be causing this patient's insomnia, we barely scratched the surface. In contrast, with other patients, I would have tried to do both types of work: supportive efforts aimed at symptomatic relief, and depth-oriented, exploratory work targeted at understanding and long-term change. In this case, however, my treatment plan was very much influenced by my notion of what would be authorized by the managed care reviewer.

Capitated systems represent another type of situation in which therapists' actions with their patients may be motivated more by another person's zeitgeist than by therapists' views about clinical care. In the current culture, therapists' actions are driven by many factors in addition to their patients' needs, including therapists' desire to make themselves marketable, need to earn a living, and wish to fit in. Dr. T., a colleague in private practice who receives referrals from an institution that has secured capitated contracts, reports that she is paid a flat per-patient fee of $250 for every patient referred to her through this institution. Whether she treats a patient for one session or ten she still receives $250. From a financial perspective, Dr. T. is clearly doing well when she sees such patients for just one session. With each additional meeting, however, her per-session profit begins to diminish such that it is in Dr. T.'s best interest to restrict the number of sessions to the lowest amount necessary. If she sees the patient twice, her hourly rate decreases from $250 to $125; if she sees the patient three times, her hourly rate drops to $75; and so forth. The patient does not know this and is completely unaware that Dr. T. is financially better off if she provides fewer sessions. Realizing her personal stake in restricting the number of sessions in as many cases as possible, Dr. T. is quite concerned about how this arrangement compromises the clinical care she provides.

Thus, even in private practice settings, the individual practitioner may no longer be thinking, working, and acting independently. A provider's thoughts and actions are very much influenced by the opinions of the policymakers and reviewers working behind the scenes. From the provider's perspective, "managed mental health care plans constrain the ability of the provider to establish whatever treatment plans he or she believes will be effective for the presenting problem" (Haas and Cummings 1991, p. 45). In the case of Charlie described above, Dr. B. felt that his opinion about the best possible treatment frame was being questioned and not given credence.

### Alice

The following clinical vignette illustrates another way in which the presence of managed care as a third party adversely affects the therapist's freedom to establish what he believes is the best treatment frame for individual patients.

> "Alice," a poor, young woman from the inner city, was referred to Dr. Y. for help with a "career dilemma." A colleague of mine, Dr. Y. had entered into an arrangement with a hospital having capitated contracts, which was very similar to Dr. B.'s agreement. He was able to see patients only as long as their insurance covered them. He agreed never to continue to treat a patient whose insurance had run out in his private practice or through some other fee arrangement. Dr. Y.'s contract with the hospital dictated that once a patient's benefits were exhausted, if further treatment was indicated, he had to transfer patients to the less expensive, less experienced hospital trainees. The rationale for this policy was that the hospital, which had secured the capitated

contract, did not want therapists skimming patients into their private practices.

Alice had just dropped out of college after a string of similar dropouts in her academic, work, and personal life. She had no job or income, her mother was unable to work due to medical problems, and her father was of little help when it came to financial or other support. Her father, who was never married to her mother, stepped in and out of her life and bailed her out of one problematic situation after another, only to repeatedly fail her by disappearing for long periods of time. In addition, Alice had numerous realistic concerns about her mother's health. The most notable feature of Alice's history was a significant pattern of multiple abandonments. As her history was highly suggestive of underlying characterological problems that could not be treated in the eight authorized sessions, Dr. Y. felt constricted by being asked to frame her problems simply as "career confusion." He believed that her problems ran much deeper than figuring out whether she should drop out of college or how to pursue her chosen career.

Given the indications from Dr. Y.'s assessment that eight sessions might not be sufficient, this was exactly the type of case he felt should have been referred directly to the hospital. Such a disposition would have enabled Alice to see a trainee with more flexibility, perhaps on an ongoing or open-ended basis. However, the nature of the health care delivery system was such that all patients having Alice's insurance type were initially referred to a clinician such as Dr. Y. Because Alice had benefits, she had to be seen first under managed care. Once those benefits were exhausted, if further treatment was indicated, she would then be eligible to apply for *another* course of treatment with a trainee, paid for by the free care system. Because it cost less, a free care funded treatment could be more open-ended.

From a clinical standpoint it was cruel to ask Alice to form yet another short-term relationship that would have to end prematurely on account of someone else's needs. This paralleled her experience with her father, who popped in and out of her life according to his whim. Whether he came or went was completely beyond her control. Further, this "solution-focused" treatment was not the type Alice was seeking. Dr. Y. felt that, in creating a treatment frame, Alice's dynamics should be kept in the forefront; given her history of abandonment, it was imperative to set up a treatment that would not repeat the problem for which she was seeking help. Given Dr. Y.'s arrangement with the hospital, for him to treat Alice was a setup for him to fail her. Treating Alice on such a brief basis constituted a therapeutic abandonment and repeated the problem for which she was seeking help.

By the third session Dr. Y. became convinced that managed care's recommendation of brief treatment for career problems was not the treatment Alice needed. He felt in a quandary because sending her back to the hospital for further treatment would be tantamount to acknowledging that he had failed as a therapist and might result in the drying up of this particular referral source. He resolved to attempt to conduct this type of treatment anyway, believing that it could be of some use to her. Dr. Y.'s need to keep his contract with the managed care company essentially pushed him to treat a patient in a way he did not feel was clinically indicated.

However, after the eight sessions approved by her insurance company, Dr. Y. still believed that Alice needed further psychotherapy. He referred her to a hospital trainee. Although he felt it was in Alice's best interest for him to continue as her therapist, Dr. Y.'s contractual obligation to the managed care plan prohibited him from making such a bid.

In a sense, Dr. Y. was caught having to offer the product the insurance company wanted to market. He felt as though he was effectively functioning as an insurance broker for the plan. He experienced the managed care company as urging him to push certain products because this is what benefited the company. Much like the vacuum salesman who gets a monetary reward for every Hoover he sells, but not for every General Electric, Dr. Y. disregarded the patient's best interest and unique needs, and tried to push a certain product. However, the managed care plan's well-being does not necessarily match the patient's best interest.

## INTRUSION IN THE PATIENT–THERAPIST RELATIONSHIP

Many therapists believe that their not feeling free to act in accord with their beliefs results from managed care's intrusion into their relationships with their patients. What was once a relationship between two individuals has now become a relationship among three or more parties. No doubt the presence of a third party in what was and should remain a two-person relationship dramatically changes the process. Interestingly, psychotherapy theorists and practitioners of many perspectives have long believed that there are many individuals present in the consulting room in addition to the patient and therapist, such as the internalized image of the patient's mother, father, and siblings, and likewise for the therapist. Now, as managed care companies' representatives often attempt to dictate to the therapist not only *how long* but also *how* to conduct the treatment, there functionally *is* another person in the room.

Even the most well-intentioned therapists cannot help but be influenced and perhaps unnerved by these intrusions into their thoughts and relationships. For instance, I once received the following note from an insurance company's psychiatrist: "Let [me] know when the patient has seen a psychiatrist for medication as she *clearly* needs this." The note came at the same time as the authorization for the first few sessions. The psychiatrist neither met with nor interviewed my patient but came to this conclusion on the basis of a brief written evaluation of mine in which I had suggested nothing of the kind. What had transpired was that an outside third person had her own agenda for my patient, which was not my patient's agenda. On the contrary, the patient had come into treatment stating explicitly that she wanted to give psychotherapy a try before considering medication. Medication had many complicated meanings for this patient, as it does for many individuals. For my part, the psychiatrist's agenda substantially affected and colored my thinking. In the interest of preserving my relationship with this insurance company, I felt pressure to work in accord with its recommendations. After receiving the psychiatrist's note, I listened to my patient in a different way, looking for any indication that medication might or might not be the solution. Because I was so busy sorting out the medication issue, I was less attuned to my patient's other communications.

There is nothing private about private practice, at least when it is practiced with a managed care patient. Private practice *is* an oxymoron in the age of managed care.

Therapists I have discussed these issues with report that the presence of a third person changes not only their thoughts and actions, but also their feelings about their work. Some of my colleagues secretly harbor so much resentment at the managed care plans for controlling them that they devise ways of getting more for their patients. When therapists successfully obtain more sessions than they were allotted, such planning has the added benefit of mollifying their frustration. Some therapists working with managed care have confessed to engaging in unscrupulous behaviors with questionable ethical implications. They speak of contemplating offering services to patients that their agreements with the managed care companies explicitly prohibit, such as continuing treatment after the insurance has been used up or altering diagnoses to secure more sessions. They rationalize their "illicit" actions with references to the patient's best interest. Other therapists report that they court and befriend managed care executives they do not like in order to obtain business. A few attempt to counter the difficulty of getting on panels in neighborhoods saturated with therapists by opening second offices in name only in a particular area that still accepts new providers on the panels. Other therapists I have spoken with profess to have expertise in specialty areas that they lack in order to get onto certain panels. In sum, many therapists report that they take pleasure in outsmarting, deceiving, or outmanipulating managed care. The conflict therapists find themselves in forces the maneuvering between what is best for the patient and what maintains their own self-interest.

### Rachel

The case of Rachel illustrates the potential dangers to patients when a therapist's contractual obligation to a managed care plan conflicts with their well-being. "Rachel" came to me in a state of terrible crisis. She was a troubled young woman making a dramatic presentation, sporting multiple body piercings, an excessive amount of make-up, and an anorexic figure. The longer I listened to her, the more trouble I realized she was in. Battered by a series of abusive boyfriends whom she felt unable to leave; destroying her body with body piercing, frequent cutting, and a daily drug habit; mired in an overly enmeshed relationship with a troubled father who refused to let her live her own life; and having occasional thoughts about ending her life; Rachel repeatedly endangered herself.

As authorized by her insurer, I saw her twice for an initial assessment. By the end of the second meeting, I had several concerns. Given her suicide risk, I felt she needed to be seen on-site at a hospital and more frequently than once per week. I believed that once Rachel withdrew from her reliance on drugs and became more in touch with her feelings, her self-destructive behavior might escalate, possibly necessitating a hospitalization. Treating her in my private office on a once-weekly basis made me uncomfortable as it seemed insufficient to ensure her safety. The insurance company denied my request for more frequent sessions. As I was not hospital-based, I forcefully communicated my opinion to the agency's triage administrator that Rachel needed a therapist who would have the flexibility to see her more frequently and in a hospital setting. Rachel was assigned, however, to yet another clinician having the same arrangement with the agency as I had. It was as if I had sent Rachel to another executioner; managed care clearly failed her. Rachel never went to see this therapist, who initiated contact with her some six weeks later. This was clearly a type of treatment that saved money for the insurance company.

What I felt would have been clinically best for Rachel from the outset would have been treatment in a hospital-affiliated clinic with emergency backup for hospitalization if that became necessary. Unfortunately, Rachel experienced my efforts as rejection and confirmation of her view of herself as "unlikable" and "too much" for others. The agency did not follow through on my recommendation, perhaps because their contract with the managed care company did not cover Rachel's being treated by a hospital-based practitioner. Since the agency did not make this referral, I felt it would then have been in Rachel's best interest, given that we had established some rapport, to continue to see me for an intensive, open-ended psychotherapy. My agreement with the agency, however, precluded my making such a suggestion as it was against the agency's rules. My hands were tied. I was frustrated that I was not able to help her, and I felt I failed yet another patient because of a procedural disagreement over how best to treat her. Two differing conceptions of the treatment of choice, mine and managed care's, were pitted against one another.

## THERAPISTS' NEED TO CRITICALLY REVIEW THEIR COLLABORATION WITH MANAGED CARE

Many therapists I have spoken with report that experiences such as this have led them to reconsider their work with managed care plans. Dr. Y. decided that he could not work with patients when his freedom was too constrained by a third party or when he experienced a conflict of interest between his needs, his patients' needs, and the insurance company's policies. For my part, after working with managed care patients for six months, I resolved not to treat any more such patients without first fully informing them of the risks to treatment, which include limitations on privacy and confidentiality, restrictions on the degree of insight to be obtained, and a focus on superficial or symptom-focused work. I realized that I could not feel comfortable treating patients when there was an extra-clinical influence that could at times undermine my clinical judgment unless I told patients from the outset something about it. I know of other colleagues whose negative experiences led them down the decision tree to the conclusion that they could not work with managed care at all. For instance, Dr. T. severed her relationship with capitated plans because she became uncomfortable with the way her financial interests and her clinical responsibilities were in direct conflict. She was concerned that her decisions about patient care were being unduly influenced by her own need to make money.

## THE PARADOX: DO NOT EXAMINE VS. TELL ALL

Curiously, working with managed care brings about a paradoxical tension between the obfuscation of the truth on one hand and the public airing of the truth on the other. Managed care companies are both too rigid and too loose about therapist–patient boundaries. In my work with managed care clients, I have found myself occasionally not wanting to know more about patients' characterological issues, childhood experiences, traumatic memories, or unresolved conflicts when there is insufficient time to deal adequately with them. I have not wanted to urge a patient to uncover painful, though truthful, material when I cannot guarantee with any degree of certainty that I will be there to help him or her work through it. I have felt disheartened knowing there is so much more a patient and I could undertake to improve the patient's well-being, while simultaneously realizing that a force outside myself works against my pursuing that path. Over time, I became aware that I was working differently with my managed care patients than with those for whom time limits were not driving the treatment. Some of my colleagues report that they too have knowingly looked the other way on occasion or helped patients seal over when they actually believed that further exploration would have been preferable.

At the same time, I have been encouraged by managed care to reveal confidential information about a patient to people outside the treatment. What was once considered a sacrosanct, private relationship between therapist and patient is sometimes thought to be public property that can be reviewed and critiqued at various intervals by one or more outside entities. At times reviewers seem interested in much more than progress toward specified goals; they inquire about personal matters, session content, and even patients' fantasy lives. Oddly enough, in several instances the truths I could not explore with patients were the very topics under discussion with the reviewer. I have experienced this incongruity as a crazy-making double bind: there is at once too much privacy and secrecy and not enough privacy and secrecy.

Even though it contradicts what they were taught, therapists who agree to work with managed care tacitly accept the premise that there is nothing private about doing psychotherapy with a managed care patient. Stern (1993) writes, "The therapist's job is to create the conditions necessary for patients to reveal, define, and work on these problems to the point where they feel comfortable continuing that work on their own" (p. 164). Such an atmosphere is created in part through the confidentiality between patient and therapist. "Third party intrusions . . . introduced by managed care" interfere with the atmosphere of safety that the therapist attempts to create and "violate [not only] the confidentiality and exclusivity of the therapy relationship [but also] the therapist's ability to provide a reliable, protected setting for therapeutic work" (p. 166).

## A CHANGE IN THE TREATMENT RELATIONSHIP

Beyond the treatment itself, the relationship between patient and therapist has been profoundly affected as well. Ideally, patients should define the therapy relationship as they need it to be. If therapists successfully create an atmosphere of flexibility and availability, they communicate that they will be present for their patients as long as they need them to be. Furthermore, treatment works best when it is driven by the needs of individual patients rather than by generally derived, formulaic policies. The fact that treatment duration, frequency, and content can be specified by others has numerous implications for the therapeutic relationship and many deleterious effects on clinical care.

One such implication pertains to the replacement of a therapeutic relationship involving intimacy with one characterized by distance and disconnection. Under managed care a relationship is not permitted to develop freely, of its own accord, without external time constraints and limitations imposed by others. The clinician begins speaking about the end of treatment from the beginning. How can a patient feel comfortable opening up when he cannot derive any security from knowing that, if he needs it, he will be supported by his ongoing relationship with a caring, understanding therapist? Perhaps some patients, notably those having problems with intimacy, actually feel more comfortable in a therapy relationship that is prescribed by managed care to be brief.

*John*

The case of "John," a patient who had a great deal of difficulty settling into treatment, illustrates this. There was nothing regular about John's treatment frame. Not only was he unable to commit to a regular weekly time for his sessions, John also refused to schedule a subsequent session during any face-to-face encounter, preferring instead to call me sometime after the session to set up our next meeting. Our mutual uncertainty about how long his insurance would cover his treatment was clearly on his mind, as he began each session by asking whether I had received authorization for him to return for yet another session.

Having just concluded a difficult phase where I had been upset about the adverse impact of managed care's intrusion into several other cases, I was more up front than usual with John about the difficulties of using his insurance to cover his treatment. I shared with him my belief that not knowing how long our meetings would go on was making it difficult for him to settle into treatment. I also acknowledged that whether we would meet again was in large part beyond the control of either of us. After five meetings, he abruptly discontinued his sessions. I was curious for a long time afterward about whether John's quitting resulted from my having been so direct with him. I wondered whether he had perceived my uncertainty and ambivalence about treating him within a managed care framework. Insofar as it provided a built-in exit, managed care's ideology matched John's "intimacy problem." Thus, rather than providing a solution to his presenting problem, managed care exacerbated it.

Paradoxically, the managed care reviewers might consider this case a treatment success for it stayed within the five-session limit. Symptomatically, John may have appeared better. Internally, however, I fear that he may have remained unchanged—in a state of turmoil.

Clearly, John, and patients with similar dynamics, would have had difficulty committing to any treatment. However, the added pressure brought to bear in managed care's authorization of sessions and placement of restrictions on his treatment seemed to make it impossible for him to settle down and establish a treatment relationship. In some ways, therapists' efforts to inform clients of their options may actually hamper the relationship between patient and therapist. Once a therapist tells a patient of the limits to the formerly private world between patient and therapist, the ever-present threat that sessions may be discontinued at any time takes center stage. This may lead the patient to keep him- or herself at some distance, never forming much of a connection with the therapist. Thus one consequence of being well informed about the limits to confidentiality and the uncertain duration of treatment is that it may limit patients' full engagement with therapists.

On the therapist's side, I, like many others, entered the profession in part because of my belief in the mutative value of relationships. In the context of being able to offer only a watered-down, time-limited version of the relationship, I, and many of my colleagues, are mournful and despairing. We have lost both a part of ourselves as well as our work. As we seek to protect ourselves from the inordinate pain associated with this loss, we transform who we are. We attempt to change our identity by using language that relabels us and redefines our professional roles. As if changing the words will eradicate the pain, we declare ourselves not "psychotherapists" but "consultants." We provide not "psychotherapy" or "treatment" but "consultation." In order to accommodate to a system in which we do not believe, we redescribe ourselves.

For me, this Orwellian revisionism has another function. It helps me manage my feelings of attachment and connection with the patient and serves to warn the patient not to get too close. The unspoken communication is that "this is not a relationship." My intention is to minimize any feelings I might have toward my patient or my patient might have toward me.

## SUMMARY

In my work as a private practice therapist participating in managed care plans I have often felt an encumbrance preventing me from acting in accord with my beliefs. In my contact with managed care patients I have experienced a dichotomy between what managed care advocates and what I am inclined to do, think, or feel more frequently than I have in my work with other patients. The pressure to resolve this tension in a way that allows me to maintain my relationship with managed care has had a negative effect on the quality of clinical care I provide. I and my colleagues have altered the treatment frame in ways detrimental to patients, embarked on short-term treatments when we believed they were not what patients needed, made clinical decisions motivated more by money than patients' best interest, and overlooked significant areas of patients' history or disturbance.

I sometimes worry that my interest in preserving my livelihood constricts me from speaking out when my opinion differs from the managed care plan's protocol. I am concerned that after many experiences in which my values and attitudes conflict with the policies of the managed care plan, I might begin to adjust or alter my beliefs. As my opinions begin to seem no longer viable in today's health care environment, my thinking might change to fit what is possible. Expanded to a global level, this could result in a frightening state of affairs in which clinicians lose the capacity to contemplate thoughts other than those sanctioned by managed care. Since there is little hope that they can be implemented, practitioners stop allowing themselves creative access to their own ideas.

Under managed care my relationships with my patients have been undeniably altered. The presence of outside reviewers who are privy to confidential information about the treatment has introduced another party into the relationship between patient and therapist. The fact that a patient's treatment can be terminated at any time by individuals outside my office, beyond the control of either me or my patient, has engendered an atmosphere of uncertainty and powerlessness. This has undermined my authority to make treatment decisions. I often find myself vying with managed care for the privileged position of being the one "in charge."

When I work with a patient who has managed care insurance, the entire issue of privacy and confidentiality changes. Curiously, in the current health care climate, the truth is paradoxically obscured at the same time that a patient's private material is broadcast to a wide audience. Not knowing how long a treatment might last leads the patient and me to collude with managed care in deciding not to delve further when there are indications of problem areas or pathology meriting further exploration. When length of treatment is partially within my control, I rarely experience this. Conversely, my needing to procure authorization for sessions means that I discuss details of patients' treatment all too openly, revealing details of sessions or dramatizing a patient's problems to an outsider unconnected with the work. When I cannot explore a patient's issues with the patient, but I then reveal them to a stranger, something is amiss. Ironically, the wrong person is being granted access to the material so that I can obtain additional time to do little more than help a patient seal over.

## CONCLUSION

What has evolved is a system in which there are two different levels of clinical care: treatment with a patient with managed care insurance and treatment with a nonmanaged care patient. Few patients are aware that there is a two-tiered infrastructure. Even fewer know that their treaters' clinical decisions are increasingly being influenced by their own pecuniary interests. As these changes have occurred insidiously, therapists are often not cognizant of the adverse ways in which their work has been influenced by managed care and capitation. If we care about delivering high quality patient care to all people regardless of their financial situation, we cannot continue to give insurance companies the power to dictate and govern clinical care.

## REFERENCES

Beauchamp, T., and Childress, W. (1988). *Principles of Biomedical Ethics*, 3rd ed. Baltimore, MD: Johns Hopkins University Press.

Haas, L. J., and Cummings, N. A. (1991). Managed outpatient mental health plans: clinical, ethical, and practical guidelines for participation. *Professional Psychology: Research and Practice* 22(1): 45–51.

Morriem, S. (1988). Cost containment: challenging fidelity and justice. *Hastings Center Report* 18:20–25.

Stern, S. (1993). Managed care, brief therapy, and therapeutic integrity. *Psychotherapy* 30(1):162–175.

# 7

# Inpatient Child Mental Health Treatment: Strategies Used to Manage Treatment

ELISA T. BRONFMAN

Child inpatient mental health services have undergone dramatic changes in the past few years. For example, on one unit in Massachusetts where I worked, the average length of a child's stay decreased from six weeks to two weeks in a few months' time. The pressure to shorten the length of stay came from three sources: managed care reviewers who would suggest that a particular child was ready for discharge, hospital administrators who knew that in order to remain "competitive" with managed care the hospital needed to boast as low an average length of stay as possible, and the unit administration that feared closure or layoffs if the average length of stay did not decrease. The adaptation to these treatment shifts was difficult for the entire staff and the rapidity of the change allowed little time to think about how the admission could remain effective for children in crisis. The shift to a shorter length of stay necessitated a change in treatment approach and required the hospital team to revise its view of what could be accomplished during an inpatient stay.

Despite the intense pressure on psychiatric units to decrease their lengths of stay, two factors have made quick discharge for children and adolescents difficult. First, resources and aftercare programs, such as specialized foster care, residential treatment, and short-term respite facilities, are in short supply, leading to fewer choices and waiting lists for the services needed by hospitalized children. Second, insurance companies and capitated contract agreements do not authorize hospitalization for children unless the level of crisis is extreme. Children who previously would have been thought of as requiring a hospital level of care are recommended for "less expensive" forms of treatment, such as foster care, respite care, or short-term residential placement, further burdening these services.

The need for psychiatric services for children and adolescents is clear. Geraty and Fox (1996) estimate that 14–22 percent of children suffer from moderate to severe psychiatric disorders. They also note that the majority of children requiring psychological intervention do not require inpatient hospitalization. They suggest that one benefit of managed care has been the development of more levels of care aside from hospitalization for children with different treatment needs. With more treatment choices, children who previously would have been hospitalized can be treated in their communities, with lower cost and less stress to families. However, the children who are now hospitalized are the children with the most severe difficulties.

When hospitalization does occur, it is considered a last resort as it is extremely expensive to the managed care companies. As a result, managed care reviews are conducted many times per week and the pressure to show quick progress is intense. In speaking to the reviewer, the clinician is asked what the hospital has "done" for the child. The anticipation of the review pressures the unit to take concrete actions, such as seeking out-of-home placement or initiating a medication trial, in order to satisfy the expectations of the plan funding the psychiatric admission. The hospital attempts to demonstrate stabilization and release the child as quickly as possible. Sharfstein (1994) links the decreased length of stay not to decreased patient symptomatology but to the use of these case reviews, which are conducted frequently, semi-anonymously, and with criteria of progress that are never specified. With the competitiveness between hospitals for managed care business, the cost of not pleasing the reviewer may be the managed care contract.

In one hospital where I was affiliated, there was pressure on all staff to provide quick interventions. One psychiatrist expressed his frustration that he often felt compelled to add medication, despite possible side effects and the brevity of his evaluation, because, in the little time available, he felt that it was "something" to add to the child's treatment. This was especially true in the case of an 8-year-old girl with severe tantrums, who was hospitalized for the first time. Although the psychiatrist believed that family systems treatment and behavioral training for the parents would be best, he was aware of managed care's watchful eye. He believed that the managed care reviewer would be more favorable to a trial of medication than a trial of family therapy. So the psychiatrist reluctantly started the child on medication. The psychiatrist remembered that when admissions were longer (even by a few weeks) he often delayed medication trials, first attempting psychosocial interventions such as behavior modification plans. His need to take an action (medication) was motivated in part by knowing that there was a limit to the amount of inpatient treatment the child could receive and also by knowing that a report would have to be made to someone who *expected* interventions like medication trials.

## Jimmy

The pressure from managed care in one case led to a desire to discharge a patient too quickly although there was evidence of the need for a longer admission. An 11-year-old boy ("Jimmy") would not stop hitting his father and mother. The police were ultimately called to the home. Jimmy, who had no past psychiatric history or legal difficulties, was evaluated in an emergency room and was admitted at an inpatient child psychiatric unit. Because of his lack of prior difficulties and his "good behavior" on the unit, contacts occurred between the managed care reviewer and the unit case manager several times a week to consider whether he required continued treatment. The unit staff remained concerned about Jimmy because of his lack of remorse toward his parents. The reviewer, however, noting Jimmy's apparent lack of aggressivity on the unit, urged discharge.

After a relatively lengthy two-week admission, a discharge date was set. In order to provide information to the newly identified outpatient team, who reluctantly agreed to take the case from a hospital unit, Jimmy was given psychological testing. During the administration of "Sentence Completion," Jimmy indicated that he had a gun and "might use it" against his parents. Suddenly the "discharge deal" that had been worked out with the managed care reviewer was in jeopardy. The reviewer expressed frustration over the failure of the discharge plan. The team treating Jimmy felt somehow responsible for discovering the homicidal ideation, as if by providing the testing they had created the problem of the gun. Although there was some relief that a dangerous situation had been averted, it was also stated overtly that it might have been better if this information had never been known and if testing had never been done.

Prior to testing, there was significant evidence that Jimmy was dangerous. He had never shown remorse for his aggressive outburst. Yet the focus of the admission had been more on finding a way to get him out than on figuring out why he had become so aggressive in the first place. The hospital staff knew that the insurance benefits would limit what could be provided for him. The truth of the situation—that a two-week admission was too short to resolve a dramatic increase in aggression—was discussed, although lengthening the hospital admission was not an option given by managed care. Ultimately, the boy was able to stay in the hospital for a few more days while the gun was searched for and found. While this was a "happy" resolution, the hospital team responded as though they would think twice before recommending psychological testing with the next child.

In order to keep the length of stay short for children admitted to psychiatric units, each hospital has had to adapt. Usually the team at the hospital comes to a shared perspective regarding the best way to adjust to a shorter length of stay. Currently, it is rare to find a unit that prioritizes individual psychotherapy as the primary means of promoting change in children. This shift away from individual therapy and toward quick stabilization has been positive in its function of returning children sooner to more normative settings. However, it has led to increased confusion about the way to promote change in psychiatrically ill children.

Given that individual therapy is not often seen as the primary means of stabilization, two other approaches have arisen: the symptom-based strategy and the systems approach. In both strategies the hospital team acquiesces to the need for a shorter length of stay and the perspective that the bulk of the psychotherapy should occur on an outpatient basis as soon as the patient is ready for discharge. In the symptom-based approach the unit staff takes the position that the symptom picture in the hospital is the best representation of the child's functioning and that the job of the unit is to stabilize the behavior on the unit. This approach tends to truncate the problem into behavioral symptoms that can be addressed through short-term hospital treatment plans. The child, rather than the family system, tends to be the target of the intervention. This approach fits well with the medical language and approach adopted by the managed care reviewers.

In the systems approach the hospital staff believes that, in order to help the child in such a short time, the focus should be on the child's family/home environment rather than on individual therapy. Attempts are made to make changes in the child's environment so that the child can better function in that environment, even with little change in the symptoms that led to hospitalization. If it is not possible to help the child function more optimally at home, a more appropriate situation is sought for the child upon discharge.

## THE SYMPTOM-BASED STRATEGY

In the symptom-based approach the staff of the inpatient child unit uses the symptom picture as the target of intervention and also as the measure of improvement. Problems are seen as primarily "in the child" in terms of discrete symptoms. Managed care reviews focus on what the child is doing in the hospital, and these behaviors are seen as dictating the timing of discharge. This approach can be particularly effective with children demonstrating the onset of new symptoms. For example, patients admitted with psychotic symptoms can benefit from medication and symptom-focused therapy. Response to treatment, operationalized as a decrease in psychotic symptoms, is then a good measure of when discharge should occur. However, the following case example demonstrates how the symptom-focused strategy can go awry.

## Jessie

An 11-year-old girl ("Jessie") was referred for an inpatient stay by her outpatient therapist because of intractable family difficulties. At the time of the referral to the unit, Jessie's mother was so enraged with her that she did not believe she could manage her at home. She believed Jessie was attempting to control the family and described her as "spiteful." This conflict was manifested in a solitary but ongoing dramatic symptom: encopresis (soiling). The family had been in therapy for one month. As part of the "homework" of family therapy, Jessie's mother had been writing a positive message each morning and leaving it for Jessie to read on the kitchen table. Following this intervention, the soiling had stopped for a few days. The mother and daughter felt excited about the change. However, the positive change in Jessie's relationship with her mother fell apart in a moment of anger. Jessie responded to a morning note by saying she did not feel worthy of the praise her mother had been giving her. The mother, believing this comment to be a rejection of her praise, became angry, and declared that since Jessie was ungrateful, she would no longer provide the morning notes. A few hours after this interaction Jessie soiled again. In the next family therapy session the mother expressed her upset about the return of the symptom. Jessie stated that she was sick of being controlled by her mother, that she could "shit" wherever and whenever she wanted and that her mother couldn't stop it.

Jessie's mother requested that the family therapist facilitate an inpatient psychiatric admission. The mother felt that Jessie was "out of control." Jessie also felt stuck, depressed, enraged, and unable to negotiate with her family. The family therapist was concerned about the entire family's rage and sense of being out of control. At the admission meeting, Jessie, her mother, and the outside therapist all framed the problem in terms of the mother–daughter conflict, Jessie's refusal to stop "shitting," and her mother's refusal to continue with the morning notes.

Jessie was admitted and remained in the hospital for a full week. Although the reason for admission was the family conflict, the symptom chosen for intervention by the inpatient unit was the soiling. The symptom-focused approach might have been more effective if family conflict had been the symptom chosen for intervention. However, the soiling was an easier, more observable choice. The treatment for the soiling consisted of daily mineral oil to address her bowel difficulties. As Jessie had no "accidents" (a misnomer in this case) while in the hospital, she was deemed ready for discharge.

Jessie was considered a successful "cure." After all, the "symptom" of soiling did not occur during the admission. The inpatient case manager did not appear to understand or anticipate the upset of the outpatient therapist upon hearing this report. It was simple: the original problem was reduced to one essential part—the bowel movements. This symptom was cured, or so they thought, by the administration of mineral oil. However, Jessie resumed her soiling behavior as soon as she returned home. Since the hospital staff's only contact with Jessie and her family was over upon discharge, they would never know about the return of the symptom and would instead consider Jessie one of their treatment successes. The inpatient case manager's report to the managed care reviewer would likewise point out the efficacy of the treatment. The problem was manageable, a cure occurred, and a good solution was obtained. Everyone was happy. Ironically, this form of treatment (mineral oil for soiling) could certainly have occurred on an outpatient basis. It was an extremely expensive method of treatment when employed on an inpatient basis.

When the time allotted for treatment is limited, it can be helpful to truncate a child's difficulties into concrete and observable symptoms. This may make it easier to focus on a workable plan. One risk is that particular symptoms can become a point of struggle. In using single symptoms alone, rather than context, a clinician may become overly reliant on patient or family report of that symptom rather than judging the entire context himself or even adequately assessing the symptom itself, as seen in the following example.

*Ricardo*

In an emergency interview a clinician was evaluating a boy for psychiatric admission. The boy ("Ricardo") was a 17-year-old who had overdosed on more than forty Tylenol. He had no prior psychiatric history. Ricardo's mother had found the empty pill bottle and had called an ambulance. Ricardo was on a medical floor because of the severity of the attempt and possible damage to internal organs. He was fortunate in having received medical treatment so quickly, as the overdose could have been fatal if undiscovered. In the interview Ricardo stated that he was sorry he had taken the Tylenol. The precipitant was his upset about a breakup with his girlfriend of six months. Ricardo's mother seemed unconcerned, stating that her son simply had a "momentary lapse." She believed that he was now safe. Ricardo appeared somewhat depressed and physically exhausted from his experience. Yet he adamantly denied suicidality. In formulating a plan, the evaluator felt trapped. Ricardo had made an extremely serious suicide attempt, but he denied that he would harm himself again. The evaluator told his supervisor, "We can't hospitalize him." The supervisor responded, "Why not?" The evaluator responded that Ricardo said he wasn't suicidal, not realizing that he had limited his evaluation to patient report alone, rather than using his own clinical observation, analytical skills, and professional judgment. The supervisor then pointed out that Ricardo had made a near-lethal suicide attempt for which he had not sought help *and* that the reason for the attempt (the breakup) had not changed. Moreover, the supervisor called attention to the fact that no one in the environment was markedly alarmed.

For a moment at least this clinician was able to broaden his perspective beyond the patient's overt report of symptoms. The evaluator realized how many times he had been called on by reviewers to report symptoms in a superficial way, although it was not what he had been trained to do in graduate school. He realized he was influenced by his expectation that the managed care reviewer for admission would ask if the boy had said explicitly that he would kill himself. The clinician had previously had this conversation with reviewers more times than he could count. In the absence of an explicitly stated "suicide threat" by the patient, he wondered what he could tell the reviewer in order to obtain a bed. The focus of the clinical interview became gaining evidence to give to the reviewer to justify treatment recommendations rather than to understand Ricardo. Even though it is unlikely that any managed care reviewer would refuse admission to a boy with such a serious suicide attempt, the clinician found that his judgment was affected by his expectation of having to respond to these questions and having to provide the "right" answers.

## THE SYSTEMS STRATEGY

Some hospitals, while continuing to assess symptoms, use a systems-based strategy to treat children. Here the hospital team believes that it is critical to change the child's environment in some way. This is accomplished by placing the child in a new living situation after discharge, by changing relationships in the existing setting, or by adding supportive services to the entire family. Maneuvering systems change is a difficult task, often requiring more time than lengths of stay allow. In addition, sometimes the only way to demonstrate the need for a child to be removed from a current living setting is to document a cycle of repeated failed placements. Systems interventions do, however, allow for multiple avenues of intervention by involving outside caregivers and parents in the plan for discharge. Consider the following case.

### John

"John," a 13-year-old refugee from Haiti, was admitted to a child psychiatric unit. A product of a rape that occurred while his mother was in a refugee camp, John was depressed and acting out. He had taken pills in a suicide attempt and had also become increasingly aggressive toward his mother. Because he appeared less depressed and had not assaulted anyone, the managed care reviewer felt after a week that John should be discharged from the unit. Even though his affect was improved, the hospital team did not want to discharge John, believing that upon return to his environment he would again become suicidal and aggressive. Two days after discharge he was readmitted with suicidal and aggressive ideation, as expected by the hospital staff. In the second admission he assaulted the unit staff. Only after demonstrating more "symptoms" in the hospital could he be considered for more intensive services. Over a period of several months John was repeatedly discharged and rehospitalized due to suicidal actions and aggressive acting out toward adults and children. Multiple hospitalizations were required before the recommendation for residential treatment was taken seriously. His condition had deteriorated considerably since his first admission. Moreover, his willingness to try new programs diminished as he expected to fail in each aftercare plan that was set up for him. John began to believe he could not trust the people who were caring for him to make good decisions on his behalf.

Given state statutes in Massachusetts, where John's treatment occurred, it could be argued that each of three different agencies (child protection, mental health, and youth services) should be responsible for his aftercare depending on the frame used to define his "problem." Often these agencies, as well as the child's health insurance, battle about who should be responsible for paying for aftercare, with each trying to shift responsibility for payment to the other. The social service agencies that provide placements to children are financially stressed, just as managed care is, leading to a need to limit the amount of service provided. Since each agency is reluctant to pay for aftercare in a multifaceted case like John's, the hospital then takes part in the cycle of repeated hospitalizations (as in the oft-stated "He'll be back"), until multiple failures and worsening of the child's condition are evident. Only at this point is a tenable plan worked out.

In the systems approach, the hospital unit works toward changing something in the child's environment. This can put the hospital in a no-win situation if it recommends that outside agencies provide services that they are either unable or unwilling to provide. For example, if the hospital finds it is not safe for a child to return home, then jockeying to secure a more intensive placement, such as residential treatment, begins. Once this recommendation is made, the insurance company often places the patient on "administrative days," lowering the reimbursement to the hospital with the expectation that the patient is "held" without treatment while waiting for the "true placement" (not paid by insurance usually) to appear.

Once the hospital staff manages to get one of the social service agencies to take responsibility for the child, an appropriate program must be identified. Even when one agency decides to take responsibility for placing a child, the problem of finding and funding a placement begins. The agency may insist that the child be hospitalized longer for stability, and to provide time to identify a placement, despite the managed care refusal to fund it. Weeks of low reimbursement to the hospital accompanied by a battle with outside agencies often ensues. The hospital staff is likely to become weary of these fights, despite a wish to change the environment for the child.

On a unit where the systems approach predominates, it is impossible to advocate for each child so as to attain all of the services he or she needs. Many children known to need more services are left "unchosen" because the hospital cannot continually battle over payment with managed care while awaiting residential placements. Hospital therapists committed to the systems approach find it especially painful to be the case managers for children who need more services than will be provided on discharge.

## THE IMPACT OF DECREASING LENGTH OF STAY

In order to respond to pressures from managed care to decrease average length of stay, hospital teams have sought treatment modalities that fit a shorter-term model. The two strategies described above provide a focus for a short-term admission. The symptom-based model provides a focal concern that is very much tied to the reason for admission. The systems-based approach focuses on changing the child's environment so that a return is possible regardless of symptoms. Whatever strategy is adopted by the hospital unit, there is a need to treat and discharge patients in ways that serve the economic interests of the hospital whose priority may be maintaining a collegial relationship with the managed care vendors that provide payment.

Unfortunately, due to limits in the "science" of hospitalization, how much time or psychotherapy is needed to treat different patients is unclear. While financial issues influenced hospital stays well before managed care, the impact of the review process has been to promote the idea of shortened stay as a mission in and of itself and thus exploits the lack of certainty about the helpfulness of psychiatric hospitalization. Managed care has capitalized on the limited information regarding the efficacy of inpatient treatment, leaving therapists with few tools to argue the need for more or less treatment for a given problem.

The inpatient therapist must also change in order to adapt to shortened lengths of stay. These changes may include decreasing the therapist's ability to "see" by ignoring obvious evidence and limiting the scope of the problems to be addressed; decreasing the therapist's sense of efficacy by repeatedly suggesting that improvement for severe, chronic, intractable difficulties should occur in a very short time; and by focusing on outside systems. None of these changes are fully acceptable to psychotherapists who value relationships highly and see them as the mechanism of human change. In the child inpatient setting, the elimination of individual therapy as the primary mechanism used for change can be experienced as a loss to the therapists.

Working on an inpatient unit can have an impact on the therapist's world view, feelings about him- or herself, and belief in the possibility of human change in therapy. Two years ago, just before I left my job as a staff psychologist at a child inpatient unit, I noticed in a glaring moment how it had changed me. I thought I enjoyed the thrill of quick admissions and discharges, and sometimes I did. I justified to myself that I was good at evaluation—figuring out the details of what was going on for the children—and that this, if nothing else, would inform and provide information to whoever would treat the child on the outside. Sometimes I felt this helped the children a lot. At other times I believed the admissions were useful only in that they temporarily removed the child from his or her environment.

I had no idea that the daily inhumanity of my world, and the futility I felt, had seeped to a deeper level inside me. I began to believe that cycles of repeated failures and extreme crises were what would lead to a remedying of a deficient environment. Although I acknowledge that working in an inpatient setting with the crises and fast pace would have been difficult even without managed care, I believe that the limitations in length of stay and lack of appropriate aftercare resources provide an extreme magnifier to this already stressful situation. This became apparent to me in an incident outside work.

One day I was walking with a friend through a large mall parking lot to get to the supermarket. As we reached the door we saw a man leaving the store with two small children. The child he held was an infant, the other appeared to be about 2 years old. The man carried the groceries and the 2-year-old toddled behind him. My friend became immediately concerned that the man was walking through this busy parking lot without holding this very young child's hand. She wanted to watch to make certain it would be okay. I was less concerned, but my friend insisted. Soon it became apparent that it was a very dangerous situation. The father was not monitoring the child at all. Cars were whizzing around. The father was several car lengths ahead of this child and not looking back.

My friend said, "I've got to do something," and ran to the lot. She walked the girl safely to her father's car. In watching this situation unfold the feeling I had was the same as when I knew that multiple admissions would be needed before a change could occur in order to justify service needs to managed care and outside agencies. I realized I had become accustomed to a pattern of waiting for situations to deteriorate to very dangerous levels before making a change. I had also developed a tolerance for waiting for the risk to elevate before seeing a positive shift. This had become my expectation not only in my job but in my life. Aspects of who I was and how I perceived the world were affected by my work. I hadn't known it until that moment.

## REFERENCES

Geraty, R. D., and Fox, R. J. (1996). Can managed care improve mental health outcomes for children and adolescents? In *Controversies in Managed Mental Health Care*, ed. A. Lazarus, pp. 57–68. Washington, DC: American Psychiatric Press.

Sharfstein, S. S. (1994). Funding, third party payers, and managed care. In *Handbook of Adolescent Inpatient Psychiatric Treatment*, ed. H. S. Ghuman and R. M. Sarles, pp. 293–301. New York: Brunner/Mazel.

# 8

## Managed Care, Psychoanalytic Psychiatry, and Hospital Treatment: A Fictional Retrospective

RALPH H. BEAUMONT

Of the various treatment modalities prevalent in psychiatry that depend on third-party payment, psychiatric hospital treatment stands out as the modality most profoundly changed by managed care in the late 1980s and 1990s. Longer-term intensive treatment of severe psychiatric disorders in psychiatric hospital units has become nearly nonexistent. Lengths of stay have been shortened in most cases to a matter of a few days. Responses among practitioners to this rather radical change in the practice of psychiatric hospital treatment have been varied. Many decry the change as a nihilistic, financially motivated undermining of fundamental clinical values by a self-serving industry whose purpose is to deny care to those who often need it and are least able to advocate for themselves. Others view the change as a favorable and more efficient reallocation of inherently limited resources that is better suited to contemporary psychiatric practice with its psychopharmacologic emphasis. Many other views, some more moderate, and perhaps some more extreme, are represented on the contemporary scene.

How can a psychoanalyst comprehend the significance of the far-reaching impact of managed care on psychiatric hospitalization? Some analysts might decline to address the question, pointing to the decreasing relevance of psychoanalytic treatment modalities and concepts to psychiatric hospital treatment. Other analysts who favor a broader clinical application of psychoanalytic ideas may be more inclined to try to address the relevance of psychoanalysis to psychiatric hospital treatment. How to approach the question in a manner that considers the full complexity of the changes in such treatment may be less than immediately apparent, however. One psychoanalytic approach to understanding phenomena not limited to the psychoanalytic situation was offered by Merton Gill, an analyst who advocated a particularly broad application of psychoanalytic methodology. In *Psychoanalysis in Transition* (1994) he wrote, "A phenomenon is not understood psychoanalytically until its subjective significance to the two participants has been explored" (p. 155).

Even if one finds this methodological suggestion compelling, the attempt to apply it to the subject at hand may still encounter insurmountable difficulties. The plethora of subjective responses to recent changes in psychiatric hospital treatment could leave one hard-pressed to derive a well-integrated understanding from the rather tumultuous mix of contemporary responses. I shall not attempt such an integration. Instead, I offer a fictional dialogue set a hundred years in the future. Perhaps this imaginary historical retrospective view can shed some light, subjectively colored though it must be, on the spirit of Gill's suggestion. The setting for the dialogue is the campus of the Harvard Business School, which has become the major academic forum for the consideration of historical trends in psychiatry. The participants are two students of the history of psychiatric economics and one of their professors. All three have recently participated in a course on psychiatric treatment in the late twentieth century in the United States. The subject matter seems to have provided the necessary ingredients for a challenging case study.

HARRIET SULLIVAN-REICHMAN (first student): In sifting through the historical artifacts of the late twentieth century, archaic and incompletely digitalized though they are, it seems clear that some remarkably primitive conflicts were still going on. On

one hand, many in the mental health community seemed
to be zealots of an early American utopian sort who believed
that mental illness could be cured if only enough psychiatric hospital treatment, including endless self-referential conversations, were provided. It was a sort of Nixon-curing-can-
cer fantasy. That movement developed momentum from
origins before World War II, peaked in the affluent '60s,
'70s, and early '80s, and abruptly declined when another
primitive group appeared on the scene. These were Puri-
tans of another variety. They were so worried about spending any money that it seemed they didn't want to conquer
mental illness, but to stamp out psychiatric treatment, including talk therapies, hospitalization, and especially talk
therapies with hospitalization. Milton, I just don't understand how such unsophisticated attitudes could have been
so rampant in public policy as recently as that. It continued
even after the information revolution when everyone had
access to the data!

MILTON FREEDBUCK REAGONERVE (second student): Remember,
Harriet, it was also the era of Arnold Schwarzenegger and
Jim Carrey as major cultural icons. Things were backward
then. Besides, I feel some sympathy with the way the managed care movement intervened with hospitals in the '80s
and '90s. It was even better than the deinstitutionalization
from the big state hospitals that started in the '60s. Lengths
of stay came down from weeks and months or more to a
matter of a few days. Where else in medicine was so much
wasted money saved? After all, there don't seem to be any
reports that the country suffered from the reduction in
hospitalization. The crime rate actually appears to have gone
down during the '90s. And look: here's a journal that compared patient satisfaction after hospitalizations of a few days'
duration with patient satisfaction after hospitalizations
of two months to two years a decade earlier. The patients
seemed more satisfied after the short stays than after the
long ones. Beyond that, there was the boom in the literary
genre of confessional hospital treatment narratives just after the turn of the century. We know it now as the infamous

psycho-gulag school. The psychiatric hospitals of the time seem to have received as much literary attention as the actual Soviet gulags. Those accounts make *Cuckoo's Nest, Girl Interrupted, Mount Misery,* and *I Never Promised You a Rose Garden* seem like beds of roses by comparison.

HSR: Now wait a minute, Milton! You're lapsing into oversimplification as usual. You're forgetting the revisionist critique of the psycho-gulag writers spearheaded by the neo-Ferenczi psychiatric critical studies movement here at the Business School in the '30s and '40s. According to their follow-up studies, both the people who wrote the psychiatric victim narratives and the others who had hospitalizations of six months' duration and longer did better on long-term follow-up. And those patient satisfaction surveys you mentioned were shown to be either negatively correlated with or unrelated to long-term outcomes. Only when there was long-term outpatient aftercare did the outcomes look good. The problem with the long stays was that people still imagined that the hospital treatments would cure patients. As with the shorter-stay patients, this led them to ignore the importance of long-term outpatient follow-up treatment of patients with severe disorders. It seems that the ones who worked through their ambivalent feelings about their intensive hospital treatments—in psycho-gulag publications or in psychotherapy—did best.

MFR: Worked through, smirked through! That was pure squeaky-wheel effect. The silent majority were miserable being brainwashed with psychobabble in those locked wards. Let 'em out early, and they're definitely happier. Read the results in the standardized total quality life space management literature of the teens and twenties.

HSR: Now that's unfair. What you're referring to is after the introduction of Zonkokinase and Somozap and the other dementalizing agents. If you want to discuss brainwashing, look at the kind of information the managed care industry of the late twentieth century tried to foist on the public. Those satisfaction surveys are pure Madison Avenue PR.

MFR: Nevertheless, the patients said they liked the shorter stays better. And there was the *Time* cover story after the turn of the century, reporting on Ken Kesey's great-nephew's short-term hospital treatment. Kesey was quoted as saying, "Big Nurse is my friend."

HSR: I don't think any discussion between the two of us is going to solve this. There's Professor Merton Couchbound. Let's see what he says.

MFR: Okay, but you'll have to explain your side. I don't understand it. Hello, Professor Couchbound. I wonder if we could ask your opinion about some relatively ancient psychiatric economic history from the late twentieth century?

PROF. COUCHBOUND: Ah, yes. A fascinating time. Like Athens. Down with Socrates, down with Freud. Up with the lowest common denominator psychiatry, democratic health care reform, and managed care. What were you wondering about?

HSR: We're talking about the historic change in the use of psychiatric hospitals at that time. My argument is that managed care and short stays were even more primitive than what came before. The data show that, despite managed care patient satisfaction surveys and the psychiatric hospital gulag literature after the turn of the century, the long-stay patients, when they had good aftercare, fared better in the long run.

MFR: What Harriet ignores, Dr. Couchbound, is the abundant documentation that patients felt better about their two- to five-day hospital stays than they ever did about those long stays.

PROF. C: Of course, of course. You're both right. I suppose they no longer teach, even in the history courses, about the concept of transference. It's been all but forgotten since the dementalizing agents became so popular and the digitalized brain techniques came along.

MFR: I'm sorry, Professor. What does electronic travel have to do with it?

PROF. C: Milton, I suppose you have no way of knowing that before travel by electronic transference became commercially available, transference was a concept in psychoanalysis. It referred to the way patients unconsciously brought past emotional investments into the here-and-now involvement with the analyst. At one time they used to talk about "transference cures." Those were symptomatic improvements based not on understanding and insight into how past conflicts influenced life in the present, but on the good feelings that accompanied hopeful, positive transferences.

HSR: So, Professor, you agree with me! The positive results from those brief hospital stays were illusions, no more real than the wish-fulfilling dreams of Freudian psychoanalysis. Since they were based only on transference, and not on insight and understanding, they couldn't last, and would inevitably collapse.

PROF. C: Perhaps so. But transference cures have not always had such a bad name. Some argued that even though they were defensive in some respects, in other ways transference-based improvements may have been indistinguishable from the corrective emotional experiences that arguably go on in all effective psychotherapy. But you're correct, of course, that the brief, transferentially based improvements that often went with short hospital stays didn't stand much chance to be worked through and consolidated. They often helped the patients into more longstanding treatments, where lasting change could occur. During the long-term treatments, patients experienced all sorts of other facets of transference. After such short treatments all bets on the persistence and durability of transference cures are off.

MFR: But Professor Couchbound, if I understand correctly, you said that I was right, and the patient satisfaction surveys were accurate. The patients were better because the hospital care helped them transfer positive feelings into the present.

PROF. C: Yes. That's how the analysts saw it. Of course, the drug people also had their explanations.

MFR: Yes, they thought the drugs available before the dementalizing agents were effective! (*HSR, MFR, and PROFESSOR C all laugh uproariously.*)

HSR: But Professor Couchbound, you said the transference cures did produce good results. What about the fact that the worst outcomes occurred with those who had transference cures in short hospital stays with little aftercare? Also, the best long-term outcomes occurred in the patients with longer hospital stays and more extensive outpatient aftercare and more obviously negative transference.

PROF. C: I suppose the hope mobilized in the early positive transferences was usually not sufficient, however necessary it may have been. Psychoanalysts seem to have used the term *transference cure* along with another phrase, *flight into health.*

MFR: That sounds like a cost-effective approach. How did they produce that, Dr. Couchbound?

PROF. C: Often, the phenomenon of flight into health at least seemed to occur quite spontaneously. Most patients didn't stay for the long term, and for them our explanations seem speculative at best. Perhaps at times they were driven by the treaters to flee, as you suggest, into some version of pseudo-health. From the relatively small number who stayed longer, we can learn in a less speculative way about how the transference cures worked. When the long-term patients looked back on their early "transference cures," they were sometimes shocked at their innocence. They described it in a variety of ways, including seduction by the treaters, denial of their problems by themselves, and dreamlike wishful thinking. Some recalled desperate efforts to convince the terrifying caregivers that everything was all right so they could escape. Whatever the description, I'm afraid it never turns out to be as simple as those managed care satisfaction surveys suggested. There's always much more to be looked into and worked through.

HSR: So it was no cure at all! Only smoke and mirrors and collusions by the treaters with the sad self-deceptions of the desperate patients!

MFR: Now that's going too far! Do you think the doctors should have tried to convince the patients that they really weren't feeling better, and that the doctors hadn't really helped?

What would that have accomplished, besides making everyone more ambivalent and more miserable?

PROF. C: You both may be right. The analysts themselves never
seemed to have been entirely clear on whether the transference cure is best understood as a dreamlike, quasi-hallu-
cination based on the fantasies of infantile wishes at long
last being fulfilled, or as the emergence of realistic and
potentially healing hope in the presence of new and
healthier object relations. But all this could be endless. If
you keep arguing about this, people will begin to think the
two of you are candidates for a dose of Vodozap, the latest
and most thorough of the dementalizing agents. (*C, HSR,
and MFR all laugh, a little uneasily.*)

HSR: You're right, Professor. They were hopelessly primitive in
the twentieth century. Goodbye.

MFR: Well, at least I can agree on that. See you later. I'm off to
my class on Takeover Techniques of Late Twentieth Century Robber Barons.

Two days later another conversation occurred on the grounds
of the Harvard Business School; nearby, practicing rowers sped down
the Charles River, sweating the most academically scented saline west
of Oxford. Enter MFR and Professor C.

MFR: Professor C., hello. It's good to see you again. I've been
having bad dreams since our recent conversation here about
twentieth century economic trends in psychiatry. That idea
of some kind of mysterious force called transference that
leaves the account books in the red struck me as no less
preposterous than Marxism. Fortunately, Calvin himself
appeared to me in my last dream with reassuring news. He
said that the free market rules in Heaven, and that we have
more graduates there than any other school. Isn't it true that
for a long time all educated people have accepted the fact
that capitalist market competition and the law of supply and
demand place necessary limits on all human endeavors,
whether in psychiatry or in mining on Mars? How could
anyone argue with managed care in twentieth century psy-

chiatry by using conjuring tricks like false transference cures? Doesn't that end up as a threat to the free commerce of the marketplace?

PROF. C: Milton, I can see that you're worked up about this. It's a rather minor episode in economic history, all things considered. You do know, I assume, that psychoanalysis continued to develop outside the third-party funded medical establishment. Rumor has it that psychoanalysis may still be practiced in some of those old neighborhoods across the river.

MFR: I had no idea! I suppose anything is possible in Somerville. But not near the undergraduate campus, I hope.

PROF. C: No, not on campus anyway. The university has seen to that. But I'm struck by your vehemence and your troubled dreams. Why do you feel that psychoanalytic free association, as it were, would be contrary to a free market?

MFR: Maybe my emotional emphasis is related to the rising rate of tuition here. I'm not sure about that. But the answer to your question seems easy. Who pays for the so-called free associations and transferences, etcetera? Why are they called "free" if they're so expensive that almost nobody could afford to pay for them? And why should someone's psychotic or neurotic failure to add value to the marketplace entitle them to greater freedom of expression in the well-appointed consulting rooms of highly paid listeners who try to spread the arcane anticapitalist practice to other disaffected free market escapists?

(*HSR enters and joins the conversation.*)

HSR: Hello, Professor Couchbound. Hi, Milton. I've started reading some dusty old books by Freud that I found in the library at Boston College since our last conversation. They're quite fascinating. But perhaps I shouldn't interrupt your conversation, which must be about more weighty economic issues.

PROF. C: Not at all, Harriet. Milton was talking about the same thing. He even mentioned his dreams. He seems to feel there was an element of hypocrisy among the analysts when they supported the method of free association in opposition to managed care and the forces of the market that produced it.

MFR: Exactly, Professor Couchbound! The psychoanalysts wanted their free associations to be paid for by others who had to put up with the unhappiness produced by their mind-bending interpretations. Thank goodness for the drugs that came along to dementalize and delibidinize those nonproductive patients!

HSR: I can't really agree. First of all, the patients who underwent analysis paid the analysts who listened to and interpreted their free associations. They didn't pay the analysts to free-associate. They paid the analysts of their own free will, in the spirit of the free market "pursuit of happiness." When President Clinton proposed a health care policy that would have outlawed the free-market private practice that psychoanalysis depended on, the plan suffered a dramatic political demise. A group started in this area, called the Coalition for Patients' Rights, seems to have contributed to the Clinton plan's end by campaigning for the freedom to choose to pay for your own doctor. But, surprisingly enough, I agree with you in a way. Free association in psychoanalysis, which I suppose is a reasonable metaphor for psychoanalytic psychiatry as a whole, never occurred without its limits. Freud's point, I believe, was not to promulgate unlimited free association. Neither did the hospital-based psychoanalysts of the twentieth century want unlimited hospital stays. Freud thought it could be particularly useful to study the spontaneous and inevitable obstacles to free association. I suppose the analytic hospital psychiatrists wanted to study the inescapable obstacles to discharge from the hospital back to what you might call the free market community. Granted that the analogy between psychoanalysis and psychiatric hospital treatment can easily be stretched too far.

MFR: I'm glad you agree with the inherent limits of the analytic approach. I think this was the basis of the managed care orientation to psychiatry that so greatly changed hospital practice. The free market would not support the false freedom of long hospital treatments with questionable analytic rationales and ephemeral results.

HSR: Unfortunately, managed care seems to have exerted its influence in a somewhat more complex way than you describe. Let me tell you about a case I came across from the archives of McLean Hospital. It was difficult to reconstruct from the data available, but this is how I put it together. A patient with alcoholism and paranoia came into the hospital after years of failed treatments, increasing symptoms, and deterioration of functioning. This occurred around the same time the hospital administration developed a policy of keeping lengths of stay less than six months in order to placate managed care companies. For some odd reason the treating psychiatrists were not informed of the policy. Perhaps they would have rebelled. The patient's bill was paid entirely by his wealthy family, not by insurance. He was discharged with great improvement after six and a half months. A number of senior psychiatrists agreed the improvement was quite remarkable. Nevertheless, the treating psychiatrist was required to submit to a prolonged legalistic review of the case by a hospital committee for vaguely articulated reasons under the threat of professional censure. The actual reason, which was never stated, was the hospitalization of greater than six months, which prompted the hospital administration's fear of losing managed care contracts. The fact that the family had gratefully paid the bill did not seem to be considered relevant. After an arduous review process, the psychiatrist was cleared. The fact that the treatment was effective couldn't be contradicted, but the ward on which the treatment took place was closed soon after. Within two years the hospital provided only short-term treatment, no more than a few weeks, despite many who were willing to pay for more. Is this an example of a free market at work? Is it an example of wasted psychiatric resources? To me it seems to expose a psychiatric establishment running scared from the managed care industry. In the course of doing so, psychiatry at times seemed willing

to compromise the quality and depth of the treatment offered to patients, including those who would willingly pay
for more.

MFR: Good business managers are always faced with the problem of maverick employees who refuse to accept the facts
of business life. Your anecdote certainly can't be used to
bolster any mega-economic argument. Besides, paranoia has
a place in a free market, as does the selection of single malt
scotches at the bar in the Charles Hotel. Would you like to
join me for one, Professor Couchbound?

Prof. C: No, thank you, Milton. Your taste is a bit steep for a
professor's salary. I am struck that you both agree on the
inherent limits of economic endeavors such as psychiatric
hospital treatment based on psychoanalytic principles. The
difference seems to be that you, Milton, in accord with the
managed care industry, would like to cope with the fact of
limits by participating in setting them. Harriet, on the other
hand, seems more inclined to see what she can learn by
observing and studying the limits that present themselves.
Milton's approach did seem to prevail as the twentieth century came to an end. Perhaps the analysts might have understood this as a not so unusual variety of identification with
the aggressor. See you both in class!

## REFERENCE

Gill, M. (1994). *Psychoanalysis in Transition.* Hillsdale, N J: Analytic
Press.

# 9

# The Marketing of Medical Psychotherapy

ELISA T. BRONFMAN

It is an exciting time to work as a psychotherapist for patients with medical diagnoses. Mental health professionals are gaining greater respect as part of medical teams and research is demonstrating the power of therapy to improve medical outcomes (Cummings 1986, Schell 1996). In addition, the pressures of managed care have been less intense in medical settings. Medical psychotherapy is often short-term due to patients' requests for goal-oriented models and the nature of the patient problems, which are frequently in the "adjustment disorder" range.

In research that markets therapy services to managed care, many studies have shown that psychological intervention decreases medical utilization, as measured by the number of visits to primary care physicians, use of diagnostic tests, and the length and number of medical hospitalizations (Borus et al. 1985, Cummings 1986, Haag 1984, Mumford et al. 1984, Schell 1996). This has been used as evidence of "cost offset," demonstrating that psychotherapy reduces overall insurance expenditure when it is provided for some medical patients (Cummings 1986, Schell 1996). Schell punctuates this point with his estimate that 60–70 percent of patients who visit primary care physicians have no new disease onset or exacerbation. He believes that when managed care vendors realize they can decrease the numbers of expensive diagnostic tests and visits to physicians, mental health services will actually be sought after rather than rejected by those desiring to control costs. The risk in this argument is that only some forms of psychotherapy, such as that for patients with medical diagnoses, may be seen as cost effective.

In the medical setting, the short-term model advocated by managed care often works well, fitting the length of hospitalization and allowing for therapy while the patient is an inpatient. In addition, medical psychotherapy is often focused around a traumatic event, such as the onset or exacerbation of illness in oneself or a family member, rather than a chronic difficulty. If the patient is an inpatient, having a person to talk to about the feelings involved who is also a liaison to the medical team can be helpful to both the patient and hospital staff members. The efficacy of this kind of inpatient medical mental health treatment is demonstrated in Mumford and colleagues' (1984) finding that with a modest psychological intervention the mean length of hospital stay is reduced from 8.6 days to 7.1 days.

In medical psychotherapy there is an immediate precipitant to a circumscribed concern. After all, who wouldn't want to talk and understand the feelings involved after learning of the need for an amputation, losing someone to death, or discovering a chronic or life-threatening diagnosis? Medical psychotherapy makes sense to managed care reviewers and patients benefit from it. In contrast, when a patient requests therapy for a more amorphous and chronic difficulty, it is not as easy for the average person to understand. When a patient or a family member is struck by illness, many people can relate. The person is seen as blameless in the genesis of the problem, unlike many long-term psychiatric patients who are seen as simply not wanting to stop their own "noxious" cycles of behavior.

## THE USE OF MEDICAL PSYCHOTHERAPY TO IMPROVE
## MEDICAL CARE AND DECREASE COST

*Willie*

A short-term treatment to facilitate surgery for an acutely ill child is easy to justify to managed care. For example, a 10-year-old boy ("Willie") who was anxious about open heart surgery was referred for outpatient psychotherapy as part of his preparation for surgery. Willie knew, as most patients do, that there was a chance he would die during the operation. However, children in this circumstance are not routinely referred for therapy. Willie was referred because he was not cooperating with medical staff. In a previous surgery, he had pulled the I.V. out from his arm and had refused to sit still for any procedure. He had kicked, screamed, and panicked during his most recent diagnostic visit. His feeling of terror was not the stated reason for the therapy referral; he was a behavior problem. Willie was also a child with many strengths, such as his excellent verbal and artistic abilities. Within a few sessions he could talk about his fears of losing control, dying, and having a serious chronic illness.

As part of the first session, Willie drew a cartoon story relating his fears about surgery. In the first frame he depicted himself sitting with his mother awaiting surgery. In the next frame he was taken away from his mother and left frightened and alone. Next he drew a room where body parts were strewn about for assembly into people. The mess and carelessness in the "body part" room were apparent. He explained that this was where he would get a new heart valve. In the last frame of Willie's drawing the doctors were using a chain saw on Willie while he was sleeping. The nurse assisting the doctor is depicted as having a "bad hair day" and not paying enough attention.

This cartoon was an avenue to understanding Willie's feelings about surgery. Once his fears were understood, a treatment plan was devised. The medical staff were alerted to changes in the plan that focused on increasing his compliance during the hospitalization. After this first session he met with his therapist and primary nurse and talked about his fears. A plan was made so that anesthesia induction could be provided with his mother present.

In the second session Willie was able to discuss some of his hopes for surgery, including to breathe better and to receive cards, balloons, and presents while hospitalized. By discussing his hopes with him, the staff could encourage positive thinking and cooperation with surgery. A short-term therapy (four sessions) enabled Willie to better cope with having the surgery and cooperate with all procedures. He felt better about the hospitalization because he managed the procedures with less conflict with both the hospital staff and his parents, who were embarrassed by his behaviors during previous admissions. He was discharged from the hospital several days before expected.

For managed care there is a financial advantage to providing this kind of treatment. In paying for four outpatient psychotherapy sessions, the cost of the patient's overall medical care was likely reduced. It is easy to imagine advocating that such interventions be provided to all pediatric cardiac patients, as money could be saved and the outcome improved. This would be very exciting and would likely improve care for many patients.

There are also dangers in this kind of thinking, however. If one form of psychotherapy is seen as a cost-saver and others are not, would managed care tend to prioritize the provision of one kind of treatment over another? Certainly, with limited resources, therapies that can prove their worth by saving rather than costing the managed care vendor money are the ones that will be supported. A battle over funds has already begun to polarize the mental health community.

The impact of these schisms on the mental health community has been dramatic in two ways. First, therapists have come to view their services in terms of cost, and have joined with the managed care view that they have little to offer if immediate progress is not observable (see, for example, Weisgerber and Mitchell, this volume). Due to the concrete nature of the problem and the clear outcome criteria specified in Willie's case, it was possible to see progress quickly. However, most issues that bring patients to mental health services do not offer such ease in evaluating the effectiveness of the intervention. This leads to doubts, even in the therapists' minds, about the worth of treatments where effectiveness is not so easily measured. Second, the battle within the psychotherapy community over which services are most helpful, now defined as the most cost-effective, has served to give ammunition to those who wish to deem all psychotherapy services as useless and subjective.

## MARKETING STRATEGIES FOR PSYCHOTHERAPY

Cummings (1986) has consistently advocated that psychologists learn to market their skills. While psychotherapists have been reluctant to do this, he argues that it is necessary to protect the guild. He has written about the real risks if therapists do not advocate for the field, stating that psychologists will become "poorly paid, little respected employees" (p. 426). There are indeed risks in both marketing and choosing not to market mental health services. If no marketing is undertaken, psychotherapy is likely to be portrayed as an ethereal practice. Without marketing, therapists appear to see themselves as "above" the real financial concerns that exist in the way health care dollars are divided. In addition, without advocates to establish the importance and benefits of therapy, it is likely that funds will diminish even further than they already have. A pitfall of marketing is that a monetary value is placed on a service that should be provided for those in need of it. The "value" of therapy may come to be seen in terms of a financial outcome that cannot always be promised or a therapeutic outcome that is not always easily evaluated.

It is clear that psychotherapy services will be further limited if there are no advocates marketing its value. The *way* of marketing is also important to consider. Mental health professionals should advocate for therapy in the medical setting because it can be helpful to people in distress. The outcome is seen in terms of benefit to people—greater ease of recovery, fewer medical visits, and shorter hospitalizations. Regardless of cost, these are good outcome measures. While saving money is a strong incentive to a for-profit insurance industry, it should not be the primary goal of mental health professionals. Joining with the concept that psychotherapy should be provided to save money on other medical expenses moves away from the perspective that psychotherapy is a valuable service in its own right.

The phenomenon of traumatic bonding is described earlier (see Weisgerber, this volume). Traumatic bonding occurs when a victim bonds to a captor because the resources are controlled by the captor and the victim subsequently begins to adopt the perspective of the captor. Marketing medical psychotherapy services as a profitmaker for managed care is a way of taking the perspective of managed care. Because psychotherapists are tied to managed care for their own survival, they risk overfocusing on the monetary aspects of therapy, both for managed care and themselves, rather than keeping patient progress as the primary concern.

Imagine using this line of reasoning with other covered services that cannot and do not claim cost saving. If a person is hit by a car, medical help is provided regardless of whether it will save on other medically covered services. It won't. It is provided because it is needed. Stern (1993) states, "Physicians don't remove a cast when a broken bone is half-healed or stop radiation treatment when the cancer is half-controlled. Likewise, we shouldn't stop psychotherapy when a patient's problem is half-solved" (p. 172). Using the argument that medically oriented therapy saves money by decreasing overall medical costs takes the focus away from the perspective that therapy can be a necessity in and of itself. Clinicians and managed care reviewers now discuss whether patients really *need* therapy or whether it is a luxury service.

The public is also aware of how all medical providers are tied to the managed care organizations that fund the hospitals and salaries. This has led to questioning about whether providers are more interested in the financial gain of all medical treatment as opposed to the personal benefit to the patient. The public's fear of managed care has become so pervasive that a popular horror novel, *Fatal Cure* (Cook 1993), has been written, which suggests that if it were financially more favorable to kill off patients rather than pay for their treatment, some doctors may be convinced to follow this treatment plan! The alliance with the patient, and general public trust in psychotherapy as a profession, may be affected by a marketing strategy of prioritizing managed care's earnings in the decision about how therapy should be provided.

## REDUCING SCHISMS IN THE
## MENTAL HEALTH COMMUNITY

The temptation to use the cost-saving potential of psychotherapy in
the medical setting did not arise in a vacuum; it came about because
of perceived threats to the funding of psychotherapy by managed care.
The finding that psychotherapy, rather than always being an expense,
can sometimes save money was seen as a powerful incentive to payers for psychotherapy services. However, the implication of this argument is that psychotherapies that are not cost saving should not
be funded.

*Sally*

In fighting for the limited health care dollars devoted to mental health care, schisms between therapists with different perspectives are magnified. At a weekly meeting for medical psychotherapists, a case was discussed. The patient ("Sally") was a
teenager with a chronic illness requiring multiple hospitalizations yearly in order to deal with acute exacerbations. Because
she was "difficult to manage," Sally was discussed several times
during her various medical admissions. She had also been treated
at another institution on an outpatient basis for severe psychiatric symptoms, including poor interpersonal skills, self-muti-
lative behavior, running away from home, and outbursts of
rage. Although Sally saw a psychotherapist three times a week
for nearly a year, she had never been hospitalized for mental
health reasons.

During her medical admissions, Sally was difficult on the
unit, often pitting staff members against one another. She refused many procedures. A psychotherapist was assigned who saw
Sally during her inpatient admissions only. This therapist focused
on helping Sally manage painful medical procedures and cooperate more fully with hospital staff. This more focal treatment
was mildly successful.

Sally then felt bonded to both her inpatient therapist and
her outpatient long-term therapist. Both psychotherapeutic in-

terventions were necessary for this very challenging patient. The focus of the two treatments was very different. However, the team of medical psychotherapists subsequently became concerned about the cost of the three-times-weekly outpatient therapy. The outpatient therapist saw the inpatient treatment as limited and tended to underestimate the potential for it to be of psychological benefit. She felt she needed to defend her use of the more frequent therapy to counteract the sentiment that her treatment was too costly. The cost of Sally's outpatient treatment became a focus of controversy by the inpatient team (in their skepticism of the frequency of treatment) and the outpatient therapist (in her defensiveness about the cost of her treatment).

Although Sally was usually quite positive about her outpatient therapy, during one admission, she was angry at the therapist and stated concerns to the medical team. These complaints were amorphous: "She's no good . . . not helping me . . . not there for me." The medical psychotherapist was sympathetic, given her concerns about the frequency of sessions, and did not explore fully the reasons for Sally's anger or the possibility that this could be a normal part of the treatment. Sally requested that the medical therapist take over her outpatient treatment. If cost of treatment had not been an issue, these complaints would likely have been seen as just a part of the context of Sally's overall relational difficulties, which were also apparent in each medical admission. She would likely have been encouraged to work out these concerns with her therapist. However, because there were concerns about the cost/frequency of sessions, the medical therapist did not discourage premature termination and agreed to see Sally weekly. Shortly after this change, the teenager's behavior deteriorated markedly and she required her first psychiatric hospitalization. The medical psychotherapist never acknowledged that perhaps the intensive (three times weekly) treatment had provided a stabilizing effect for Sally. While therapists from different orientations have often had difficulty seeing each other's perspective, introducing money as a factor serves to increase this schism and further polarizes therapists into their respective camps.

## CONCLUSIONS

In the short run, marketing medical psychotherapy services as cost saving may lead to additional monies for mental health. In the long run, focusing on money as a determination of what should be provided threatens to erode the ways in which therapists consider the range of services that are needed for all patients. Schisms within the field are likely to develop between therapists who provide treatments that save money and therapists who provide treatments to a "more costly" clinical population. In addition, looking at psychotherapy as cost saving to other medical interventions relegates it to a position as an adjunctive service rather than as a treatment needed in its own right.

It is exciting to be able to demonstrate the efficacy of medical psychotherapy in treating focal problems. It is also a strong vantage point in leveraging managed care to *want* to give monies. However, since not all mental health services are cost saving or readily amenable to measures of efficacy, using these arguments may ultimately limit rather than expand psychotherapy services.

## REFERENCES

Borus, J. F., Olendski, M. C., Kessler, L., et al. (1985). The "Offset Effect" of mental health treatment on ambulatory medical care utilization and charges. *Archives of General Psychiatry* 42:573–580.

Cook, R. (1993). *Fatal Cure.* New York: Putnam.

Cummings, N. A. (1986). The dismantling of our health system: strategies for the survival of psychological practice. *American Psychologist* 41(4):426–431.

Haag, A. (1984). Psychosomatic consultation–liaison service in a medical outpatient department. *Psychotherapy and Psychosomatics* 42:205–212.

Mumford, E., Schlesinger, H. J., Glass, G. V., et al. (1984). A new look at evidence about reduced cost of medical utilization following mental health treatment. *American Journal of Psychiatry* 141(10): 1145–1158.

Schell, B. J. (1996). Chronic disease and psychotherapy: part I. *Psychotherapy* 31(1):21–25.

Stern, S. (1993). Managed care, brief therapy, and therapeutic integrity. *Psychotherapy* 30(1):162–175.

# IV

## The Impact on the Training and Development of Therapists

# 10

# Forming an Identity as a Psychotherapist: Training under Managed Care

## PAMELA WOLF AND E. CATHERINE LOULA

Managed care has necessitated many adjustments in the conduct of psychotherapy. While it has emerged as an attempt to solve difficult economic problems, it brings with it a host of others. These difficulties include a preponderance of brief, short-term, solution-focused treatments; manualized care governed by universal guidelines that may not be in the best interest of the individual; and an overwhelming number of treatment decisions influenced by the profit interest of the insurance company.

Adaptation to managed care has in many cases resulted in innovative treatment strategies and more efficient use of time. However, as has been amply argued (see, for example, Loula, Mitchell, and Wolf, this volume), these adjustments have entailed certain sacrifices and compromises that may not be in the best interest of either the

We would like to thank Karen Weisgerber, Ph.D., for her invaluable contributions to this chapter. Without her time and assistance, this chapter would not have been possible.

patient or the therapist. With respect to therapists, perhaps those most greatly affected are those currently in training. Sacrifices are made in the formation of a fully evolved professional identity, the learning process, appreciation for theory, exposure to learning-focused activities, and the development of mentoring supervisory relationships. These are not simply issues of education; the ways in which managed care influences training determine the future of psychotherapy, in that training ultimately shapes the professionals of tomorrow.

Psychiatry and psychology training programs are in a difficult position. They must remain viable and hence respond to realistic economic imperatives. On the other hand, they need to offer excellent training and model integrity. These aims are not always compatible. The danger in such programs, as in the field as a whole, is that a training necessity may come to be viewed unquestioningly as a luxury even when it is not. As such, these programs may be especially vulnerable to compromising excellence in their effort to adapt to the requirements of managed care.

The conflict between striving for excellence and providing the greatest profit margin may fuel a polarization between ideal and actual components of training programs as follows: (1) professional identity development versus professional identity foreclosure; (2) learning a process versus acquiring a set of skills; (3) appreciation for theory versus focus on pragmatics; (4) exposure to training-focused versus income-focused experiences; and (5) supervision versus support. In each case the ideal value is at risk of being sacrificed. In a variety of ways, these compromises arise from the capitulation to various pressures associated with managed care such as limited time for treatment, changes in the financing of training programs, and demoralization in the training environment.

Throughout this chapter we will draw upon interviews conducted by the authors with psychiatry residents and psychology interns at several major East Coast medical centers. While the anecdotes included in the chapter are not generalizable to the experience of all trainees, they exemplify some of the problems that ensue when training institutions adapt, as they must, to the demands of managed care. Managed care's impact on training is an indirect result of the influence of economics. Cutting funds results in compromises in training. Before turning to a detailed description of the compromises taking place in the training environment, we will briefly review the impact of the many recent changes in funding for training.

In the past, federal and state training grants helped subsidize a significant proportion of training activities. This is no longer the case. These grants have been reduced drastically due to state and federal fiscal deficits. Additionally, as teaching hospitals (where the majority of such training occurs) typically charged higher treatment rates to cover the cost of the education they provided residents and interns, indemnity insurance plans that covered patient stays at these hospitals indirectly subsidized training. Federally granted incentives for these hospitals to provide free care to patients lacking sufficient resources also contributed to offsetting the cost of training. In states that are heavily penetrated by managed care, hospital rates are now negotiated in a continuing attempt to keep costs down. As managed care companies obtain lower hospital rates in exchange for agreements to use particular hospitals, other insurance companies demand lower rates as well. In this competitive era, insurance companies are no longer willing to pay the higher rates of teaching hospitals. The net result is that the cost of supervision and didactics can no longer be indirectly absorbed through higher hospital fees. In addition, many insurance companies, as well as Medicare and Medicaid, which in the past covered treatment rendered by trainees, have begun to refuse reimbursement for the services provided by them. As a result of these developments, the previously ubiquitous conflict between training and economic solvency is now intensified.

Due to reductions in funding, training programs must support themselves, which means that they must be income-generating. While in the past hospitals were able to absorb much of the cost of training, today an unprecedented number of training decisions are being made with an eye to the economic bottom line. This boils down to one fact: trainees must provide services that not only cover the cost of training itself, but provide revenue to the hospital. There is, however, a catch-22: earning money for the hospital means less time conducting psychotherapy with patients and more time spent on revenue-generating services, such as testing, assessment, and consultation. To further complicate matters, there are fewer sites available to train new psychologists and psychiatrists than ever before as fiscal pressures have forced hospital closures, consolidations, and the trimming down of all training activities. These fiscal realities lead to therapists being trained less and less in therapy per se, and more and more in lucrative skills such as assessment and consultation.

While there have always been harsh fiscal realities that compromise training, managed care is the most recent solution to be promulgated. As an industry, managed care thrives only in that it offers the least expensive source of health care delivery to employers who are seeking to reduce the cost of offering health benefits to employees. As more employers have contracted with managed care, its impact on the entire health care delivery system in the United States has grown exponentially, and managed care in its various forms (HMOs, PPOs, capitated systems, and other forms of management) has become the single most influential force in health care delivery today. The managed care environment presents a major threat to training, as elements long considered critical to training are sacrificed for the sake of turning a profit. The economic realities of the managed care era have thus impacted training and the development of the psychotherapist of the future in myriad ways.

## PROFESSIONAL IDENTITY DEVELOPMENT VERSUS PROFESSIONAL IDENTITY FORECLOSURE

The training years usher in a developmental process during which one forms a professional identity, a process that continues long after the completion of training. Becoming a psychotherapist includes much more than learning the techniques and modalities of treatment through clinical service or academic classes. Bilsker and Marcia (1991) have described the ways in which identity formation emerges out of the exploration and selecting of new identities and the simultaneous repudiation of old commitments.

A professional identity is formed in part through a gradual process of sitting with and trying on different professional selves. The characteristics, therapy style, and personality of teachers become guideposts against which the trainee internalizes admired qualities and rejects disliked ones. The trainee looks to his or her mentors and supervisors for feedback and guidance about the "goodness of fit." This is not unlike Erikson's (1968) conceptualization that the developmental task of consolidating a secure identity requires "the selective repudiation and mutual assimilation of childhood identifications and their absorption in a new configuration" (p. 159). Over time, trainees come to feel at one with their professional selves. They find a level of comfort with various treatment modalities, theoretical approaches, and ways of thinking about people, and are able to match them to their characters and temperaments.

Just as a pair of new shoes may feel uncomfortable, stiff, and awkward, stepping into the role of psychotherapist initially feels somewhat foreign. While the trainee might try on the shoes of a supervisor, the fit is not quite right because they bear the mold of another person's feet. Over time, the shoes become his own: well-worn, soft, and comfortable. They blend into the rest of the wardrobe, no longer standing out.

Senior, well-respected clinicians report that this process of identity formation takes time and cannot be rushed. When interviewed about his psychotherapy training at Worcester State Hospital in 1948, noted psychiatrist Arnold Modell said:

> The thing that was wonderful about those days . . . [was that] you were not overwhelmed with service functions. We had all the time needed to study our patients. . . . One found an interesting case and simply immersed oneself in the treatment. . . . If people had any question about primary process and the meaning of the unconscious, all they had to do was have one schizophrenic patient and they were convinced. [cited in Hunter 1994, p. 353]

Having ample time to let things evolve of their own accord is essential. However, it is much more than time and an absence of distraction that facilitates the understanding of patients. Havens (1993) believes that the ability of trainees to be with patients without an agenda is of the utmost importance. He describes how initially frightened psychiatry residents were by the patients they were treating at state hospitals. The trainees dealt with their fears by referring to their patients in pathologizing medical terminology, saying such things as "snarling, terrified, wrapped in stories of assault and madness, talking ragtime if they talk at all, the patients seem inhuman" (p. 139). Over three or four months, these "odd couples," the therapist and patient, become the "best of friends" (p. 140). It is in this agendaless, timeless context that "the crude dress of hostility and bizarreness falls away and a naked soul speaks. . . . The young therapists almost stumble on the person in the patient" (p. 140). Developing the capacity to find the *person* in the patient may be one of the core developmental achievements in training.

The process of trying on different professional selves can be emotionally and cognitively chaotic, an "'identity crisis' where everything once held as self-defining becomes disequilibrated" (Stephen et al. 1992, p. 285). Many of the trainees we interviewed described feeling out of sorts or regressed. Seashore (1997) has described this identity crisis, including the breakdown of many of the trainee's relationships and the complete turning upside down of all that was once stable. Some trainees quit the profession at this early point in their training, perhaps because of this internal upheaval. They are faced with an overwhelming number of decisions about how to be with a patient, which theoretical orientation to embrace, how to listen and understand, and which clinical path to pursue. As beginning psychotherapists, trainees experiment with varying levels of activity: directing, questioning, opening up, closing down, interpreting, making links to the past, or remaining in the present, and have difficulty finding the way that feels most "right" to them. Painful yet unavoidable, both personal and professional identity crises signal that development is occurring.

An inevitable concomitant to the process of forming an identity is discomfort. While trainees often struggle with the internal upheaval they undergo as their own identity develops, they may experience a particular conflict between their beliefs and values and what training sites, adapting to the demands of managed care, ask them to do. They have to juxtapose their academic graduate programs' prioritizing the development of relationships and careful, time-consuming thought about treatment with their teaching hospitals' demands for quick action and ready solutions to complex problems. Many of the trainees we met with experienced their two central training experiences, the theoretical and the practical, as at odds. This conflict may result in their gradually compromising their views about what was previously important to them in their work with patients. One resident who began her short-term inpatient rotation valuing depth-oriented, exploratory inpatient work joked: "After a few months, you take on the goal of 'get 'em out'—well, the whole culture around you thinks like that, so you end up thinking that way too." The managed care culture, in which rapid assessment and efficient management are prized, had eroded her enthusiasm for and interest in knowing her patients.

In their efforts to cope with these conflictual feelings and ally themselves with the largest employers of health care professionals, many of the trainees interviewed reported that they felt impelled to specialize early in their professional development, before they had had an opportunity to develop a thorough knowledge base from which to be able to choose a specialty. Seeking to identify themselves as specialists having a unique expertise in a competitive, exclusionary health care environment, some trainees prematurely pigeonhole themselves into certain professional corners out of anxious desperation. Being desirable to managed care is highly practical, and often encouraged by those senior in the field. Yet committing oneself to something before having had a chance to learn about various ways of thinking is akin to "psychological foreclosure" (Bilsker and Marcia 1991), the "unquestioning acceptance of parentally defined values ... [involving] commitment without exploration" (p. 77). As this often takes place before one has acquired a broad knowledge base, the commitment to one way of being occurs without the benefit of actually having made an informed choice. Anxiety about being marketable and competitive encourages trainees to commit themselves early in the discovery process to one way of being, and managed care now offers a convenient solution: a premature foreclosure of professional identity as a time-sensitive, solution-oriented psychotherapist. The natural unfolding of a mature, evolved professional identity is thus hampered.

For example, a psychology intern training to be a child therapist reported that relatively early in his training, he came to be thought of by his staff as an "infancy expert." This occurred, however, during his very first child rotation. The intern became confused about whether he really *was* an infancy expert or whether he was cast in this role because that was what his department needed. Fiscal pressures to provide reimbursable assessment services for which he did not have a thorough training base led his staff to market him as an infancy specialist to patients. The identity or label he was given felt so foreign to him on the one hand, yet so gratifying on the other, that he lost the capacity to know if in fact he was gifted at infancy work; furthermore, he could not discern whether this type of work even brought him satisfaction. Nevertheless, when the intern completed his training, anxiety about his professional future drove him to market himself as an infancy expert providing rapid assessment and consultation for which managed care was willing to pay. He became willing to suspend doubts about what he did not know in order to have a viable professional identity, and his training colluded with this. The economic pressures from managed and capitated care, therefore, can accrue in such a way as to limit patient contact, force premature specialization, and constrict the developmental process of coming to know oneself as a therapist.

## LEARNING: A PROCESS ORIENTATION VERSUS A SKILLS ORIENTATION

Perhaps one of the most important lessons of training is learning how to learn. Like widening the angle of the camera lens to take in more of the landscape, training encourages a way of thinking that involves opening up one's thinking to include more possibilities. Across various theories of psychotherapy, exploration rather than certainty is prized. Training has traditionally encouraged wonder, curiosity, and inquiry. Math students learn how to prove geometry theorems, not rote memorization of rules, because the process teaches an approach to problem solving and conceptualization. Likewise, therapists are taught how to approach a *person* rather than simply to review a symptom checklist. In both cases it is learning a way of considering and thinking through a problem that is most important.

Psychotherapy training has traditionally taught therapists that alone they do not have answers, but that they are to work together with their patients to discover them. As reality is relative to each person's point of view, and there are many possible personal realities, it is impossible for any one person, therapist or otherwise, to learn which is the correct view for a given person. The therapist acts in accord with the perspective that "the individual has a sufficient capacity to deal constructively with all those aspects of his life which can potentially come into conscious awareness. . . . [The] counselor accept[s] . . . the client as a person who is competent to direct himself" (Rogers 1951, p. 24). Similarly, Winnicott (1971) stated, "I interpret mainly to let the patient know the limits of my understanding. The principle is that it is the patient and only the patient who has the answers" (pp. 86–87).

In the face of learning this broadening, ambiguous approach, the trainees we interviewed often found themselves longing for certainty and clarity. With its guidelines and protocols, managed care offers trainees a way out of their discomfort. The development of formulaic treatment approaches and guidelines or a "skills orientation" assuages the anxiety of sitting with a complex person and coming to know—or realizing how difficult it can be to know—them. Also, the current health care environment's emphasis on rapidly demonstrating observable results often supersedes the "not knowing" described above. Action supplants curiosity and offers a shortcut through the difficulty of learning. Many of the trainees we interviewed stated that they frequently felt they should tell the patient what to do to fix the problem given that they had only a few sessions with which to work.

Stern (1993) suggests that managed care encourages therapists to believe they "know" something prematurely. He warns that in this context therapists may feel pressured to formulate treatment plans too rapidly and initiate interventions in the first session or two. Such exigencies may jeopardize therapists' being open and receptive to new data. He further believes that the time pressures associated with managed care threaten to disrupt the unique connection between patients and therapists that enables patients to tell their stories. "If therapists feel pressured into early closure regarding the nature of a patient's problem or become prematurely committed to a particular line of intervention, it is likely they will lose the patient (literally or affectively) along the way" (p. 165). It is one thing to choose to work this way; it is quite another never to be taught to work any other way.

Clinical training has shifted—away from teaching ways of thinking and understanding—toward teaching practical applications of formulaic, empirically derived treatments and skills. What is taught is what the market will bear and, as such, training has been co-opted by the pressures of managed care. Some authors even advocate this development. Charous and Carter (1996), for example, have written about the need for training programs to shift their focus toward short-term treatment, "mental health care economics," and "the ethical and legal practice of psychology in a managed competition system" so that their graduates remain competitive in the workforce (p. 634). "To produce competent practitioners, graduate schools need to teach both the technical aspects of brief therapy as well as to provide training in the area of administrative problems, managed practices, and so forth" (p. 632). The focusing on administrative issues and managed care techniques during training, albeit useful and necessary, comes at the expense of encouraging a tolerance for ambiguity and uncertainty. To be schooled solely within the frame of managed care induces the acceptance of these treatment guidelines—such as shorter sessions, fewer meetings, and medication as a first-line intervention—as a fundamental treatment algorithm rather than simply one model of patient care. When an attitude of questioning and exploration is removed from the education of psychotherapists, the integrity of training is compromised.

Many fields require that their practitioners have a broad base of knowledge or expertise from which to draw upon. Such expertise is acquired through substantial firsthand experience, observation, and didactics during a period of formal or informal training. For a psychotherapist, expertise is built through learning the art of diagnosis, understanding etiology, knowing how and when to intervene, and appreciating the consequences of interceding in various ways, at various times, and with various people. In the era of managed care and capitation, the need for trainees to rapidly provide an income-generating service truncates the development of such expertise, substituting instead a set of routinized skills. The pressure to produce quick results leads to reflexive action rather than critical thought. A patient would be ill advised to consult a cardiologist who had not also been trained to listen to the lungs, examine the circulatory system, and consider the influence of diet and stress. Similarly, a patient would be ill advised to seek out a psychotherapist who had been trained, as Charous and Carter (1996) suggest, in only one model of intervention that is based on economic needs rather than clinical interest.

Under siege due to the tightening of resources, trainees often feel the need to focus their own educational objectives to be in accordance with the managed care perspective. Many of the trainees we interviewed felt their academic programs were failing them by not teaching enough about what to do in the era of managed care. One graduate student in psychology wished that his doctoral program offered more short-term therapy courses because he anticipated that ultimately he would be reimbursed only for short-term treatment. Although he believed that learning various theoretical perspectives and a number of treatment modalities including intensive therapy would best help his expertise as a psychologist, he felt pressured to learn how to pragmatically apply short-term approaches in managed care settings. He was adamant that he did not want to "waste" time learning a theoretical body of knowledge that the market would prevent him from using. His focus was on what to do with patients, not how to think. As such, much that we prize so highly in the endeavor of psychotherapy is being lost. The opportunity to come to know over time, to follow one's inclinations, and to form conclusions after a thorough, critical appraisal of a variety of plausible hypotheses, theoretical perspectives, and treatment models are all at risk.

## APPRECIATION FOR THEORY VERSUS FOCUS ON PRAGMATICS

The 1997 study materials for the National Licensing Exam in psychology (Association for Advanced Training in the Behavioral Sciences) call attention to the ways treatment is no longer ideologically or theoretically driven:

> Since the inception of managed care in the '90s, the treatment authorization and utilization review procedures of this system have forced clinicians to formulate treatment plans with clear and measurable behavioral outcomes in order to get reimbursed for services provided. The practice of psychology, *once ideological and theoretically based,* is now primarily based on empirically justified treatments. Treatment interventions according to the guidelines of managed care companies must match the diagnosis of the patient, not the theoretical orientation of the clinician, and are time-limited in scope. [p. 3, italics added]

The presence of this paragraph in the licensing study guide materials is profound. It makes a strong statement that the economic pressures of managed care have indeed transformed the profession.

Theory, defined by the *American Heritage Dictionary* (1976) as knowledge that is "distinguished from experiment or practice" (p. 718), usefully aids in navigating therapists through a maze of potential options. It serves to organize data, make predictions, and explain behavior. Having a theoretical base from which to work helps trainees develop a body of knowledge they will rely upon when making clinical judgments throughout their careers.

In the era of managed care, theory has erroneously come to be thought of as synonymous with an intervention, a treatment recommendation, or a technique. The emphasis on pragmatics has blurred the distinction between theory and practice. In actuality, theory is neither intervention, treatment recommendation, nor technique. Rather, theoretical formulations are an approach to help practitioners understand the problem and begin to decipher which interventions will be most helpful.

In today's training climate, knowing how to implement a singular treatment is often more highly valued than understanding a person from several different conceptual vantage points. Schooling in treatments that relied on hypothesis generating, testing, and working through has given way to manualized, mandated therapies created to globally describe a class of individuals, but never meant to be applied uniformly from one patient to the next without a critical evaluation of individual need. Formerly, clinicians worked to find the right theoretically derived treatment approach to fit a particular patient; now, however, the patient's problem is made to fit the managed care approach. It literally becomes a "managing" rather than an understanding of patients—managing the behavior, the symptoms, the support system, and the activities of daily living.

When individual therapists are trained to follow manualized guidelines, they are no longer trained to think critically for themselves. The deprofessionalization of the field ensues, for graduate-level practitioners or medically trained psychiatrists are not needed to implement formulized treatment programs. Training mental health professionals, then, evolves into an education that is not so different from teaching skills to technicians.

In one such case a psychology intern was conducting an evaluation of a female patient who had presented to an emergency room in the throes of a manic episode. After determining that this grandiose and delusional patient was unable to care for herself or her children, the intern decided it was necessary to hospitalize her. The intern worked hard to understand the nature of the patient's distress, and thought carefully about how to formulate the case. She then called several inpatient units only to get turned away time after time because the hospitals did not accept the patient's insurance. As emergency room work was a core component of her training experience, she was making the calls in front of her supervisor. Although feeling frantic internally, the intern was methodically and clearly presenting the case to yet another intake coordinator when her supervisor whispered: "Just ask them if they have any beds," as though seeking placement was the training issue at hand instead of accurately formulating a patient's presenting issues. The trainee abruptly interrupted her well-planned presentation and bluntly posed the question. The intake coordinator on the other end was taken aback by the pointed query. He tersely chastised the trainee, saying, "You need to watch your presentation." In an instant, "training" was reduced to how to correctly word a presentation so that an inpatient admission would be obtained. Training had devolved into minding manners and coming up with correct phraseology to persuade a hospital to accept a patient.

## EXPOSURE TO TRAINING-FOCUSED EXPERIENCES VERSUS INCOME-FOCUSED EXPERIENCES

Historically, teaching hospitals have struggled to find a balance between training and overloading trainees with income-generating clinical responsibilities. Training sites have been cautioned against taking advantage of trainees by demanding an undue amount of direct clinical service. For example, a psychology internship program must "demonstrate that interns' service delivery tasks and duties are primarily learning oriented and that training considerations take precedence over service delivery and revenue generation" (American Psychological Association 1995, p. 15). "The intern's primary role is as a trainee, and service goals must not erode training goals" (American Psychological Association 1979, p. 22). Likewise, Accreditation Council for Graduate Medical Education guidelines (1983, 1987, 1997) mandate that residents' clinical responsibilities should be few enough to allow them to immerse themselves in the study of their patients and have time for other educational activities.

Yet demands for service delivery are increasing dramatically as hospitals bear more and more of the financial burden of training. Some training sites have begun docking the trainees' already low take-home stipend if they fail to see a designated number of patients. Other training sites use subtle shame and public humiliation to motivate trainees to keep their hours of service delivery up to snuff by circulating reports on the number of patient visits and other billable services rendered by each trainee.

Financial pressures have changed the type of clinical work trainees do. Trainees' presence on one service rather than another may stem not from its being a good learning environment, but from potential costs saved. Having relatively inexpensive mental health trainees (compared with their more expensive counterparts from the medical staff) perform highly compensated services for which the hospital recoups the difference makes the hospital money. Many of the trainees interviewed reported that rather than treat fewer numbers of patients with a broad set of problems on an ongoing basis, they frequently see many patients with a more restricted range of problems for consultation or brief treatment. This type of work is more lucrative for the hospital. Psychiatric residents on inpatient units reported that they were increasingly making psychopharmacologic interventions, aftercare placements, and supportive efforts. Decisions about the nature of trainees' clinical work are made with one eye on the financial solvency of the training institution rather than the variety and depth of the training experience. As a result of the changing nature of their clinical work, the trainees interviewed felt they were spending fewer hours conducting psychotherapy and more time doing management work.

The internship or residency experience has evolved to become an experiential cornerstone of clinical training. Yet, ironically, in the current environment, "therapists" receive little training in how to conduct therapy. However, in these fiscally conscious times, the training years are the only time interns or residents would have an opportunity to receive training in the conduct of psychotherapy.

## SUPERVISION VERSUS SUPPORT

Training guidelines for both psychology interns and psychiatry residents (American Psychological Association, Accreditation Council for Graduate Medical Education) emphasize the importance of supervision, stating that training should offer students the opportunity to learn how to function as competent, knowledgeable, professional psychologists or psychiatrists "in the context of appropriate supervisory support [and] professional role modeling" (American Psychological Association 1995, p. 18). Supervision affords trainees the opportunity for a review of their patients, an examination of interventions, and an investigation of difficulties and therapeutic impasses. The process of grappling with these issues with a more experienced and seasoned clinician helps trainees develop the facility to monitor their own interventions. Much more than knowledge and wisdom is imparted during supervision; supervision offers the opportunity to learn through a relationship. As the patient learns through his or her relationship with the therapist, the trainee learns through his or her relationship with the supervisor.

However, with the widespread prioritizing of revenue-generating activities, time for the supervisory relationship is often sacrificed. Supervisors are typically present only on a brief or intermittent basis to offer support. The nature of what hospital staff do has changed so dramatically that their teaching and mentoring function now bears little resemblance to its previous form. One training director lamented that over the past ten years the primary focus of his department meetings has shifted from training to service delivery. Supervisors often do not have time to teach, nor do they have time to provide empathically attuned responses that help trainees develop professional identities of their own. Rather, supervisors frequently have a diminished ability to be psychically or physically available to take up their roles as teachers and mentors, as they are often burdened with increased service delivery requirements of their own.

To ensure the survival of training programs in the ever-changing zeitgeist of HMOs and capitated contracts, staff are preoccupied with balancing administrative, clinical, and teaching duties. Supervision becomes a luxury—a nonbillable hour—to be compromised, as opposed to a cornerstone of training to be protected. Trainees interviewed at several training sites complained about their supervisors' lack of availability and spoke longingly of their wish for more regular supervision time. Some trainees felt they needed a specific reason, such as a patient emergency or a management quandary, to justify the use of their supervision hour. An extreme example of this came from one training site where supervision was thought necessary only to correct for deficits in trainees not up to par.

In addition, many of the trainees interviewed believed that the nature of supervision had become largely supportive, aimed at helping them and their patients adjust to the realities of the managed care era. One intern, who had to drop a number of his psychotherapy cases due to their lack of profitability, pithily summed up the nature of his supervision: "Supervision is not about learning who can benefit from psychotherapy and how; it's about who can handle it if they get dropped." In this situation supervision became "case management": helping the therapist in training consider what other resources his patients might have as he evaluated who among the group could be "dropped." Simple problem solving thus replaces the former learning of an ideology through a supervisory relationship.

As economic exigencies erode the training environment, hopelessness about the field, low morale, and a sense of loss necessarily influence what supervisors convey to trainees. Some of the trainees interviewed reported being encouraged to consider different careers, others have been encouraged to move to other parts of the country where psychotherapists are more in demand. Many of the interns and residents reported being asked by those more senior to them, "Why are you going into the field now when things are so bad?" As fiscal pressures for managed care mount, supervision as well as treatment becomes problem-focused. When supervision becomes more supportive than educative, and so infrequent and unreliable as to compromise its being thought of as a mentoring relationship, one of the most valuable learning tools of the profession is lost.

## SUMMARY

The rapidity of changes brought on by managed care, while perhaps inevitable and unavoidable, creates a climate that is not conducive to learning a broad-based fundamental way to approach caring for patients. The problem is not with managed care itself; the problem lies in the ways in which training programs scramble to adapt to the ever-changing landscape of the fiscal pressures resulting from managed care. In their efforts to adapt to these requirements, training programs are especially vulnerable to compromising excellence. Core elements vital to training are frequently sacrificed for the sake of increasing efficiency and profits. Making training decisions in these fiscally conscious times is an insurmountable challenge. Training programs, therefore, are in an unenviable, untenable position.

Managed care and capitated systems have stepped up the competition for health care dollars. Hospitals are scampering to gain favor with the managed care plans in order to guarantee a steady stream of revenues. The system has evolved such that the managed care companies are in the uniquely powerful position of dictating and directing the flow of health care dollars. In the majority of cases, these dollars are allocated to the lowest bidder. Hospitals cut costs wherever they can, which often requires making sacrifices that formerly would have been unthinkable.

The implications for training are enormous, as training costs money that cannot be directly returned through patient fees. Someone has to be willing to pay for it. Over and over again, training is being left out of the equation. While not earmarking funds for training may save money in the present, it will eventuate in a system of poorly trained mental health care professionals. Clinicians will envision and be able to implement only one model of treatment, perform rapid assessments rather than understand their patients, and follow uniform guidelines instead of engaging in critical thinking. Perhaps what will unite the practitioners of tomorrow is the absence of a solid foundation in theory.

To ensure the health of this country in the future, psychotherapists in training must not sit by idly while much that they value about their profession is chiseled away. Action in the face of this needs to be taken while there are still those around who know and remember what it is like to have choices. The most significant deleterious effect of managed care on training is the possibility that it might eradicate, for the next generation of therapists, the knowledge that there are *multiple* ways of understanding and responding. Should this come to pass, we will all lose.

## REFERENCES

Accreditation Council for Graduate Medical Education. (1983). *1983–1984 Directory of Residency Training Programs.* Chicago: American Medical Association.
——— (1987). *1987–1988 Directory of Graduate Medical Education Programs.* Chicago: American Medical Association.
——— (1997). *Graduate Medical Education Directory, 1997–1998.* Chicago: American Medical Association.
*American Heritage Dictionary of the English Language* (1976). ed. P. Davies, New York: Dell.
American Psychological Association. (1979). *Criteria for Accreditation of Doctoral Training Programs And Internships in Professional Psychology.* Washington, DC: APA.
——— (1995). *Guidelines and Principles for Accreditation of Programs In Professional Psychology.* Washington, DC: APA.
Association for Advanced Training in the Behavioral Sciences. (1997). *Oral Workbook* 2, 43rd series. Ventura, CA: Psychology Licensure Review.
Bilsker, D., and Marcia, J. (1991). Adaptive regression and ego identity. *Journal of Adolescence* 14:75–84.
Charous, M., and Carter, R. (1996). Mental health and managed care: training for the 21st century. *Psychotherapy* 33:628–635.
Erikson, E. H. (1968). *Identity: Youth and Crisis.* New York: Norton.
Havens, L. (1993). *Coming to Life.* Cambridge, MA: Harvard University Press.
Hunter, V. (1994). *Psychoanalysts Talk.* New York: Guilford.
Rogers, C. R. (1951). *Client-Centered Therapy: Its Current Practice, Implications, and Theory.* Boston: Houghton Mifflin.
Seashore, C. (1979). *In grave danger of growing.* Unpublished paper.

Stephen, J., Fraser, E., and Marcia, J.E. (1992). Moratorium-achieve-
   ment (Mama) cycles in lifespan identity development: value orientations and reasoning system correlates. *Journal of Adolescence*
   15:283–300.
Stern, S. (1993). Managed care, brief therapy, and therapeutic integrity. *Psychotherapy* 30(1):162–175.
Winnicott, D. W. (1971). The use of an object and relating through
   identifications. In *Playing and Reality*. London: Tavistock.

# 11

# Holding On to the Center: Challenges of Psychiatric Residency Training in the Era of Managed Care

BERNARD M. EDELSTEIN

Recently a group of residents was discussing with me their concerns about managed care and how it is affecting their training experience. One resident expressed a wish that his psychiatric training not focus on trying to make him marketable at the expense of teaching him the complexities of how to understand and work with patients in a deep way. "If, when I finish my residency, I need to vacuum my office," he told me, "I'll vacuum my office, but I don't need to practice vacuuming now. If five years from now someone comes to me and says, 'My house has some structural damage, can you help me to repair it,' what will I tell him, I'm sorry but I only know how to vacuum?"

His concern speaks to the difficulty of psychiatric training at the close of the twentieth century, the anxiety of those residents who choose to become psychiatrists because they wish to help explore the inner lives of their patients, and the concern of all those in training, that they finish training with skills that will be valued, and that will allow them a place as valued physicians.

In the past decade psychiatry has been at the center of two revolutions: (1) an explosion of neuroscientific knowledge that has brought exciting new understanding of major mental illness as well as hopeful new treatments; and (2) the advent of managed care with its insistence on symptom management as the sole model of psychiatric care, and its message to subscribers, "If we don't cover it, it isn't a problem." In the media and in academic journals, these two dramatic factors have been conflated into a single phenomenon that threatens to turn psychiatry into a mechanistic antipsychological discipline. Commonly, policymakers and clinicians do not differentiate between treatment choices that grow out of new pharmacologies— which add an important dimension to an established therapeutic core—and treatment choices that are aimed at decreasing the intensity and frequency of patient–clinician contact exclusively as a means of cost saving.

Managed care aside, neuroscientific advances have led to an increasingly ambitious curriculum for training psychiatric residents. Residents' knowledge base must include a growing sophistication about biological mechanisms. The challenge for psychiatrists and for the residents they teach is to integrate psychological models with biological ones. The hazard is the devaluation of psychological thinking, the possibility that we will no longer ask our residents to get to know their patients. In the context of the managed care revolution, this danger greatly increases.

As a psychiatric residency training director, I struggle with the question of how to hold on to what is central in training residents. What are the core values we wish to communicate to those who are newly entering the field of psychiatry? How do we maintain our psychological-mindedness as we teach about the frontiers of neuroscience? As the values of insurance companies enter increasingly into the academic world, how do we help our residents to maintain a sense of clarity, to realize that caring effectively for patients is not the same as making financial decisions? Some of these questions are specific to psychiatric training; however, educators throughout the mental health system wrestle with the issue of how attitudes toward treatment and training have been challenged by the loud voice of those representing first and foremost an economic perspective.

If we believe that what is central to training psychiatrists involves an understanding of the therapeutic relationship, then we must admit that in the current climate of managed care, our ability to teach that understanding is severely threatened. We must consider how compromising this central aspect of training will affect our current residents and future generations of psychiatrists.

## BACKGROUND

A review of the literature on the subject of managed care and its effect on psychiatry residency training includes a variety of outlooks and a range of philosophical orientations, yet all of them address the changes that are being wrought by managed care as a fait accompli; the authors write about how we will live in this new medical economic reality, what we must give up, and how we might preserve some remnant of our identity.

A review might begin with a 1991 article by Dennis Staton entitled "Psychiatry's Future: Facing Reality." Staton predicted that the 1990s would bring marked curtailment of reimbursement for psychiatric services. He is critical of the psychiatric profession for promoting care that is overly expensive and of unproven efficacy. In a position that is repeated by others in later articles, Staton argues that the psychiatrist must be attentive to the limited resources available for treating psychiatric illness. He sees academic psychiatry as having perpetuated an irresponsible and unrealistic vision of what psychiatrists can and should do. He urges a change in how psychiatrists are trained, a change that reflects a shift in emphasis from the relationship between the psychiatrist and his patient to the relationship between the psychiatrist and the larger needs of society.

In "Clinical Skills for the 1990s: Six Lessons from HMO Practice," Sabin (1991) describes an approach by which psychiatrists can achieve "clinical effectiveness and professional satisfaction" in a mental health treatment environment characterized by "cost containment, hard nosed attention to outcomes, practice audits and treatment guidelines" (p. 605), and he suggests that the skills he outlines will be required for psychiatrists practicing in the 1990s.

Another point of view, however, is held by Gabbard (1992), whose "The Big Chill: The Transition from Residency to Managed Care Nightmare" points to the difficulties encountered by newly trained psychiatrists as they make their way into clinical practice. While their training experience emphasizes development in the context of traditional presumptions about "the sanctity of the doctor patient relationship, and the privilege and responsibilty of clinical decisionmaking" customarily afforded the physician, newly graduated residents encounter a health care environment in which "physicians are no longer in charge [but are] beholden to health care brokers and case managers" (Gabbard 1992, p. 120). Gabbard describes the demoralization that grows out of this shift from training to practice, and makes recommendations about how training programs can help prepare residents for some of the realities of managed care.

In "The Moral Myopia of Academic Psychiatry," Sabin (1993) responded to Gabbard's article, writing that psychiatrists have a "responsibility to look beyond the individual patient to consider the health of society." He further asserts that in failing to prepare residents for a managed care environment, "academic psychiatry suffers from a serious case of moral myopia" (p. 175).

A series of articles in 1995 reflect the growing influence of managed care on the theory and practice of psychiatry. These articles lament changes in psychiatric practice brought about by managed care and address adaptations by the profession, specifically in the training of psychiatrists, that will preserve some aspects of psychiatric care in a landscape they see as permanently altered. Meyer and Sotsky (1995), along with Beigel and Santiago (1995), suggest that psychiatrists must consolidate and protect their role by establishing themselves as leaders on the multidisciplinary team. They propose that psychiatrists are uniquely able to treat the severely and chronically ill, those with complex medical and psychological problems, and to integrate biological and psychological interventions. Verhulst (1996) focuses on the importance of preserving a role for psychotherapy in the psychiatrist's work. He describes a dual role for the psychiatrist, combining narrative and medical methods, and warns that "when the medical model is not complemented with a narrative approach, diagnostic errors and iatrogenic complications are likely to occur" and that "the patient's disorder should not be disconnected from the patient's story"(p. 201). Robinowitz and Yager (1996) observe the growing breadth of the psychiatric curriculum associated with the expanding knowledge of neuroscience and competing types of psychotherapy training. In that context they refer to a concern by some educators "that the more recent graduates of residency programs are much less adept at communicating with patients and formulating problems along broad biopsychosocial lines" (pp. 593–594). They go on to reflect on the difficulties that managed care has introduced into psychiatric education and make recommendations about how managed care might best be integrated into training, including the usefulness of learning three or four brief psychotherapies, and how to utilize them creatively.

In their 1995 article entitled "Wagons Ho: Forward on the Managed Care Trail," Summergrad and colleagues (1995) describe the effects of managed care on psychiatry training at a busy teaching hospital. They reflect on the ways in which managed care has interfered with the process of training: they offer recommendations on how best to preserve a meaningful training experience and how to avoid demoralization among faculty and residents. Unlike many of the preceding articles, they ultimately conclude, as I do in this chapter, that it remains an essential part of psychiatric education to teach an understanding of depth psychology, and that training in long-term psychotherapy is a central part of residency, even if that training is not reimbursed by managed care.

An extreme view is held by Detre and McDonald (1997), who argue that the economic restrictions imposed by managed care, in combination with the increasingly biological basis of psychiatry, have created an environment in which psychiatry ought no longer exist as a discrete specialty, rather, that psychiatry and neurology should combine their clinical and academic missions by creating a new consulting specialty of "clinical neuroscience." In two responding commentaries, Sharfstein (1997) and Olfson and Weissman (1997) describe multiple existing and evolving roles for psychiatrists, a need for psychiatrists to care for suffering patients that transcends the economics of managed care and that extends beyond the research laboratories of neuroscientists.

## THE PSYCHIATRIST'S ROLE IN MANAGED CARE

The problem, by now well known, is that over the past decade principles of the free market have increasingly been applied to American medicine. This has led to conflicts between decisions about medical care that are patient centered and those that are economically driven. In the realm of training the problem is compounded. Trainees who are learning about normal development, psychopathology, the subtleties of assessment, and the complexity of the doctor–patient relationship are confronted by economic imperatives that threaten to confuse the process of learning about patient care. Practicing psychiatrists, supervisors, and teachers, also confronted by the preempting of decisions about patient care by single-minded attention to cost, are at risk of second-guessing their own worth; their conflict is readily transmitted to their students.

The academic mission has also been constrained by direct decreases in funding. The insurance industry, as represented by managed care companies, is not interested in paying for teaching or research, nor, one could argue, should that be their responsibility. The question that has emerged as hospitals have had to manage on slimmer and slimmer budgets is whose responsibility is it?

What do we see as the psychiatrist's role and what do we wish to teach our residents? It seems apparent that a psychiatrist would bring to a treatment the most sophisticated psychotherapeutic and psychopharmacologic skills possible. This means passing on the acquired knowledge of generations of teachers and clinicians, a knowledge that allows us the chance to understand the full complexity of our patients' illness, and to treat it as fully as we can. Physicians have been confused and angered by the expectation espoused by insurance companies and a handful of policymakers that they compromise their therapeutic skills in the name of ideas about fiscal responsibility, ideas that do not necessarily represent the feelings or needs of their patients. If, in the 1980s, the American public expressed anxiety about the rising cost of health care, that is far different from claiming that our patients want to address that anxiety by rationing health care, or that they expect their doctors to stop short of providing the best care they can.

For the psychiatrist, giving up the role of psychotherapist means giving up what is for many the core of their knowledge, and a central way in which they feel they can help their patients. Verhulst (1996) makes a distinction between the humanistic physician, for example, a warm and empathic surgeon, and a psychiatrist, who uses what Verhulst calls the "empathic-narrative approach" as a central aspect of inquiry and cure. If we devalue the process of psychotherapy, of exploration and working through, and rename it as an attitude of warmth and respectfulness—an attitude that should no doubt be a part of any physician's approach to his patients—then we will be training humanistic pharmacologists and leaving behind a crucial means of understanding and relieving suffering.

Becoming a psychiatrist has for generations meant learning how "to sit with patients," to understand their predicament from the inside, to help them learn how to know their own experience rather than having to live at a distance from it. This has meant developing an intuitive sense of empathy into a skill; if empathy is a melding of identification and compassion, how can one make use of it in the patient's service, and what sorts of difficulties might one encounter as one enters into the patient's experience? A psychiatrist who uses the *DSM-IV* as a guide to diagnostic thinking may either use that manual to approach the patient from the outside, as a constellation of symptoms that a patient may endorse, or as a way to build a framework with which to get to know the patient from the inside. The former keeps the psychiatrist at a distance, from which he may make a diagnosis. The patient, however, is unlikely to feel he or she can enter into a deeper understanding of his or her experience. The latter, which we hope to teach our residents, allows an opportunity for therapeutic change.

It is the responsibility of a psychiatric residency to teach residents about the spectrum of mental illness, to provide the resident, for example, with an opportunity to treat acutely psychotic patients as they are admitted to an inpatient unit, and to see the course of their illness over time; to evaluate a patient in the emergency room, and to experience the challenges and rewards of working with that patient in a psychotherapy.

## INPATIENT PSYCHIATRY: THE AILMENT

A patient with borderline character pathology might be admitted to an inpatient unit during a period of crisis in an outpatient treatment, or when adversity in daily life tips the patient's delicate balance so that he or she becomes more hopeless or suicidal. If sufficient containment is provided by the hospitalization, the patient may learn more about how to understand and to tolerate his or her internal struggle. Caring for such a patient, a resident would learn about the intensity of that struggle, about the way in which that struggle affects caregivers on the unit, and about how a period of intense inpatient treatment can provide the containment and hope needed to sustain the process of healing. There is the associated moment of recognition when that resident reads Main's (1957) classic article "The Ailment" and appreciates Main's ability to articulate the phenomenon of splitting on an inpatient unit, what it represents about the patient's internal world; how the patient's passions are experienced by the staff; the liabilities of being the object of those passions; and how the staff, alert to such liabilities, might provide effective interventions.

This process requires that the hospital staff and attending psychiatrist, who acts as supervisor to the resident, have the freedom to go through this complex process with the patient, and in turn to teach the resident about it. The alternative, which has become all too prevalent, is one in which the patient is encouraged to pull himself together, to recant his expression of suicidal thoughts, and to be discharged as soon as possible. Our patients, particularly those with borderline and narcissistic conflicts, wanting to satisfy and gain the approval of their psychiatrists, will compliantly agree to the expectations, and little in the way of genuine treatment will occur. Indeed, false compliance among those who can least afford to be compliant, may be the greatest danger for our patients in the age of managed care. For the resident whose patient is admitted and discharged with only a superficial contact, a central part of the training experience disappears. Rather than learning about the process that Main describes, the resident learns only about how to avoid regression and how to set limits. The psychiatrist who is trained in such a setting will have a major deficit in understanding and will have no way to learn an essential lesson about psychopathology and treatment.

It is no wonder that residents seem at times afraid to get to know their patients, afraid to establish a relationship with their patients, afraid to raise the expectations of their patients too high, afraid to argue with an attending psychiatrist if they feel a patient is being discharged too early. In the current environment, residents remark that they feel like bad doctors. Attending psychiatrists, pressured to manage cases aggressively, struggle to find time to teach. Faculty lament that residents seem unable to describe a patient or to formulate a case, that presentations sound like quotations from the *DSM-IV*, that a feeling of frustration leads immediately to thoughts of the need for a change in medication. Does our current model of inpatient care mean that psychiatric units can no longer provide adequate training in the most basic of the clinician's skills? If so, then as a training director I must ask if it is being provided elsewhere.

## THE EMERGENCY UNIT EXPERIENCE

In other settings as well there is a push in the current environment to rush to closure. In the emergency room residents see patients who walk into the hospital, or are brought in by family members, friends, employers, or the police, urgently seeking intervention. An empathically skilled interviewer who is able to help create an atmosphere of sufficient safety, and who expresses a genuine curiosity about the patient's predicament, may lead the patient to a powerful sense of relief, or hope, usually as a first step in identifying what change needs to occur and how the patient–clinician pair may begin to bring about that change. Being effective in this setting means having an eye and an ear on medical versus psychological factors, listening to one's own affective responses, and managing a significant amount of anxiety. In short, it is a complicated business.

As the insurance climate has changed, such emergency room visits have increasingly come under the scrutiny of managed care-based reviewers. Emergency room clinicians are asked to present patients to anonymous, often minimally trained reviewers. When presenting a clinical case, clinicians find that reviewers are interested in yes or no answers to a series of stock questions, that address suicide risk, homicide risk, and psychosis in a way that all too often oversimplifies or even caricatures the process of assessment. Residents complain that they feel devalued by reviewers, that they spend hours negotiating with insurance companies, and that they feel they have little recourse if there is a difference of opinion between the resident and the reviewer.

Caught in the web of administratively justifying and arranging hospitalization, residents may grow cynical about the crucial role they can provide in the emergency room. Patients complain that clinicians seem preoccupied with extracting from them answers to questions about suicide risk rather than in hearing their story. Again, an essential arena for a trainee to learn and experience the complexities of assessment has been transformed in such a way as to often devalue the central tools and methods that we struggle to teach our residents.

## OUTPATIENT PSYCHOTHERAPY: LEARNING THE ESSENTIALS

Training in outpatient psychiatry has also been affected by the growth of managed care. Learning about transference, about being the object of a patient's unconscious wishes and fears, is a most challenging aspect of psychiatric training, and one that can best be learned in the context of a psychodynamically oriented outpatient therapy. At a recent meeting of a case conference, a resident presented the case of a young man whom she had been treating for six months in weekly psychotherapy. The patient had used the treatment to explore his conflictual relationship with his mother and to attempt to find a way to bring about a satisfactory separation, something that had been quite difficult for him. Shortly after beginning therapy, the patient had cut off all contact with the mother. After six months of silence, mother and son had had a tearful reconciliation. The patient resolved to leave the therapy, his home, and his current career aspirations; to move back to his hometown; and to live with his parents. I suggested that the therapist try to help the patient stay in the treatment, to think about alternatives to the choice between a complete break with the mother and returning to his parents' home, and to explore transference feelings toward the therapist, including the possible unconscious fantasy that the patient had to choose between his therapist and his mother.

My comments provoked a debate among the residents. Some felt that my proposed intervention represented an infringement on the patient's role as an autonomous adult. I suggested that we ought to consider the role that transference was playing in the treatment and the unconscious struggles that were contained in the patient's dilemma about his autonomy. I proposed that working as a psychiatrist meant respecting the patient's consciously stated needs and wishes, while also helping the patient to identify those that were unconscious. Some members of the group spoke about their discomfort with this scenario, and with being the object of a patient's transference.

This episode represented to me a developmental process in learning the art of psychotherapy. The process involves having the freedom to explore with patients the complexity of their inner lives and to come to understand that process, with the help of supervisors. Ultimately it means becoming comfortable with the ambiguities and uncertainties contained in the role of a psychiatrist. When the managed care company sends a message that going deeper and exploring transference is unnecessary, the developmental process of becoming a therapist cannot occur. Such a rupture in training threatens the ability of the next generation of psychiatrists to care for their patients.

There is no substitute for a foundation of training in long-term psychotherapy, and residency training programs must make a commitment to provide a core experience in long-term psychotherapy. Yet most managed care companies do not allow residents to treat their subscribers for either brief or long-term psychotherapy. Programs committed to providing this experience have had to sponsor treatments for which there is no reimbursement in order not to be restricted by the limitations imposed by managed care.

With the changes on inpatient units and in acute hospital settings, residents may come to understand that the only setting in which they can learn about the complexities of the therapeutic relationship, and in fact see a patient get better, is in outpatient treatment. Perhaps even more insidious than restricting resident access to patients is the message to practicing psychiatrists that shoring up patients' defenses and offering them superficial skills to deal with the external world, rather than addressing their inner lives, constitutes an acceptable psychotherapy. This devaluation of the practice of psychotherapy, and the drastic limitations on how the psychiatrist might hope to help his or her patient, lead to demoralization in those who are practicing and teaching. If residents are denied access to patients, and teachers and supervisors are left feeling that the essence of their knowledge is no longer worth conveying, then a training program's ability to continue teaching some of the basic skills of our profession is deeply challenged.

An increased pressure to teach brief psychotherapies has emerged as an anxious response to managed care's insistence on time-limited treatment. As with decisions about how and when to use new medications, the issue of when a brief treatment is clinically indicated has become blurred when it is economically mandated. A number of brief psychotherapies have been developed and an increasing body of outcome research has suggested that some are efficacious in treating certain disorders, particularly when the goal is to treat a circumscribed symptom. But psychiatrists and residents alike are more impressed by the message that if one wants to be on a managed care panel one must be skilled at time-limited psychotherapy, and that the practice of long-term therapy is viewed in the modern economic arena as a liability. Indeed, an article by Blackwell and Schmidt (1992) refers to a study in which, of 163 residency training programs surveyed, a majority did not require any experience with long-term psychotherapy.

Our increased sophistication about neurobiology and, by association, neuropharmacology has led psychiatrists to feel a strengthened identification as physicians. Indeed, this expanded role has to some degree led to a decrease in the traditionally perceived distance between psychiatrists and physicians of the other specialties. A shared language has emerged in which internists and surgeons can speak comfortably with psychiatrists about *DSM-IV* diagnoses and drug interactions. To the extent that this change has diminished the anxiety that nonpsychiatrists may feel about psychiatric patients and their treaters, it is no doubt a good thing. The difficulty lies in the possible illusion that psychiatric illness can be understood and treated by a checklist, and that psychological conflict can be resolved with the right combination of medications. This is a risk similar to one that can seduce the internist, that the physician can draw a sense of efficacy and satisfaction by ordering the right blood tests and looking for abnormal values. For psychiatrists, our helpful new tools are helpful only if they do not lead us to foreclose on understanding the complexity of our patients, to rush to certainty, or to steer away from the natural anxiety of swimming in deep waters.

## HOLDING ON TO THE CENTER

As stated in the introduction to this chapter, managed care, with its emphasis on rapid evaluation and symptom control, greatly increases the risk that psychiatrists will move toward a more superficially comfortable and woefully incomplete vision of their role and of what they have to offer their patients. This risk is that much more palpable for those in training. Establishing an identity as a psychiatrist has historically meant grappling with uncertainty, tolerating the conflicts of our patients and the feelings they stir up in us. Residents in training today appear more focused on their identification as physicians than in the past. An increased sense of identification as physicians may be a positive development; it would no doubt be helpful for psychiatrists, for other physicians, and for our patients if psychiatrists were to feel more integrated into the medical fold. The liability is that this increased integration might take place at the expense of crucial parts of our training and of our identity as psychiatrists.

Well-trained psychiatrists must know, because they have experienced it with their patients, that the process of change utilizes the power of the unconscious and the complexities of the therapeutic relationship. With that foundation in place we can also expose our more senior residents to a range of psychotherapy approaches, including the brief psychotherapies. Ultimately I feel it is our job to train psychiatrists who are knowledgeable about psychological process and who have had experience working with patients across the diagnostic spectrum, with a range of treatment modalities that integrate the psychological and the biological.

In training psychiatric residents, we are training not only the next generation of clinicians, but its teachers. If we do not share the gift that was given to us, to think with psychological complexity, and if we teach them only to be managers, administrators, and businessmen and women, then what will they share when it is their turn to teach?

If, in the name of an experiment in economic expediency, we do away with the psychodynamic backbone of our treatment and training programs, in a generation or two we will have lost the accumulated wisdom of our teachers. Unlike the wisdom that is contained in books on theory and technique, the wisdom that is passed on in the mentoring exchange between supervisor and resident is contained in the transmission of a personal knowledge about the nature of psychological change that comes with years of experience.

In the current environment, in which managed care exerts a powerful effect, we as clinicians and teachers are at risk of feeling that what we were trained to do, and the sense of mission and commitment that we have brought to our work, is not of value. The danger is that we will begin to devalue ourselves and each other, and to transmit to our patients and our students a sense of bitterness or cynicism. Above all else we are role models to our students. We must look to ourselves and our colleagues to keep attuned to what is genuine, meaningful, and lively in our clinical work, and to be clear at each step what is in the best interests of our patients as distinct from what are the financial/economic choices we make. We must then attempt to reconcile the two in a way that will allow us to maintain a sense of excitement and hope in our work. If we can pass along that wisdom to those we are training, we will have done the job we set out to do.

## REFERENCES

Beigel, A., and Santiago, J. M. (1995). Redefining the general psychiatrist: values, reforms and issues of psychiatric residency education. *Psychiatric Services* 46(8):769–774.

Blackwell, B., and Schmidt, G. L. (1992). The educational implications of managed mental health care. *Hospital and Community Psychiatry* 43:962–964.

Detre, T., and McDonald, M. C. (1997). Managed care and the future of psychiatry. *Archives of General Psychiatry* 54:201–204.

Gabbard, G. O. (1992). The big chill: the transition from residency to managed care nightmare. *Academic Psychiatry* 16(3):119–126.

Main, T. F. (1957). The ailment. *British Journal of Medical Psychology* 30:129–145.

Meyer, R. E., and Sotsky, S. M. (1995). Managed care and the role and training of psychiatrists. *Health Affairs* 14(3):65–77.

Olfson, M., and Weissman, M. M. (1997). Essential roles for psychiatry in the era of managed care. *Archives of General Psychiatry* 54: 206–208.

Robinowitz, C. B., and Yager, J. (1996). Future of psychiatric education. *The Annual Review of Psychiatry* 15:581–604.

Sabin, J. E. (1991). Clinical skills for the 1990s: six lessons from HMO practice. *Hospital and Community Psychiatry* 42(6):605–608.

———— (1993). The moral myopia of academic psychiatry: a response to Glen O. Gabbard's "The Big Chill." *Academic Psychiatry* 17(4): 175–179.

Sharfstein, S. S. (1997). The futures of psychiatry. *Archives of General Psychiatry* 54:212–213.

Staton, D. (1991). Psychiatry's future: facing reality. *Psychiatric Quarterly* 62(2):165–176.

Summergrad, P., Herman, J. B., Weilburg, J. B., and Jellinek, M. S. (1995). Wagons ho: forward on the managed care trail. *General Hospital Psychiatry* 17:251–259.

Verhulst, J. (1996). The role of the psychiatrist: defining methods, theories, and practice in the time of managed care. Academic Psychiatry 20(4):195–204.

# V

## The Social and Cultural Impact

# 12

## The Normalizing Effects of Managed Care on Psychotherapy[1]

PETER GILFORD

Within the last half-century, psychotherapy has grown from a cottage industry of largely independent, fee-for-service practitioners to become a health benefit to which virtually all Americans may now be entitled. Professional psychology's historical allegiance to the medical paradigm and to the methods of positivist science have granted it political legitimacy, widespread cultural acceptance, and the warrant necessary for entrance into the domain of health care financing. Yet, despite its acceptance in American society, clinical practice has been undergoing a period of considerable instability and upheaval due to changes in funding strategies, the imposition of accountability measures, and shifts in access to mental health services. Mental health treatment is increasingly being represented as a standardized, scientized aspect of medical care, and sold to the public and corporate employers through managed care arrangements under

1. An earlier version of this chapter was presented at a symposium entitled "Social and Cultural Influences on Clinical Practice" at the 1996 meeting of the American Psychological Association in Toronto, Canada.

the all-encompassing term "behavioral health care." The impact of these changes is said to be responsible for what former American Psychological Association president and managed care advocate Nicholas Cummings has called the "greatest resocialization of professional psychologists since the World War II era" (Cummings 1995, p. 10).

The regulation of psychotherapy administered through managed care arrangements has forced clinicians to reconsider the essential nature of their work. What exactly is it that we do? To whom are we ultimately accountable? On what methodological foundation do we define and evaluate therapeutic success and failure? How should we conceptualize psychopathology? Should mandated guidelines structure and focus the therapeutic hour toward defined goals? Do we utilize transference without an exploration of its meaning, ignoring its potential to inform us about how power, authority, and domination affect a patient's presenting problem and relational understandings? Are the positive changes we observe in our patients a result of the persuasiveness of our prescriptive authority, the consequence of applying the correct technique, or due, fundamentally, to a trusting relationship developed over time and maintained in a supportive, safe environment that nurtures self-discovery? And last, what is our image of the healthy self? What is the normative image of human being that guides our work?

Core aspects of psychotherapy, including the importance of temporal understanding, the role of human relationship in healing, the development of trust, and empathic intuition, have, to a considerable degree, been held apart from the realities of the marketplace and reductive commodification. But outside the therapy office, in the world of health care politics and corporate power, these and other long-established elements of clinical work are denied significance. With the regulations of managed care companies, the increased pressure for accountability, and the impending "templating" of psychotherapy, the future of clinical practice and the identity of psychological discourse are uncertain.

## HOW PSYCHOTHERAPY CONSTRUCTS THE SELF

What follows is based on the central assumption that psychotherapy has political impact in the way that its theories and practices construct a particular configuration of the self—one usually complicitous with the needs of market capitalism (Cushman 1990, 1995, Kovel 1980, Sampson 1981, 1988). Psychotherapy's usefulness and importance to Western society has grown in the last century, but its sociopolitical function has largely escaped critical appraisal; psychotherapists are no less immune to economic, guild, and ideological pressures than other professionals, and thus have a vested interest in defending rather than transforming the social order. Nevertheless, those clinicians and social scientists who have studied the impact of psychological understandings on society argue that psychological discourse[2] has reflected and constructed a particular image of personhood, one that plays a significant role in the perpetuation of the political and economic status quo.

For example, Bellah and colleagues (1985) identify how the therapeutic ethos has encouraged the atomistic individualism that permeates American culture and reinterprets the ideology of democracy. Cushman (1990, 1995) conceives of an "empty self," one derived from psychotherapy theories and encouraged by advertising. Constructed by the needs of capitalism, this empty self constantly needs to fill itself by purchasing and ingesting material goods. Greenberg (1994) explores how the popular psychology literature on "codependency" remaps the proper behavior in respect to individual boundaries in relationships, recapitulating and perpetuating the staunchly individualistic cultural conditions from which such relational problems arise. Herman (1995) examines the evolution and impact of the interrelationship between psychological research, discourse, and practice and American political culture, revealing through historical analysis how each has relied on the other to achieve and justify their political agendas. Kovel (1980) argues that the relationship between psychological discourse and the aims of capitalism displaces the true social and political causes of psychological suffering and

---

2. The terms *psychological discourse, psychology,* and *psychotherapy* are used interchangeably in this chapter. This usage is intended to refer to the discipline in its entirety as well as to the specific aspects of therapeutic action and process, including how therapists think about, understand, and formulate patient difficulty and the means to its amelioration. Psychological understandings and explanations should be understood in their impact on the culture at large.

locates them within individuals instead of in society. In addition, Prilleltensky (1989, 1994) argues that the moral, political, and social implications of applied psychology and its theories strengthen the social status quo and perpetuate social injustice. Similarly, Sampson (1981, 1988) argues that psychology's subject is a sociohistorical, cultural product that fits the existing structures and arrangements of contemporary Western society.

The preceding writers take a sociohistorical view of psychological knowledge and practice, and argue that the institution of psychology and its diverse schools of thought have had a defining impact on our moral understandings of what it means to be correctly human. They maintain that psychological ideas and practices have profoundly penetrated our everyday private lives and thoughts, and that therapeutic explanations put forth specific moral visions of how we ought to consider ourselves and understand the motives and consequences of our actions. Using interpretive methods, they base their analyses on the idea that the reality of the self is a social construction.

This understanding is anchored in the philosophical viewpoint of social constructionism, which has its roots in the phenomenological position articulated by the philosopher Martin Heidegger (1962). Heidegger's phenomenology stresses the idea that human subjects are formed by the historical cultural practices in which they develop, and the social world is understood to be both constituted by and constitutive of the person. When we focus on the social origins of assumptions about ways of being, our attention is directed to "the social, moral, political and economic institutions that sustain and are supported by current assumptions about human activity" (Gergen 1985, p. 267). Through a social constructionist analysis, it is clear that normative psychology has been, and continues to be, a powerful discourse that helps to sustain existing sociopolitical arrangements, circumscribing and implicitly shaping the moral meanings we impart to all human activity and thus prescriptively shaping our modes of self-reflection.

With the arrival of managed care and its limitations on treatment, the potential of psychotherapeutic work to resist or challenge the status quo has essentially been eliminated. Managed care regulations force the loss of an implicit moral vision of psychotherapy as an emancipatory process because the goal of such regulations is to codify, delimit, define, measure, and make determinations of value. The process, in effect, becomes a product, the therapist, a provider, and the patient, a consumer. The emotionally distressed and vulnerable individual who seeks treatment through managed care channels must swiftly communicate his or her problems and submit to formulaic technical intervention based on a predetermined, specified treatment. Long, complex stories are forcibly reduced to shorter, simpler ones. There is little time to encourage patients to question the normative assumptions of culture, gender, class, and other socially determined understandings that constitute their suffering.

We must ask ourselves: What exactly is lost when understanding is delimited through the imposition of restrictions based on predetermined intervention strategies? What comes to pass when patients must trust quickly and with an innocent dependence on the ethics and moral authority of the therapist? Without attending to the power relation that manifests in the therapy hour through resistance and transference–countertransference dynamics, dialogue and mutuality are replaced by an insidious, directive domination. Dialogue becomes monologue and intersubjective understanding is replaced by technicist intervention.

The final result of such an approach to healing suggests a configuration of self that is docile, easily dominated, and therefore politically expedient. Psychotherapy's potential to empower individuals to uncover and question the social conditions contributing to their distress and to develop strategies to challenge existing understandings is nullified by the strict regulations imposed by managed care companies. For patients, what is lost in the therapeutic process is the potential for the development of what Joel Kovel (1988) calls "critical intelligence." Defined as "consciousness exhibited by maximum inner freedom," Kovel states that such an intelligence "recognizes the determination of any practice by the social order of which it is a part; and in so doing, moves to transcend that order . . . critical intelligence differentiates, and distinguishes sharply between surface and depth, actuality and potentiality" (pp. 158–159). For therapists, especially those whose work is informed by psychodynamic theories, what is lost is a conception of the therapeutic process as an unfolding dialogue, the focus and goal of which is determined exclusively by patient and therapist rather than by bureaucratic decree.

## HOW MANAGED CARE CONSTRUCTS PSYCHOTHERAPY:

The term *managed care* is so evocative for many mental health professionals that its definition bears closer examination. Broadly defined, managed care corporations act to regulate the cost of care through patient treatment preauthorization, monitoring of treatment progress and outcome, and computer profiling of therapists to ensure their compatibility with managed care treatment philosophy and fiscal goals. Designed, marketed, and sold to large corporations, managed care-administered mental health benefits coexist within general health care plans or are attached as "carve outs" that are either sold to companies specializing in the administration of mental health care or are administered as part of an overall health benefit such as that found in a health maintenance organization. In the simplest sense, managed care constructs psychotherapy by the limits set out in a specific benefits package (e.g., fifteen sessions per year). Treatment authorization and denial is commonly based on a definition of medical necessity. This allows companies to approve or deny treatment based on a checklist of criteria, with coverage (i.e., treatment) limited by the definition of what constitutes a treatable condition. However, as will be argued, managed care's construction of psychotherapy is considerably more far-reaching than simply the regulation of treatment access and length.

Proponents of managed care argue that psychotherapy should be an empirically based science of "behavioral medicine" or "behavioral health care." The change in nomenclature reveals the message—mental health treatment is to be concerned with behavior and viewed through the lens of medicine. Supporters also argue that dynamic therapies—those that emphasize the centrality of transference work—are exploitative in that they encourage the dependency of patients on therapists. Moreover, they claim that such dependence can never be therapeutic and is based solely on its economic benefit to practitioners rather than on long-established clinical and theoretical understanding. Proponents frequently argue that outcomes research fails to support the belief that longer-term treatments are of superior effectiveness, and that, regardless, only a small segment of society can afford longer-term treatment, leaving the mental health care needs of the majority unmet (Austad 1996, Sabin 1996). The unconscious and transference may be interesting therapeutic concepts, but for managed care bureaucracy they are considered clinical "noise" (Pigott 1997), their utility limited solely because they cannot be easily operationalized into reliable, objectively observable, discrete, measurable phenomena.

For the proponents of managed care, causation and intervention equals confidence, the capacity to make determinations of worth through replicability, reliability, and validity—the hallmarks of science. As social constructionist Kenneth Gergen (1995) has stated, "empiricism itself operates much like a fundamentalist religion: if one fails to embrace its tenets, the state of grace is denied" (p. 394). In general, those who staunchly maintain the belief that psychotherapy should be a scientific practice based on a positivist tradition of truth production find the regulations imposed on psychotherapy by managed care a welcome relief. They perceive it as a much needed correction to the complex, top-heavy, technically unreliable psychotherapy that has appeared to be accountable to no one other than its practitioners, and even then only to those who hold a similar theoretical position. But it is the practitioners who directly experience the unremitting gap between theory and praxis, and for many this rift has always been necessarily humbling. For many it has also served as a fulcrum to deeper levels of understanding. As managed care policies attempt to transform practice into impersonal technical maneuvers based on formulaic understandings, this gap is sure to widen.

A view of managed care informed by the perspective of critical theory would describe it as the institutionalized endpoint of means–ends determinations in late industrial capitalism. It is the contemporary manifestation of what Max Weber (1946) described as the continued expansion of rationalization and bureaucratization, the synergy between the thrust of modernity and capitalism—the "iron cage" of a formal cost-benefit rationality. The ideological character of "managed" "care" fuses aspects of the market and of bureaucracy that are incompatible—market competition and rational management.

Therapists find themselves unknowingly caught in the middle of another inherent conflict in managed care, between the rational aims of "management" and the moral intent of "care." While the ideology underlying management is firmly embedded in the lexicon of economics, the moral ideal of "care" is generally thought to be a human interest held apart from the harsh realities of the marketplace. Therapeutic caring has traditionally been concerned with the individual life, while management is associated with the supervision of agents and action toward an impersonal end. Managed care might best be conceptualized as the culmination of the progressive industrialization of psychotherapy; it involves the regulation, measurement, and production of emotional well-being and social order, and, through rigid empirical methods, the standardization of a "caring" human connection (Herman 1995, Kovel 1980).

Thus we can see that the managed care paradigm imposes the ideology of management on therapy and on the self. Through standardized treatment guidelines tailored to diagnostically related groups, with the treatment goal being the reduction of specific problem-symptoms, the patient is to be *managed* out of therapy as quickly and cheaply as possible, and must then "manage" independently (Shulman 1994). If the old therapeutic maxim was "It's the relationship that heals," the new one would seem to be "it's the relationship that steals" with its suggestion that any dependency in psychotherapy exploits the patient, robs the insurance company, and unfairly distributes social resources.

## THE OBJECTIFIED SELF

The goal of all psychotherapy under managed care is the reduction of symptomatic distress in the shortest possible time using the least expensive intervention. Managed care relies on an implicit objectification of the self to achieve this goal, with the therapeutic subject perceived through the lens of reductive methodologies based on universal claims about the nature of human suffering and of human being. The underlying assumption is that our selfhood can be apprehended in the same manner as our physical being. Not suprisingly, this is consistent with the discipline's presentation of psychotherapy as a neutral scientific practice that treats ahistorical, objective illness. Because of this, the emergence and growing hegemony of managed mental health care should not be understood as the true cause of the mental health profession's crisis. Rather, it is the result of the discipline promoting itself and gaining legitimacy on the same epistemology and methodological foundation as the natural sciences. Due to psychology's historical association with the medical model, explanations of human action are shifted from a moral model to a causal-determinist one. Further, this model decontextualizes human suffering by failing to consider the person as a dynamic social agent "defined by what class, community and history" have meant for him or her (Kovel 1980, p. 86). This has led to a degree of objectivism that serves as an exemplar of an excess of technical reason, which philosopher Charles Taylor argues "forgets the patient as a person, takes no account of how the treatment relates to his or her story and thus of the determinants of hope and despair" (Taylor 1991, pp. 105–106). It is an objectification that distances, perpetuates the disengagement of an allegedly neutral observer, and then reifies and freezes such observations as expert knowledge. Under the control of managed care, this scientistic justification should be understood as an exercise of power and a form of domination that cultural genealogist-philosopher Michel Foucault argued attaches an identity and imposes a law of truth on the person, making him a subject and "subject to" (Foucault 1983).

Nevertheless, therapy *is* a social practice that reflects the prevailing cultural modes of organizing and understanding human experience, and it attempts to heal a self that is no stranger to the distortion and injustice of objectifying practices (Cushman 1990, 1993, Foucault 1980). Therefore, attempting to heal the self without a critical consideration of the cultural etiology of its psychological distress will only perpetuate the very conditions from which it suffers. To heal the self through the same technicist mind-set that has so greatly contributed to its fragmentation and displacement will only normalize the conditions of its dis-ease. This is not to say that our scientific technological world hasn't improved the quality of life in many significant ways, but there is also evidence that it has produced much psychological suffering, and the "world" as so constituted remains left out of most psychological formulation. And, unfortunately, an industrialized psychotherapy in an era of accountability will, like the medical profession, become increasingly specialized, resulting in an even more fragmented conception of self. As treatments are tailored to an increasing number of putatively discrete symptom-based diagnostic categories, fragmentation seems to be the unavoidable result.

For example, concurrent with mandated limitations on treatment, the nature of mental disturbance is increasingly understood as a biochemical imbalance requiring only pharmacological intervention. Locating and defining the determinants of mood, even of character, neurochemically, then, reconfigures the self in the name of efficiency, improved functionality, and relief from symptomatic distress. As human suffering becomes reductively decontextualized—ahistorical and apolitical—symptoms lose their symbolic, cultural, and even personal meanings.

Human beings are not objects. A distressed self in need of healing must be understood, and must come to self-understanding, in relation to the cultural background of distinctions of worth. When this mode of understanding is obstructed, as can be seen in the regulations for psychotherapy by managed care, the self can only adapt. As Herman (1995) succinctly states, "If psychological knowledge is to mobilize people for progressive change, rather than equip them to endure new variations on old injustices, the dichotomy between internal and external transformation will have to be rejected as false and useless" (p. 16).

## MEASUREMENT

Psychology has evolved based on its ability to measure, but the discipline continues to have difficulty coming to terms with the philosophical problem of separating fact from value. Managed care policies further obscure and perpetuate the political consequences of this issue through a reliance on the use of intake screening and simplistic outcomes measurement. Broadly speaking, measurement not only helps produce and define the self in contemporary society, but also maintains it under a form of surveillance. At present, due to advances in information technology, collecting and reducing large amounts of raw data to impersonal statistical inference is now accomplished quickly and easily, making objectification through measurement even easier. Added to growing concerns about confidentiality, this reductive process only further disengages the source of the data itself—

the suffering individual whom the therapist encounters—from what Taylor (1991) calls "the moral background of benevolence" (p. 106) which is required to enframe an action to its moral ideal.

For instance, imagine how accumulated psychological information such as therapeutic outcomes or functional status indices correlated to diagnostic-related groupings could be used for dubious purposes. Stored in proprietary corporate databases and epistemologically depoliticized, such information could well be used as a marketing tool by managed care companies to corporations purchasing mental health benefits for employees. This is not unlike a manufacturer making claims about product quality by citing longer mean time before failure—only the product in this case is human "functionality."

The use of psychological measurement is not unique to the ascendance of managed care. As noted, it has a long history in the legitimation of psychological knowledge. However, its significance in a critical understanding of managed care is the perpetuation of an aura of scientific objectivity that simplifies psychological distress and locates it inside a decontextualized self, with moral positions about what it is to be properly human disguised in the means of assessment. Measures of functionality, personality, psychopathology, and intelligence do not gather objective data about an ahistorical, acultural self. Rather, their mode of assessment frames the intelligibility of their results (Danziger 1990, Shedler et al. 1993). Put another way, our existing knowledge, beliefs, and theories predetermine what we perceive, as well as what we measure and how we measure it. Our theories must always live in their metaphysical presuppositions, never to be detached from their philosophical and epistemological uncertainties. In fact, their uncertainties give them life and significance.

This reductive objectification of individuals parallels the dangerous trajectory of a kind of political arithmetic in which the uniqueness of an unknown, unpredictable self is an increasing threat to the future—as is the uncertainty that is seen to increasingly require management for the smooth functioning of modern society. Measurement technologies in the hands of managed care corporations serve as an exemplar of what Foucault (1979) identified as the means by which constant surveillance enables power to be used with maximum efficiency.

## TIME-SHIFTING

The therapist's office has traditionally been considered a contained place, a haven, closed off from the hustle and bustle of the social circulatory system and apart from the dehumanizing trends of modern society. It was a place where, through the process of telling one's story, one might discover oneself. The quickened pace of modern life, however, has now permeated the therapeutic enclosure as therapists are forced to do more, faster, with less. Therapy has been downsized and becomes another strategically organized activity reproducing the cultural zeitgeist.

The waning of the sense of historical time seen in the culture at large is aptly symbolized by managed care's requirement for brief treatment. Psychotherapy can no longer be carried out under the patient's or therapist's sense of time. Instead, therapy operates solely under fiscal time—time determined by limits imposed solely by economic incentives. Time is of the essence, and the therapist becomes the monitor of this fiscally constrained temporality by directively focusing the therapeutic hour on the attainment of specific goals. This limits understanding of psychological distress and the means to its amelioration to a level that ignores and diminishes the interconnectedness of past, present, and future. It is quicker—and cheaper—to forget than to remember.

However, in systems of accountability that link subjective distress to objective standards of assessment and treatment, a subjective sense of time has little place. And in a world that is increasingly technologically organized and scientifically understood, subjectivity becomes ever more circumscribed. Looking through a postmodern lens, when the story-course of a human life is simply a constructed narrative, it can then be quickly reconfigured. With the imposition of a constricted therapeutic structure subjectivity will eventually conform, because technical methods are recognized as rational, neutral, and they embody expert truth—facts, not values. Because psychological understandings implicitly normalize human experience, the forced time-shift explicit to managed care practice requires a submission of subjectivity in a way that impacts the contemporary notion of a true and free self, its cultural construction and political uses notwithstanding. Subjectivity, however, must be set free in order to do its political work.

## NORMALIZING EFFECTS

Normalizing occurs by the definition of common goals and procedures and agreed-upon examples of how human activity should be organized and understood (Dreyfus and Rabinow 1982). In this respect, all forms of psychotherapy can be said to have normalizing effects. That is, as a social practice psychotherapy has had a significant influence on the configuration of the contemporary self. What has been proposed thus far is that under managed care, how psychotherapy functions as a political technology of the self (i.e., its normalizing function) is extended to dangerous extremes, becoming a means not of emancipation but of control, encouraging an unquestioning adaptation.

An example of managed care's normalizing effect is that it contributes to the configuration of a self that is both subject and object. This exacerbates another form of surveillance, one Foucault (1979) called "panoptic," in which the self becomes subject to its own psychological interrogation and monitoring. Managed care practices extend the normalizing functions of psychotherapy by destroying its potential as an emancipatory process and moral discourse, one that can help individuals reflexively transcend the political uses of subject–object, internal-external dichotomies. In the era of an industrialized treatment of normalized selves, the realm of freedom is invisibly diminished and the means of control extended.

Some therapeutic traditions, particularly those that focus on the therapeutic relationship, have countered the normalizing functions of psychological understandings by modeling an ethic that rejects totalizing claims, values historical connections, and deconstructs disguised ideology camouflaged as ontological truth. These traditions have, to some degree, resisted objectifying the therapeutic subject by focusing on therapeutic process and the evolving dialectic of the therapeutic relationship. A dialectical understanding at least attempts to demystify power in the therapeutic interaction by acknowledging and interpreting its manifestation over time.

Certain forms of psychotherapy have also implicitly subscribed to aspects of a form of "dialogical knowing," echoing hermeneutic philosopher Hans Gadamer's (1975) idea of the genuine conversation. The unfolding of the narrative reality of the self is here furthered by a therapeutic stance of unknowing, an open curiosity and present-ness to the uniqueness of the other's subjectivity. However, holding this therapeutic stance is not possible where accountability is highly formalized and defined by something outside the intersubjective reality created by patient and therapist. Inarguably, these therapeutic ideals and the theories that underlie them are derived from the same sociohistorical context that has given rise to managed care, and so must also be viewed as arising from discursive practices[3] that legitimate other forms and arrangements of power. But these ideals function as an important cultural counterpoint and resistance to the status quo as they contain the potential to question the dominant ideologies that constitute—and posit—a self in need of healing.

Ironically, it is the very success of psychotherapy in American society (an unobstructed psychotherapy) that has brought about its industrialization—and the compromising of patients' needs and therapists' ideals. But to practice these therapeutic traditions and to be guided by these ideals inescapably requires time, and time constraints may be the central means by which managed care practices normalize. It is of critical importance to consider what will happen to the normalizing effects of a psychotherapy so obviously beholden to the arrangements of power that fund its practice. What will become of the self that such a psychotherapy constructs is of even greater importance.

Psychological knowledge must be understood as a discursive formation. Otherwise it will not be seen to have a normalizing function that helps to maintain existing arrangements of power and privilege. A political, that is, *critical* intelligibility for therapeutic discourse is dependent on identifying the ideologies that are supported by it, and must operate from what Paul Ricoeur (1981) has called a "hermeneutics of suspicion." This is essential for the development of a critical psychology guided by emancipatory values.

The issues brought up by managed care psychotherapy serve to reignite a much deeper and longstanding debate within the discipline,

---

3. Foucault (1979, 1983) argued that discursive practices such as psychotherapy inescapably involve knowledge claims that give expression to both resistance *and* legitimation to existing arrangements of power and privilege.

the debate about what it is to be human. This is a moral argument that the rhetoric of science conceals. Here, perhaps, lies something latent in the managed care crisis—the possibility that this argument can be genuinely addressed. But, as I have been suggesting, this debate cannot rely on objective laws, pure subjectivity, or the totalization of theory. It must rely on a moral dialectic furthered by interpretive understandings of the cultural practices that construct us.

## CONCLUSIONS

Foucault looked at reform as an entry point, a symptom or sign that often revealed a disguised normalizing of an existing cultural practice. Managed mental health care is a powerful reform, and, as I have argued, forces the loss of an emancipatory moral vision. It moves psychotherapy in a regressive direction epistemologically, away from the awareness of postmodern and constructionist challenges to psychological knowledge and toward an "innocent knowledge" that denies the connections between means of understanding and their social and political uses. Therapy is a discursive formation, a practice and logic of discovery that produces things—forms behavior, prescribes being, advocates and prohibits certain modes of self-understanding. It is a body of knowledge *and* a power responsible for a specific "politics of truth" (Foucault 1980). As clinical practice is increasingly subsumed by the ethos of the consumer marketplace, the therapeutic community must become aware that it is in the midst of a significant and observable reconfiguring of the self—a remaking of the psychotherapeutic subject.

Because psychotherapy theories manifest specific ideological commitments and moral positions, the popularity or dominance of any theory of therapy must be understood as implicitly, and usually unknowingly, advocating a specific moral ideal of what it means to be human, leading to a particular configuration of self. This is why the current transformation in mental health care should be understood as a moral reform, shifting the meaning of managed care's transformation of therapeutic practice to a broader, sociopolitical perspective. If a different configuration of self is indeed being transmitted through psychotherapy practice as defined by managed care, then what are its parameters? What is its shape, and what are its sources of definition?

Current arguments about the future of psychotherapy, including its accessibility, the extent of its coverage as a mental health benefit, and the form in which it should be delivered, must be understood as moral and political debates about the self. Without this understanding, and with the continued representation of psychotherapy as a scientific, value-neutral enterprise, the resolution of the dilemma confronting the profession in its struggle with the forces of industrialization will be determined by the repression of what postmodern perspectives reveal—that there is no objective discovery of truth that will tell us how to act or to be. Psychotherapy can no longer claim to be an applied science that delivers objective knowledge. If the mental health profession ignores this and believes in "innocent knowledge" as it is exemplified by managed care regulations, then the future of psychotherapeutic discourse and practice will most certainly be in the service of something other than "truth." It will be a truth claim embodying nothing more than the will to power.

## REFERENCES

Austad, C. S. (1996). *Is Long-term Psychotherapy Unethical?: Toward a Social Ethic in an Era of Managed Care.* San Francisco: Jossey-Bass.

Bellah, R., Madsen, R., Sullivan, W., et al. (1985). *Habits of the Heart: Individualism and Commitment in American Life.* Berkeley: University of California Press.

Cummings, N. A. (1995). Impact of managed care on employment and training: a primer for survival. *Professional Psychology: Research and Practice* 26(1):10–15.

Cushman, P. (1990). Why the self is empty: toward a historically situated psychology. *American Psychologist* 45:599–611.

——— (1993). Psychotherapy as moral discourse. *Journal of Theoretical and Philosophical Psychology* 13(2).

——— (1995). *Constructing the Self, Constructing America.* New York: Addison-Wesley.

Danziger, K. (1990). *Constructing the Subject.* New York: Cambridge University Press.

Dreyfus, H. L., and Rabinow, P. (1982). *Michel Foucault: Beyond Structuralism and Hermeneutics*, 2nd ed. Chicago: University of Chicago Press.

Foucault, M. (1979). *Discipline and Punish: The Birth of the Prison*. New York: Vintage/Random House.

—— (1980). Truth and power. In *Power/Knowledge: Selected Interviews and Other Writings by Michel Foucault*, ed. C. Gordon, pp. 109–133. New York: Random House.

—— (1983). Why study power: the question of the subject. In *Michel Foucault: Beyond Structuralism and Hermeneutics*, 2nd ed., ed. H. Dreyfus and P. Rabinow, pp. 208–216. Chicago: University of Chicago Press.

Gadamer, H. G. (1975). *Truth and Method*. New York: Continuum.

Gergen, K. (1985). The social constructionist movement in modern psychology. *American Psychologist* 40(3):266–275.

—— (1995). Postmodern psychology: resonance and reflection. *American Psychologist* 50:394.

Greenberg, G. (1994). *The Self on the Shelf: Recovery Books and the Good Life*. Albany, NY: SUNY Press.

Heidegger, M. (1962). The question concerning technology. In *Martin Heidegger: Basic Writings*, ed. D. F. Krell, pp. 287–317. New York: Harper & Row, 1977.

Herman, E. (1995). *The Romance of American Psychology: Political Culture in the Age of Experts*. Berkeley, CA: University of California Press.

Kovel, J. (1980). The American mental health industry. In *Critical Psychiatry: The Politics of Mental Health*, ed. D. Inglesby, pp. 72–101. New York: Random House.

—— (1988). *The Radical Spirit: Essays on Psychoanalysis and Society*. London: Free Association Books.

Pigott, H. E. (1997). Computer decision-support as a clinician's tool. In *Managing Care, not Dollars: The Continuum of Mental Health Services*, ed. R. Schreter, S. Sharfstein, and C. Schreter, pp. 245–263. Washington DC: American Psychiatric Press.

Prilleltensky, I. (1989). Psychology and the status quo. *American Psychologist* 44:795–802.

—— (1994). *The Morals and Politics of Psychology: Psychological Discourse and the Status Quo*. Albany, NY: State University of New York Press.

Ricoeur, P. (1981). *Hermeneutics and the Human Sciences*, ed. John Thompson. New York: Cambridge University Press.

Sabin, J. E. (1996). Is managed care ethical care? In *Controversies in Managed Mental Health Care*, ed. A. Lazarus, pp. 115–126. Washington, DC: American Psychiatric Press.

Sampson, E. E. (1981). Cognitive psychology as ideology. *American Psychologist* 36:730–743.

——— (1988). The debate on individualism: indigenous psychologies of the individual and their role in personal and societal functioning. *American Psychologist* 43:15–22.

Shedler, J., Mayman, M., and Manis, M. (1993). The illusion of mental health. *American Psychologist* 48(11):1117–1130.

Shulman, M. E. (1994). Managed care and health care reform: appreciating the full threat. *Psychologist/Psychoanalyst* 14(2): 5–9. Publication of Division 39 of the American Psychological Association.

Taylor, C. (1991). *The Ethics of Authenticity*. Cambridge, MA: Harvard University Press.

Weber, M. (1946). Bureaucracy. In *From Max Weber: Essays in Sociology*, ed. and trans. H. Gerth and C. W. Mills, pp. 196–244. New York: Oxford University Press.

# 13

## *The Corporatization of Psychotherapy: A Study in Professional Transformation*

### DAVID PINGITORE

$M$ental health services in the United States are undergoing a profound reorganization in purpose, administration, and delivery best exemplified by the emergence of managed care. The corporatization of mental health services represents the transformation of professional work in the postindustrial era, yet efforts by mental health professionals to understand this transformation highlight their conceptual limitations in understanding the most profound changes to have occurred in their work in the last thirty years. This corporatization is best understood as a routine feature of how, when analyzed together, all professions represent a system in itself (Abbott 1988). This social-systemic perspective considers professionalization to be the possession and successive development of expert labor that responds to social and cultural forces that emerge from within and outside the system as a whole (Abbott 1989).[1]

---

1. Studies that rely on the principles of general systems theory often over-contextualize the data available (Candib 1990), emphasize internal harmony within a given social system at the expense of analyses of political or psychological con-

In response to corporatization, mental health professionals are investigating how the dramatic changes in health care economics have transformed many aspects of our work (Austad et al. 1988, Berkman et al. 1988, Broskowski 1991, Cummings 1995). Despite their efforts, this work is hampered by a deeply ideological outlook regarding the organization of the U.S. economy and the social role of mental health services. Corporate and public policies concerning the future administration, financing, and social role of mental health services are accepted as a fait accompli. This accommodationist outlook is further hampered by a reflexive parochial identity whereby individuals view themselves principally as psychologists, for example, or even more generally as "psychotherapists." Their adherence to this identity ultimately prevents them from understanding the complex interconnections between their status as providers of unique and expert labor and the overarching economic, social, and cultural systems that allow therapy to function in this country. It is ironic that individuals who are authorities on human behavior lack the analytic tools necessary to fully understand the transformation of their work and their professional selves.

The corporatization of psychotherapy also challenges the views held by those mental health professionals and academic critics who link psychotherapeutic work with a broader social agenda (Alford 1989, Cushman 1991, Kovel 1981, 1988, Richards 1984). Using a variety of methods, including neo-Marxist, feminist, psychoanalytic, and poststructuralist, these commentators have uncovered a dialectic involving the work of psychotherapy and its relationship to prevailing social and economic structures that extends the tradition of the Frankfurt school, and its critical social theory. This dialectic hinges on the recognition that while psychotherapy helps patients liberate a portion of their own lives, it simultaneously embodies social con-

---

flict (Pingitore 1994), and generally conceive of social and political hierarchies as historical absolutes (Friedman 1987). Yet even under these conditions, Abbott's (1988) use of a systemic formula works, because he gives credence to historical context and the reality of social and political conflict. If there is one glaring omission in his analysis of the professional system, it is in failing to consider the role of unconscious individual and group dynamics to explain both the work that individual professionals perform and their relations between and among each other.

trol features necessary for maintaining economic and political hierarchies (Giddens 1991, Kovel 1981, 1988, Lichtman 1982, Wolfenstein 1993).

Yet such accounts of the subversive nature of psychotherapy were written before mental health services were more fully corporatized and the managed care model gained ascendancy in the private sector. In the context of encroaching corporatization and attempts by mental health professionals to understand this development, a critical sociology of the work performed by this group is urgently needed. This perspective is vital because as members of this profession we are faced with vast changes in our work and accompanying identity.

## PSYCHOTHERAPY'S NEW WORLD ORDER

Over a period of decades, mental health service delivery gradually took on the organizational structures that now constitute this industry. In 1960 only 13 percent of the population had encountered the mental health establishment, and reimbursement for psychotherapy as we now know it was virtually nonexistent. Yet the combined efforts of corporate financing, public policy, and professional development contributed to a culture in which in 1980 26 percent of the population either unilaterally sought, or had been placed under the treatment of, mental health professionals (VandenBos et al. 1991).

Much of the impetus for the increase in the numbers of psychotherapists was initiated by an interventionist public sector in the 1960s and early 1970s. The increase in mental health service delivery by the federal government was, quite simply, part of a larger dynamic of economic expansion, public policy experimentation, and cultural optimism regarding individual and group opportunities during a period of American political and economic preeminence in the world. The profession's work was also sanctioned by cultural institutions as one method to assist individuals and families in negotiating the intimate experiences of modernity itself, commonly labeled "the stress and demands of everyday life." By the late 1970s this interventionist approach was replaced by the contracting of many services provided by public institutions and a dramatic decrease in the funding of mental health services. While access to services was the social and political agenda that legitimated the expansion of services in the postwar period, cost containment is now the cornerstone for private and public policy in health and mental health services.

The current transformation or, as some would argue, the dismantling of mental heath services is part of a national effort to better manage American industry. Corporate profits have soared in the 1990s (Labate 1992). This increase has been the result of a number of factors, including productivity increases, cost reductions due to technological innovation, and a steady downsizing of the labor force. Reducing mental health costs—through copayments, deductibles, or reductions in the duration of services or fees paid to providers—is part of this total strategy by U.S. industry to increase profitability.

Some mental health professionals have maintained the scope of their work in the face of cutbacks through a revision and redefinition of their work. One example of this flexibility in the face of change has been the transformation of alcohol treatment from inpatient to outpatient modalities. Professionals in the drug and alcohol fields have been able to maintain their legitimacy in the face of budget cutbacks and a retrenchment in the therapeutic goals for psychotherapy. They have accomplished this goal by effecting a merger of two previously separate professions (alcohol and drug counselors), aligning with a third profession (criminal justice practitioners), and shifting the location of treatment (from inpatient to outpatient), thereby cutting costs. Their work has also coincidentally addressed the economic and political concerns of politicians, corporate and public sector administrators, and a segment of the general public by providing services that hold out the promise of containing behaviors that threaten social stability. The result has been a near-doubling in treatment units during the 1980s even in the face of cost containment (Schmidt and Weisner 1993).

Researchers in psychology, psychiatry, and public health have also responded to the contraction of traditional mental health services. They have assembled an impressive body of data to clarify the misperception that mental health costs are expanding in an unjustified manner, and that psychotherapy services provide few financial or organizational benefits to employers or third-party payers. Labeled the "medical offset" literature, these reports provide striking evidence of how a variety of psychotherapy services drastically reduce overall medical costs in both outpatient and inpatient settings (Kessler et al. 1985, Orleans et al. 1985, Shemo 1985) as well as promote employee productivity (Hirsch 1995). Yet employers remain skeptical of a treatment that is not defined by its providers as a "medical necessity" (Zimet 1986). Nor have mental health professionals, to meet the demands of industry, developed a political calculus that effectively combines the issues of cost containment, clinical effectiveness, and wide cultural legitimacy such as that offered by their competitors in the medical community (Stein 1991).

The need for mental health professionals to carve out new work highlights a significant ideological task that confronts the profession. This task involves developing a survival strategy that includes as one of its goals a definition of "mental health" acceptable to those institutions who control its financing, legislation, and cultural legitimation. This reframing of mental health work tasks is increasingly difficult because a corporatized mental health delivery system may authorize treatment for a situation that is viewed by all parties as a necessity (e.g., chronic alcoholism), but makes it far more difficult to pay for the treatment of something as unmeasurable as alienation (Herron et al. 1994).

The future remains uncertain for psychotherapists who work in the traditional treatment format of unlimited length and cost, and who therapeutically engage with patients in a manner beyond a reduction of medically defined symptoms. For steadily encroaching on psychotherapists' traditional work routines is a central social dynamic in contemporary society, namely, the rationalization of time itself under the conditions of capitalism. The development of managed care is symptomatic of the overall collapse of unconscious and existential time to the administrative and financial imperatives of commodified time (which is measured only in monetary units) and is a cornerstone of a free market economy. In effect, the growth of brief psychotherapy in our field is another example of how the reorganization of time is a fundamental feature of all modern social institutions (Giddens 1991).

## PSYCHOTHERAPY AND THE SYSTEMS OF PROFESSIONS

Studies in the sociology of professions offer a number of models to understand the social character of mental health work. These include functionalist and structuralist models, the "power literature" of the 1960s and 1970s that focused on the professionals' social control function, and, lately, cultural theories, which document how professional work becomes legitimated and enacted in the wider culture. The corporatization of psychotherapy highlights social and cultural changes that help shape the process of development within all groups that possess expert labor known as professionalization (Abbott 1988). Technical, scientific, organizational, and ideological changes within one profession (such as health care financing and administration) affect phenomena in another profession (psychotherapy). The professional system is best understood as a network of labor processes, social institutions (such as public bureaucracies that administer mental health service delivery), and cultural values (for example, efficiency in the promotion of goods and services). In the professional system, there are internal differences within a given profession (e.g., psychiatrists versus marriage counselors or female therapists versus male administrators), as well as external social forces that shape a profession in a given era. Examples of external forces include federal budget priorities, corporate downsizing trends, and society's continuing cultural ethos of technological rationality and organizational efficiency.

Four trends in the practice of psychotherapy convincingly demonstrate its corporatization. First, the control of the work of psychotherapy, previously in the near-exclusive hands of the clinician, has now been expanded to include other groups such as corporate benefits managers and managed care personnel. As a result of this development, multiple professions are in conflict with one another over the control of the administrative, clinical, financial, and ideological content of psychotherapy.

The entry of administrative and managerial professions into the psychotherapist's domain has created disequilibrating and conflict-laden scenarios in our daily work routines. This development intensifies interprofessional rivalries and has dramatically weakened the link between a profession's work and its claims to being a group with expert and exclusive services. Psychotherapists' claims to the unique hold on the work of diagnosis, treatment, and inference in the clinical encounter are under attack by health care administrators, entrepreneurs, and even colleagues from within their own ranks.

This attack represents the most crucial challenge to the presumed expert labor of psychotherapists. Diagnosis, treatment, and inference represent the core staples of the work of psychotherapy. However, the parameters of the corporatization process increasingly require that diagnoses be made routinely when treatment begins. This approach is in contrast to the fundamental rules and aims of most psychotherapies, which do not require the clinician to organize diagnosis, treatment, and inference in such a hierarchical manner. Furthermore, the practice of psychoanalysis provides therapists with equally compelling, and different, diagnostic formulations for presenting problems (Perry et al. 1987, Pine 1985).

The role of inference is undertaken by psychotherapists when the connection between diagnosis and treatment is obscure (Abbott 1988). Virtually every therapist has responded in an inferential manner with a hunch, impression, or feeling to therapeutically engage with a patient during a session. Yet the use of inference as a professional tool is on the decline, and its demise is best witnessed in the routinization of medical tasks. From the perspective of administrators, managers, and researchers, too much clinical inference in practice makes the therapist's claims to effectiveness hard to legitimate on economic grounds.

The second trend involves changes in the tools and procedures that constitute the craft of psychotherapy. Changes in the tools include the expansion of instrumentation for diagnosis, treatment, and outcome evaluation research. Other developments include the expansion of automated processes for billing and administration, and the introduction of a new round of scientific management techniques (Eckert 1994) to achieve cost control and consumer satisfaction. Changes in the psychotherapists' work routine also include case manager's control and monitoring of treatment planning, the introduction of predetermined treatment protocols explicitly designed for individuals who suffer from particular disorders.

Taken together, these changes reflect conventional patterns of mechanization that have traditionally affected workers. Some therapists now experience an intensification and degradation of their work as managed care companies require them to see scores of patients (Philipson 1993). Therapists also experience the gradual immiserization, or dismantling, of the content of their work as routine service provision is split off from its reflective and intellectual aspects (Larsen 1980, Philipson 1993). Yet the mechanization of psychotherapy is in one crucial respect quite unlike similar developments that occurred earlier in other professions. The modernization processes that are now transforming psychotherapists and their work are no longer exclusively in the service of urbanization, nation building, or even professional development, but rather reflect the administrative streamlining of services in a global economy.

The third trend is that a division of labor is evident in the practice of therapy. Of course, a division of labor has always existed in the profession as psychoanalysts and psychiatrists have held a preeminent position through their role as therapists, supervisors, and consultants to other mental health workers. In the present climate corporate priorities have intensified this division of labor. The work of treatment planning is now made by administrators and utilization review personnel in some settings. Mental health professionals now also work within an internationalized health delivery system, exemplified by a worldwide corporate ownership of hospitals that is expanding in scope. There is also an increasing split along gender, generational, and racial/ethnic lines whereby junior-level positions are increasingly held by women, recently licensed professionals (Philipson 1993), and ethnic minorities.

Finally, corporatization has fostered within this profession an alienation from work in terms at once organizational, technical, political, and psychological. Political alienation, the experience of being systematically unable to influence the course of one's professional work, has been noted in the published accounts of psychotherapists who now work in managed care and other corporate settings (Hirsch 1995, Philipson 1993). In the traditional process of professionalization individuals traverse the educational and training path to become independently licensed practitioners, develop a specialty, and hence, have a "career." This process engenders in many of us a sense of entitlement and financial reward that is now increasingly blocked by the corporatization of our work. The results are a cruel assault on an individual's sense of professional self (Larsen 1980).

The corporatization process has also led some commentators to question whether a nascent proletarianization is underway (Abbott 1988, Larsen 1987, Philipson 1993) whereby entrepreneuring therapists are transformed into salaried workers. This argument originated in part from New Left theorists' belief that educated workers would constitute a "new working class." In theory, this new formation would effectively confront corporate structures and policies in the public arena and pave the way for substantive social transformation (Aronowitz 1991, Gouldner 1981, Larsen 1980). Yet following the demise two decades ago of the New Left, and the subsequent rise of conservative political governments in Europe and the United States, this radical transformation of the social role of educated workers has not occurred to the degree forecasted. The work performed by mental health professionals helps constitute it as a class in itself, such that other professions do not perform similar functions (Braverman 1974). However, professionals as a group neither defend the efforts for legal protection by other professionals nor coalesce in a collective fashion to defend themselves against corporate or governmental employers. Hence, they have not developed the consciousness or organizations that would constitute it as a class in itself (Abbott 1988, Braverman 1974).

The deprofessionalization in status and role of many psychotherapists resonates with the general theory of educated labor's proletarianization (Abbott 1988, Larsen 1980, McKinlay and Stoeckle 1994). What is unique about the proletarianization of psychotherapists is its uneven development. Younger and recently licensed psychotherapists may be more vulnerable to these changes. The system of graduate education and clinical training also contributes to a decided advantage in the marketplace to university-trained clinicians over those without a doctorate or from the so-called professional schools (Robiner 1991). More important, the origins and implications of proletarianization are not fully understood by many professionals who have commented on the recent changes in their work (Cummings 1995, Shore 1993, Wylie 1992, Zimet 1986). What is absent from these accounts is a politicized perspective that links the harrowing changes now underway in our profession with the various transformations in economic policy and social developments outlined above.

## CONCRETE ABSTRACTIONS

The dismantling of certain professions as a result of economic and social changes is a reoccurring dynamic in American history. Examples include the demise of homeopathic physicians in their struggle with allopathic physicians in the nineteenth century, and the defeat of neurologists at the hands of psychoanalysts and psychiatrists during the 1920s. This trend continued after World War II when general practitioners were eclipsed in their battle with surgeons and specialists (Abbott 1988, Starr 1982). The fierce interprofessional rivalry between mental health groups that results from corporatization ensures that there will be winners and losers in the course of the struggle for survival.

Professional rivalry can be understood as efforts to control work in the public and private arenas through the successive development of cognitive structures that attack old problems in new ways; structures of knowledge and practice that sociologist Andrew Abbott has termed *abstractions* (Abbott 1988).[2] Abstract knowledge systems serve as the foundation for any professional's work, and professional rivalry is best understood as a struggle between competing systems of abstraction. Psychotherapists now face from three separate fronts an assault on the abstractions regarding the purpose, course, and value of their work.

---

2. As Abbott notes in this regard, "[A]bstraction is the quality that sets interprofessional competition apart from competition among occupations in general. Any occupation can obtain licensure (e.g., beauticians) or develop an ethics code (e.g., real estate), but only a knowledge system governed by abstractions can redefine its problems and tasks, defend them from interlopers, and seize new problems— as medicine has recently seized . . . hyperactivity in children, obesity, and numerous other things. . . . [T]he degree of abstraction necessary for survival varies with time and place in the system of professions. . . . What matters is abstraction effective enough to compete in a particular historical and social context, not abstraction relative to some supposed absolute standard" (pp. 8–9).

The first of these assaults is directed from our fellow clinician-colleagues. For example, the theorists of planned brief therapy (Budman and Gurman 1988) radically undermine the arguments for the viability of long-term therapy by proposing a new meta-psychology for the role of time in psychotherapy. They assert that for the vast majority of patients positive treatment outcome peaks somewhere in eight to ten sessions. In other words, the planned and prescriptive use of time at the onset of a psychotherapy in and of itself is the optimal variable in patient improvement (Budman and Gurman 1988).

Second, psychotherapists now must contend with the findings from researchers in the psychotherapy process and outcome field. These researchers have raised a number of important questions for the profession, such as what characteristics (or variables) in the patient–therapist interaction help construct positive therapeutic change. Equally challenging to the profession has been these researchers' willingness to question whether psychotherapy can be effective simply with nonspecific factors (such as empathy), or whether it can be implemented in the absence of any interpersonal context simply via technique (Strupp 1986).

Finally, the psychotherapy profession is confronted with the abstractions, often reflective of mere ideology, generated by the market economy itself. These abstractions reflect the myriad economic, technical, and cultural patterns of late capitalism (Jameson 1991). Through the information industry these abstractions are commodified via a global network of industries, decoded and repackaged for everyday discourse by an information/entertainment complex, and then made available to the general population. Perhaps the most compelling abstraction to be developed in our era has been the proposition that a person's cognitive, emotional, and developmental aspects are fundamentally enhanced as a result of work with computers (Turkle 1985). In the era of complex telecommunications industries and the information superhighway, the marketplace offers services that can (presumably) enhance many individuals' quest for immediate and unlimited gratification. The social role of psychotherapy as a practice to increase self-awareness and well-being is quickly being eclipsed by relationships founded on the person–machine interface.

## THE SOCIAL ENVIRONMENT FOR PSYCHOTHERAPY

The most serious political consequence resulting from the corporatization process is that mental health professionals are increasingly called
upon to use any technique at their disposal to sequester experience
(Giddens 1991), such that deeply personal existential and political
questions are addressed primarily through an increasingly narrow
professional worldview. Because of the unique character of our work,
we must help individuals and families adjust to the demands and
opportunities of modern society. The ongoing debate over the respective benefits of brief versus long-term psychotherapy also exemplifies the profession's need to clarify the effectiveness of its work in
changing social circumstances. This effectiveness must be addressed
in both practical and ideological terms. The ideological function
involves the ability of mental health professionals to more effectively
provide "preventive adjustment" (Abbott 1988), often for the expressed purpose of maintaining social harmony in an era of declining economic opportunity for most Americans.

In addition to these changes in the character of mental health
work, other externally derived social changes are propelling the corporatization of psychotherapy. First and foremost, there is the dominant position of large-scale organizations as a fact of industry itself.
One of the characteristic features of corporate settings is vertical and
horizontal integration of services. A characteristic of organizational
culture is a frame of mind that puts a premium on "measuring things"
(Abbott 1988). In this context the introduction of brief treatment
and detailed treatment protocols flow naturally from this characteristic of large organizations.

The social environment in which psychotherapy functions also
includes an increasing use of technology in health (Faltenmeyer
1992) and mental health care. Examples include the use of comput-
erized systems and networks to coordinate research on a worldwide
scale (Azar 1994a,b), to evaluate clinical trials and outcomes (Faltenmeyer 1992, Sleek 1994a), and even to serve as an adjunct to the
psychotherapy process (Sleek 1994b). New psychotropic medications
continue to be developed in university settings and the pharmaceu-
tical industry, with the latter's capacity to engage in research and
development, production, and marketing.

Other developments that indirectly affect the profession follow technological innovation and organizational change. One of these is the commodification of knowledge. As Abbott (1988) notes, commodification relegates expertise to the position in which it "can be bought and sold without the involvement of jurisdictional authority" (p. 146). Examples include self-help books for health and mental health problems, diagnostic algorithms in medicine, and statistical packages such as the mass marketed SPSS (Statistical Package for the Social Sciences) programs to aid research psychologists in treatment evaluation. In the self-help literature on mental health topics alone, the number of publications has increased by nearly 50 percent in the last seven years (American Psychological Association 1994).

The net effect of these changes is to reduce the psychotherapist's professional autonomy and claims to exclusive control of skills that were once defining characteristics of the profession. The demystification and marketing to the public of previously obscure psychological knowledge may have decidedly liberating effects for individuals who cannot afford mental health services. Yet the impact of this development on the employment stability of individuals who have essentially only one job skill—the practice of psychotherapy—is profound.

The limited goals of psychotherapy under managed care are also being met by rival professionals who now confront mental health workers. Epidemiological studies conducted over the past twenty years have convincingly demonstrated that the majority of Americans receive psychotherapy not in a systematic fashion by private clinicians, but in bits and pieces by primary care physicians (Kessler et al. 1987, Narrow et al. 1993, Orleans et al. 1985). Primary care physicians once represented a de facto mental health system in the 1970s. Today they represent competitors in the provision of mental health treatment, a significant referral source for therapists, and the effective gatekeepers for people's access to psychotherapy in most health care plans now in operation. This administrative feature is another characteristic of psychotherapy's corporatization. It represents a division of labor whereby physicians are accorded the work of diagnosing who has a mental problem amenable to an assortment of psychotherapies, and then prescribing the treatment via a referral. The provision of mental health services through the primary care network relies on its own technology of intervention that includes standardized procedures and a specialization of services.

Finally, the ability of psychotherapists to rely on human capital or expertise alone to enhance professional legitimacy continues to be undermined by the increasing role of physical capital in work settings. Mundane examples such as computer billing services and voice mail administered by phone companies reflect the continued encroachment of corporate structures into the daily routines of mental health professionals. These examples illustrate the fact that psychotherapists' relationship to major corporations and the market economy has always had a double-edged quality to it. By participating in corporate settings as well-positioned clinicians or administrators, or by purchasing the commodities necessary to run a small business, psychotherapists have greatly enhanced their productivity, income, and prestige. Nonetheless, this participation has come with a strategic political bill that is now due. Mental health professionals are losing degrees of economic independence and political influence and authority as a direct result of their integration into the market economy and corporate structures. The disgruntled responses of therapists to the cost-cutting strategies undertaken by corporations and the state represent a form of sour grapes, the complaints of individuals who believed that a system devoted to the extraction of profit from all forms of work would somehow never touch their own particular service.

## LEVERAGING OUR SOULS?

In an era dominated by rivalry and competition, many mental health professionals reject the values and political agendas of social movements that could aid their empowerment. Members of the ecology, feminist, gay, and lesbian, and the labor movements have articulated critiques of corporatization relevant to the issues of health care delivery. They have also developed compelling versions of how society can emancipate itself from crippling forms of consciousness and social interaction by offering alternative ways of relating to ourselves, other people, and the natural environment (Kovel 1991).

These perspectives would further enable us to recognize the three social dynamics crucial to the current mental health care crisis. These dynamics are (1) the globalization of industrial economies that has precipitated the shrinking of mental health budgets, (2) the societywide cultivation of competitive individualism that hampers collective action by professionals, and (3) the deeply ideological nature of many media and professional accounts of the health care delivery system that fail to link social and economic dislocation with individual malaise (Lerner 1995).

In the program of health reform from above, we are being coerced into embracing bottom-line balance sheets as more important than the aims of the clinical encounter. Aggressive self-promotion of therapy as a commodity, indistinguishable from other such services, becomes the only legitimate way to represent our work. In positioning itself to succeed in a rapidly changing health care economy, psychology is abandoning therapies with a long tradition of reliability for the sake of a share in the market. We are being asked by many leaders and other colleagues of our professional organizations, as well as administrators in managed care companies, to invest our most important and personal identifications with this work, to "leverage" our souls, for the sake of possible future financial rewards. At the same time, the reality of mental health work under managed care has led to drastically reduced income and the erosion of control over the conduct of psychotherapy for many professionals.

The work that is most readily under attack is the conduct of long-term psychotherapy. In spite of this attack, the previously mentioned social movements that can contribute to our understanding of human psychology and serve as important allies are relegated to a secondary status by many of our colleagues in favor of forms of mental health work that are marketable, reimbursable, and profitable to corporations. The challenge for mental health professionals in the future is to try to maintain a commitment to the best principles of traditional practice, incorporate new approaches that really improve patients' lives, and engage in the political process of building coalitions with our allies so that traditional practice is neither destroyed nor irrevocably replaced.

Corporate capitalism and state institutions have helped build the mental health professions in ways that have significantly enhanced the scope and social function of the latter's work. Yet under the impetus of a number of necessities, including profit maximization, business and government are recasting the terms of their relationship with this profession. The profession's track record in legitimating psychotherapy independent of market values and restrictive state policy is marked with few instances of independent action. It remains for mental health professionals to decide to what extent their work with patients will remain as an independent relationship, and not as an alliance ultimately subservient to the demands of others.

## REFERENCES

Abbott, A. (1988). *The System of Professions: An Essay on the Division of Expert Labor.* Chicago: University of Chicago Press.

Alford, C. F. (1989). *Melanie Klein and Critical Social Theory.* New Haven, CT: Yale University Press.

Aronowitz, S. (1991). *The Politics of Identity.* Minneapolis: University of Minnesota Press.

Austad, C. S., DeStefano, L., and Kisch, J. (1988). The health maintenance organization–II: implications for psychotherapy. *Psychotherapy* 25:449–454.

Azar, B. (1994a). Research made easier by computer networks. *APA Monitor* 25:16.

———— (1994b). Computers create global research lab. *APA Monitor* 25:1, 16.

Berkman, A. S., Bassos, C. A., and Post, L. (1988). Managed mental health care and independent practice: a challenge to psychology. *Psychotherapy* 25:434–440.

Braverman, H. (1974). *Labor and Monopoly Capital.* New York: Monthly Review Press.

Broskowski, A. (1991). Current mental health care environment: why managed care is necessary. *Professional Psychology* 22:6–14.

Budman, S. H., and Gurman, A. S. (1988). *Theory and Practice of Brief Therapy.* New York: Guilford.

Candib, L. (1990). Naming the contradiction: family medicine's failure to face violence against women. *Family and Community Health* 13:47–58.

Cummings, N. A. (1995). Impact of managed care on employment and training: a primer for survival. *Professional Psychologist* 26(1): 10–16.

Cushman, P. (1991). Ideology obscured: political uses of the self in Daniel Stern's infant. *American Psychologist* 46:206–219.

Eckert, P. A. (1994). Cost control through quality improvement: the new challenge for psychology. *Professional Psychology* 25:3–8.

Faltenmeyer, E. (1992). Let's really cure the health system. *Fortune,* March 23, pp. 46–50.

Friedman, J. (1987). *Planning in the Public Domain.* Princeton, NJ: Princeton University Press.

Giddens, A. (1991). *Modernity and Self-Identity.* Stanford, CA: Stanford University Press.

Gouldner, A. W. (1981). *The Future of Intellectuals and the Rise of the New Class.* New York: Oxford University Press.

Herron, W. G., Javier, R. A., Primavera, L. H., and Schultz, C. L. (1994). The cost of psychotherapy. *Professional Psychology* 25:106–110.

Hirsch, L. (1995). Adapting to health care reform and managed care: three strategies for survival and growth. *Professional Psychology* 26:16–26.

Jameson, F. (1991). *PostModernism, or the Cultural Logic of Late Capitalism.* Durham, NC: Duke University Press.

Kessler, L. G., Cleary, P. G., and Burke, J. D. (1985). Psychiatric disorders in primary care. *Archives of General Psychiatry* 42:583–587.

Kovel, J. (1981). *The Age of Desire.* New York: Pantheon.

——— (1988). *The Radical Spirit.* London: Free Association.

——— (1991). *History and Spirit.* Boston: Beacon.

Labate, J. (1992). The world economy in charts. *Fortune,* July 27, pp. 61–80.

Larsen, M. S. (1980). Proletarianization and educated labor. *Science and Society* 9:131–175.

Lerner, M. (1995). The assault on psychotherapy. *Family Therapy Networker,* Sept./Oct., pp. 44–52.

Lichtman, R. (1982). *The Production of Desire.* New York: Free Press.

McKinlay, J. B., and Stoeckle, J. D. (1994). Corporatization and the social transformation of doctoring. In *Beyond Crisis: Confronting Health Care in the United States,* ed. N. F. McKenzie, pp. 271–284. New York: Meridian.

Narrow, W. E., Reiger, D. A., Rae, D. S., et al. (1993). Use of services by persons with mental and addictive disorders: findings from the National Institute of Mental Health Epidemiological Catchment Area Program. *Archives of General Psychiatry* 50:95–107.

Orleans, C. T., George, L. K., Houpt, J. L., et al. (1985). How primary care physicians treat psychiatric disorders: a national survey of family physicians. *American Journal of Psychiatry* 142:52–57.

Perry, S., Cooper, A. M., and Michaels, R. (1987). The psychodynamic formulation: its purpose, structure, and clinical application. *American Journal of Psychiatry* 144:543–551.

Philipson, I. J. (1993). *On The Shoulders of Women: The Feminization of Psychotherapy.* New York: Guilford.

Pine, F. (1985). *Developmental Theory and Clinical Process.* New Haven, CT: Yale University Press.

Pingitore, D. P. (1994). American culture in American medicine: the case of family medicine. *Science as Culture* 4:167–211.

Richards, B., ed. (1984). *Capitalism and Infancy: Essays on Psychoanalysis and Politics.* London: Free Association.

Robiner, W. N. (1991). How many psychologists are needed? A call for a national psychology human resource agenda. *Professional Psychology* 22:427–440.

Schmidt, L., and Weisner, C. (1993). Developments in alcohol treatment. In *Alcoholism, Volume II: Ten Years of Progress,* ed. M. Galanter, pp. 369–396. New York: Plenum.

Shemo, J. P. D. (1985). Cost-effectiveness of providing mental health services: the offset effect. *International Journal of Psychiatry in Medicine* 15:19–30.

Shore, K. (1993). Mental health in the Clinton plan. *Health/PAC Bulletin,* Fall pp. 28–30.

Sleek, S. (1994a). Technology is helpful adjunct to therapy, *APA Monitor* 25:22.

——— (1994b). Therapists turn to computers to measure treatment effects, *APA Monitor* 15:24.

Starr, P. (1982). *The Social Transformation of American Medicine.* New York: Basic Books.

Stein, H. (1991). *American Medicine as Culture.* Boulder, CO: Westview.

Strupp, H. H. (1986). Psychotherapy: research, practice, and public policy (how to avoid dead ends). *American Psychologist* 41:120–130.

Turkle, S. (1985). *The Second Self: Computers and the Human Spirit.* Greenville, NC: S. S. Publishers.

VandenBos, G. R., DeLeon, P. H., and Belar, C. D. (1991). How many psychologists are needed? It's too early to know! *Professional Psychology* 21:441–448.

Wolfenstein, E. V. (1993). *Psychoanalytic-Marxism.* London: Free Association.

Wylie, M. S. (1992). Toeing the bottom line. *The Family Therapy Networker* 16(1):30, 75.

Zimet, C. N. (1986). The mental health care revolution: Will psychology survive? *American Psychologist* 44:703–708.

# 14

# Our Human Condition:
# What We Don't Talk About
# When We Talk About Managed Care

CHARLES MORGAN AND STEPHEN A. RUFFINS*

> In the desert
> I saw a creature, naked, bestial
> Who, squatting upon the ground
> Held his heart in his hands,
> And ate of it.
> I said, "Is it good, friend?"
> "It is bitter—bitter," he answered;
> "But I like it
> Because it is bitter,
> And because it is my heart."
>
> —*Stephen Crane*

---

*We would like to emphasize that the order of authorship here is arbitrary and that the work that follows reflects a fully cooperative effort.

## INTRODUCTION

This book as a whole considers the traumatic nature of the relationship between therapists and managed care companies, exploring the often unconscious and mutually reinforcing wishes, needs, and vulnerabilities that link provider and payor in problematic ways. In this chapter we attempt to explore the broader contexts out of which this relationship has arisen, exploring the linkages, traumatic and otherwise, from the perspectives of history and culture.

Manifestly, we all view managed care as a means of fiscal management, a solution to rising health care costs. Less explicitly, but as significantly, managed care appears to represent a means for arbitrating the standards and criteria, as well as the quantity, of care. As redoubtable as some of these aims may be (Miller and Farber 1996), in their current incarnation in managed care, one finds innumerable contradictions, cross-purposes, and paradoxes (Miller 1996) . In accounting for some share of these anomalies, we are less interested here in managed care's beneficial or benighted qualities, but prefer to examine it as a phenomenon reflective of the culture at large and for whose creation we all share some responsibility.

We have divided this chapter into three main sections. In the first, we make note of the anxiety that arises from humankind's capacity for self-reflection and the resulting search for truth and certainty. We see psychotherapy as another in a long line of ways mankind has developed for managing uncertainty and doubt. Psychotherapy struggles as to its goals and methods, dividing along lines of philosophical and scientific inquiry. In the second section we explore these distinctions; in the third, we look at managed care and its relationship to our desires for certainty, our interests in psychotherapy, and the problems it reflects and encompasses in our complex and diverse society.

## DRIVING FORCES

*Vulnerability, Certainty, and the Need to Know*

Human beings enter the world naked, helpless, vulnerable, and dependent. In this we resemble other creatures of the animal kingdom.

Unable to feed or protect ourselves, we are reliant on others. Early on, however, human creatures develop a capacity foreign to other species: the capacity for reflection. Thus we grow cognizant of our nakedness, of our helplessness, of our reliance. This is our human condition. We are able to recall history as well as imagine the future; our every moment is caught in an unremitting dialectical relationship with our past and future. We now become subject to truly human emotions such as regret, hope, bitterness, desire.

Our capacity for awareness and reflection, for memory and imagination, fuels a kind of fundamental self-concern or anxiety, an angst or dread, as we forever suffer with the unshakable knowledge of our dependence and vulnerability (see, for example, Becker 1973). This is not the anxiety of zebras confronted with the intimation of lions. Their strategy is action, perhaps largely preprogrammed, but certainly unimpinged upon by reminiscence or remorse. The anxiety related to self-reflectivity, this by-product of the cognizance of our dependence and vulnerability, concerns not action per se, but meaning and judgment. Without that self-reflectivity, our need to know and control would be similar to that of the lion from whom the zebra has escaped: we would execute a change of strategy free of memory's judgment and unburdened by any sense of regret. But we are inexorably self-reflective and thus always weighted with anxieties, feelings, and ambivalences that leave us yearning for respite, for certainty and control (Beres 1980). Certainty about what will happen to us, predictability about the world we find ourselves in, can provide a sense of comfort and safety, however elusive or ephemeral. As Emch (1944) has written, the unknown represents a universal source of tension. We seek to interpret it through myth or master it through science. We seek certainty through knowledge, whether of the cosmos, the species, or the mind. It should be noted that the quest for knowledge can have unintended, even humbling, consequences. Copernicus's proof that the heavens did not revolve around the earth, Darwin's tying of humankind's lineage to the apes, and Freud's undermining of the belief in the psyche's supreme rationality, all heightened humanity's anxieties and brought forth vituperative assaults because of their decimation of old certainties.

In any case, our profoundly human desire for knowledge has as its source, in part, the fantasy that to know is to be protected, to be saved even. To know is to reduce vulnerability, to mitigate helplessness, to fend off death. Knowledge becomes the balm of our deepest anxieties, expressed across the interacting domains of present, past, and future. We may fantasize that if we knew enough *now*, we would feel more in control of present events. Or if we had only known *then*, we could have averted some catastrophe or created some benefit. And if we learn enough *from now on*, we can preclude future failings or losses. This characteristically human reflection on what could have been, should have been, and might yet be—from wistful wanting, for example, to vicious self-reproach to fantasies of possibility—provides the feel of self-correction, a kind of psychical gyroscope of the self. But it is often, in fact, our wistful attempt to substitute a wish for the reality of our unresolvable and irreparable uncertainty, the anxiety that no a priori knowledge can vanquish.

## Pathways to Knowing

Religion, philosophy, and science represent three characteristic means by which humankind has sought to wrest knowledge and certainty from the darkness of the inexplicable. Belief in an omniscient, superordinate force, a higher power, provided an early source for explanatory comfort. This religious method at times grew necessarily dogmatic and exhortative as worldly forms of explanation offered alternatives to mythic modes. Speculation on the human condition led increasingly to the more organized form of inquiry called philosophy, which evolved as a more human-centered means for wrestling with questions of ultimate causality, of truth and reality. And as the material world revealed its complexities under the scrutiny of human inquiry, science offered facts as a potent and appealing avenue to certainty and mastery, along with technology as the means to their execution.

Whether in a covert or overt manner, all cultures, and at times all nations, struggle with a certain question: Does the management of the human condition become effected through an inexorably progressive move from the dogma and faith that is religion, through the speculative inquiry into ultimate causality that is philosophy, to the nirvana of the more complete certainty of established facts that is science? Or might the management of the human condition, for us as individuals and for cultures and nations as collections of "us," lie within a matrix of the three, the diminution of any one effecting a surrender of some important adaptive response to the passivity of not-knowing in the face of human self-reflectivity? That is, in order to help us manage our varying states of not-knowing, do we (or when do we) need a priest or a shaman, a behavioral technician, a teacher, a physician, a philosopher, a psychologist, a scientist, or some combination of all of the above? And what modes of human inquiry best help us manage our dependence on and vulnerability to the materiality of the universe and its mechanisms, including our world of interpersonal relationships? Through time, across generations, and around the world, the answer has and does vary. In general, Western culture has followed a developmental trajectory that has given preeminence to science.

## The Particularity of Science and American Science in Particular

Although there are certainly a variety of scientific practices in the United States, for the most part what might be termed *normal science* in Kuhnian terminology follows particular European proclivities toward measurement and universalism, constructing powerful systems of organization through privileged positivistic methods that implicitly derogate particularity and nuance (Fox 1996). Fitting well within the American penchant for pragmatism and utilitarianism, the achievements of mainstream American science have been impressive, from combating disease to propelling mooncraft. But as Fox Keller (1985) and others have written, the central methods of our science derive from ways of looking at the world that dogmatically elevate certitude, mastery, and control. Paradoxically, in a nation priding itself on individualism, we privilege scientific pursuits that claim as their legitimate object that which remains unchanging and normative, thereby relegating individual differences to secondary status (Geertz 1973).

The very notion that science itself may be linked to particular sets of values and beliefs and that its methods can be no more rational or perfectable than its practitioners is an idea of relatively recent origin. Scientific methods and discoveries all derive from and gain power from their situation in particular cultural practices at particular moments in time (Geertz 1973, Gould 1981). A science bent on control and mastery may be reflecting in part its own struggle with uncertainty in the face of social complexity. A modest example might be our often driven attempts to seek the genetic basis for social disorders, such as criminality. On the other hand, the fairly recent "discovery" of the benefits of Asian medicinal practices, for example (whose scientific successes, within an empirically based methodology, can be measured in millennia!), gives some suggestion of our deeply historical need to exclude alternative ways of knowing (Gergen et al. 1996). Naturally, the exclusion of alternative data and interpretations heightens the certainty of the data we privilege. After all, every mode of knowing grows out of our particular human need to master uncertainty, but is driven in its own particular ways by the needs and complexities of particular cultures in particular periods of history.

## The Case of Psychology

Psychology is the most recent body of knowledge and inquiry to liberate itself from the purview of philosophy and claim its status as an independent science. Struggling to find its identity, psychology claims its methods to be those of the "hard" sciences, debating variously at times over the "true" object of its inquiries, whether behaviors or processes, the unconscious or cognitions (Gergen et al. 1996, Jacobson and Christensen 1996). Psychology means, etymologically, "word of the soul" (to whom Eros is wedded in everlasting bliss). It may not be surprising then that psychology finds itself in the inherently conflictual position of trying to elucidate word of the soul through the methods of material science. Psychology's status often seems to depend on its adaptation to mainstrean scientific expectations, even as its subject matter may require methods of inquiry as diverse as human nature itself (Kipnis 1994, Marecek 1995, Riger 1992). Is psychology "word of the soul" or the "study of human behavior"? Is it an inquiry into human consciousness or the study of cognitive processes? Is it the exploration of the human condition or the explication of symptoms and signs? (We pose these questions in dichotomous terms, not only as a reflection of current debates but to clarify competing positions. Our view, however, is that psychology requires a diversity of methods and modes of inquiry, reflective of its status as "word of the soul," as the science of the human mind.) The problems become more complex when we consider psychology's applied arm: psychotherapy.

## THE PSYCHOTHERAPIES

I have nothing to do with the origin of the primary mental powers, any more than with life itself.

—*Charles Darwin*

Control over people's minds is the main thing happening today.

—*Chuck D*

As the realms of the spiritual, the philosophical, and the scientific became increasingly separate in the West, the tasks previously assigned to the roles of priest and minister devolved as well. Each realm became represented by its own "wise men," its own community of knowers and interpreters. Each realm developed its own specified programs of identifying, educating, and credentialing these "wise men" who consequently became empowered to perform the rituals and to interpret the approved theological, philosophical, or scientific doctrine to the people. Each realm suffered or welcomed alternative interpretations within the group and splintered, grew, transformed, or died as a result of internal conflict or as a result of its skill in managing its boundary with the outside world.

In the West, the particular uncertainties posed by the social transformation of the late nineteenth century—the rapid spiral of scientific progress, the profound transformations effected by technology and capital on the family and community life, the genesis of ethnic and capital globalizations—engaged in a reciprocal interaction with the various ways of knowing, deeply influencing and being influenced by them. The increasing marginalization of religious life, the isolation of philosophy into the academy, and the increasing isomorphism between science and "facticity" (Latour and Woolgar 1982) were also part and parcel of these social transformations, leaving much of Western society with a paucity of resources for assisting its citizens in reckoning with human experience itself, with their feeling states, their personhoods, their inner worlds.

As academic psychology attempted to gain its foothold as a legitimate science at the turn of the century, psychoanalysis in Europe and behaviorism in the United States developed as alternative nonreligious, nonphilosophical, nonpolitical, but "scientific" solutions to the exigencies and slippages of everyday life. Both physicians of the mind and nonmedical psychotherapists began to come into their own at this time. This secular priesthood rapidly expanded its domain to include the self, human behavior, cognition, emotion, the psyche, parenting, education, socialization, and all manner of human functioning, the development and regulation of which had previously been the exclusive purview of religion or the state. Whether derived from the academy or from medicine, psychotherapy had the patina of science, and hence a seductive legitimacy. At the same time, a scientific rationale critiqued, enveloped, and effectively displaced the prior, traditional forms of managing uncertainty in response to the problems incumbent on our capacity for self-reflectivity, our human condition. (The spread and variety of contemporary "therapies" may be more reflective of the breakdown in traditions of emotional management, rather than evidence of ever-better solutions.)

Arising from a more philosophic base, psychodynamic-based therapies focus less on circumscribed symptoms or problematic behaviors than on the meanings of personhood within the larger context of human nature and the particular context of personal history. Based on positivistic scientific studies, cognitive-behavioral therapies attempt to ameliorate clearly defined symptoms through education and practice. "Conditions" seems to best characterize the object of the former; the object of the latter can be described as "symptoms" and "behaviors." Both these general lines of applying psychology describe themselves as empirically based and both heavily rely on inquiry for their data gathering, which confounds their distinction to some extent. And the idiosyncratic quality of the psychotherapeutic encounter makes generalizations problematic. However, we can trace within the major trends of the clinical application of psychology the separate lines representing the scientific and philosophical traditions.

## Conditions versus Behaviors

Psychotherapies drawn from the religiophilosophic traditions have sought to ease human suffering through nonjudgmental, confessional, interpretive modalities. In the tradition of priestly tasks, these psychotherapies have sought to help patients locate their difficulties within the spectrum of human concerns, reckoning with loss, change, tragedy, unhappiness, existential struggles, family woes, problems in living, and the like. Freud's definition of the task of psychoanalysis exemplifies this view. At one point Freud noted that the best the psychoanalyst could do was to help turn the patient's neurotic misery into ordinary unhappiness. Humanistic, relational, self-psychological, existential, analytic, and psychodynamic therapies tend to promote as essential to beneficial treatment such factors as the therapy relationship, the verbalization of feelings, and the illumination of unnoticed (or unconscious) ways of being. At their best, such therapies take a modest view of an individual's plight, uncertain of when, whether, or why a person might ultimately change, however certain they may be of the likelihood of change. In the psychodynamic therapies, for example, there is a presumption that some significant aspect of a patient's psychological struggles lies outside of immediate conscious knowing. Indeed, it is the unknown (exemplified by the unconscious) that is seen as containing, often in some conflictual paradigm, the motive forces behind problematic behaviors. For the classically psychodynamic therapist, symptoms are largely the signal for less readily perceivable and more complex intrapsychic (or sometimes interpersonal) phenomena. Manifest phenomena are seen as keys to latent phenomena, and latent phenomena, uncovered through attention to the seemingly irrational, become the source for insight and transmutative interpretation. Therapies in the philosophic tradition offer the opportunity for inquiry that can proceed forward into the manifest as well as backward into the latent and unseen. By offering patients the opportunity to examine a wider perspective on their struggles, these therapies allow for the possibility of unforeseen pathways to change. However, such possibility is not without consequences, as it carries with it the uncertainty of choice and the potential paralysis of freedom.

Psychotherapies following from Western scientific traditions have sought to render human suffering into scientifically measurable units from which could then evolve empirically clear technical interventions (Barlow 1996). Beginning with the behaviorist theorizing of Watson, then Skinner, and evolving into the contemporary work on cognitive processes, such therapies assume chains of discoverable causal links motivating problematic behaviors. Interventions may consist of disruptions in those causal links, retraining in patterns of thought and behavior, and similar educative practices. In the cognitive-behavioral therapies, for example, there is a presumption that patients suffer from deficits in knowledge and/or skills. Troubling symptoms or behaviors are carefully defined so that interventions can be specifically focused and changes can be readily measured, in keeping largely with the classical scientific method. Through the increased awareness of behaviors, instruction on their reduction, and the practice of reduction skills, for example, patients may learn to control and master the targeted problems. However, by focusing on what is manifest and circumscribing human characteristics into operationable measures, these therapies tend to militate against any thorough reckoning with the cultural meanings or social structures that may give rise to particular symptoms or behaviors. Thus change tends to move only in the direction of social adaptation. Obviously, this is more accommodating to our wishes for clarity and certainty.

The problem of "difficult" or "resistant" patients poses complexities for each tradition of treatment. In the psychodynamic therapies there is an assumption that at least on an unconscious level a patient has ambivalent feelings about change, that repetitively self-destructive behaviors may serve some complex need, and that their amelioration may require special interpretive efforts and some open-ended period of working through. There is nothing anomalous then in the encounter with patients who are resistant to change. The therapist, by assuming conflict, accepts the refractory nature of human desire. Indeed, it is this very refractoriness that becomes the object of therapy, that is, the ways in which patients stand in the way of their own manifestly wished-for development. By starting with the assumption of human complexity, the object of the therapist's task becomes in part an exploration of the human condition.

In the cognitive-behavioral therapies, the assumption is that the patient suffers from a deficit in knowledge—a skills or learning or experiential deficit. When the therapist encounters refractoriness to the treatment, he or she assumes the existence of some as yet unknown behavioral reinforcer or negative cognition that keeps the behavior in place. The focus of the treatment may then shift to discovering the problematic behavior or cognition on which subsequent technical operations can then be performed to remove or transform it. Even so, these methods have a difficult time accounting for patients who continue to resist change or sabotage learning or for whom education does not lead to expected transformations. It is here that history—the patient's assumptions about him- or herself—confounds the learning task. Change, then, becomes not simply a matter of learning or practicing, but shows itself as one element in a complex field of wishes, fears, and desires. The permutations of personality and the human condition resist the rationalities of a behaviorally derived science.

## The Problem of Diversity

> If we want to discover what man amounts to, we can only find it in what men are: and what men are, above all other things, is various.
> —*Clifford Geertz*

In a homogeneous society, one could elicit general agreement on what constitutes mental health and what endeavors one might apply to its enhancement. For example, if there were a community belief that strong intimate relationships were the cornerstone of psychological well-being, then there could be general agreement that therapy would be provided to anyone unable to form such a relationship. For the most part , a relatively brief adaptation-oriented therapy might suffice. But what if yours is a society of diverse ethnic, racial, or economic groupings, with a variety of beliefs not only about the value of intimate relationships but about how such relationships are constituted? If the therapeutic interventions are based on scientific studies of the majority population, then it becomes problematic whether the adaptational expectations of that treatment would be helpful. In fact, it is unclear whether any manifest behavior carries sufficient uniformity across groups of individuals, however defined, to be amenable to generalized treatment interventions.

The human condition is constituted by its diversity of meanings, and human society is constituted by its diversity of peoples. A scientific method that looks for immutable certainties can do so only by the exclusion of what is chaotic, uncertain, diverse. In constructing an office building we require scientific certainties, but in exploring human nature we can only be humble in the face of its immeasurable inexplicability. We need a science of pattern and nuance, otherwise we are left with only a partial perception of who and what we are, dictated rather than illuminated by the very tools of our observation (Geertz 1973).

## MANAGING CARING

We cannot posit direct or absolute causal reasons for the rise of managed care; however, it is obvious that rising health care costs contributed to a climate that appeared to necessitate action. It is clear that, in mental health at least, independent companies rose up to take advantage of this pecuniary cultural moment and to develop ways of limiting expenditures, mainly by reducing payments to providers and limiting the number of psychotherapy sessions. Given that the average number of psychotherapy sessions was relatively low to begin with (estimates range from six to ten sessions) (Miller 1996), the main limitation on sessions would be for those who were engaged or might engage in a more open-ended or long-term treatment. Given, also, that much of the money saved was simply transferred into the profits of managed care and insurance companies, the claim that managing psychotherapy was somehow good for the public has a certain disingenuousness. And finally, of course, given that the cost of psychotherapy is a very small portion of overall health care expenditures (and that a fairly robust literature indicates that psychotherapy reduces utilization of other health services) (Miller 1996, Seligman 1995), we begin to realize that the specific rationales for managed mental health care cannot begin to capture its raison d'être as a social phenomena.

## Managed Care as a Reflection of the Culture

From the taming of the wild West to the creation of the atomic bomb, American culture operates under the assumption that nothing lies beyond its capacity for knowledge, penetration, and control. Uncertainty and ambiguity do not fit comfortably in America's views of itself. For this reason, for example, our inability to resolve the fundamental racial conflicts between black and white Americans continues to create an unbearable cognitive dissonance that gets expelled through such irrational means as constructing scientific proofs of inferiority or promoting utopian separatisms. Similarly, to the extent that the psychotherapeutic endeavor reckons with humankind's chaotic, unmanaged, unconscious side, it broaches realms of mystery and meaning that conflict with American assumptions about our capacity for individual control, about our fundamental clearheadedness and rationality. In this context, then, managed care can be seen as an attempt to move away from the more chaotic, unconscious sides of human nature to that which is more efficiently understandable and remediable.

Managed care can also be viewed as a product of our contemporary penchant for efficiency through corporatization and our concomitant concerns with money management and profit making. As we increasingly apply market rules and expectations to social tasks, the distinction between public and private means of control grows ever narrower. In this ethos, then, goals are equated with profits, and the need for profits guides not only the allocation of funds but the determination of what is to be valued. From the manufacture of toilet paper to the building of skyscrapers, this can be a magnificently creative paradigm, but its utility in the public sphere, of art and libraries, of medicine and education, is less clear. Whether psychotherapy works as a for-profit institution merits serious debate.

Within the context of these money issues, the familiar American conflict between autonomy and dependency also arises. In the larger

250   IMPACT ON TRAINING AND DEVELOPMENT

culture this has been exemplified in the furious debates over welfare, resulting in comprehensive political efforts to move a greater portion of the determination of welfare needs from individuals to financial overseers. Managed care, too, can be seen as an attempt to undercut the dependent relationships between therapists and patients, to "free" patients, like welfare recipients, from their unmanaged dependence on others. Indeed, a newsletter sent to practitioners on the panel of one managed care company explicitly derided psychotherapies that used the therapeutic relationship per se as a vehicle for exploration and change. Any focus on the therapeutic relationship was deemed regressive, unhelpful, and not based on scientific principles.

Another rallying cry of managed care companies—as well as many psychologists, to be sure—is that treatments be "scientifically based." In keeping with general cultural assumptions, this tends to mean a science as practiced in the sphere of the natural sciences, an experimental science of replicability and generalizability, what Kuhn characterized as "normal science." Historically, Americans have not been inclined to pay for applied religious or philosophical endeavors; therefore, psychotherapies that make their application to human suffering within traditions developed out of religion and philosophy beg the question of who should pay for them. Psychotherapies more in keeping with our conceptions of mainstream science are funded with less ambivalence. But the more complex question remains as to which scientific practices are best suited to reckoning with the complexities of psychotherapy and the psychotherapy relationship, and even whether one scientific tradition is sufficient for an understanding of the diverse ways diverse peoples resolve psychological struggles (Fox 1996). A recent book on the cognitive-behavioral treatment of anxiety disorders of African-American patients suggests something of the dilemma of attempting to generalize principles of psychotherapy from sample populations within traditional scientific designs. We would need a book on cognitive-behavioral treatment of anxiety disorders among gays, among lesbians, among older Caucasians, among Unitarians, or military officers, or children of working class fathers, and so forth, if we insist on using a scientific method, derived from the natural sciences, to capture and explain the diversity of human expression in American culture. We suggest that at least some of what besets the human psyche may be too variable and diverse to entrust to any single scientific method. It is not unscientific, but in fact Darwinian, to suggest that only an ecology of methods can hope to capture the variability of the human spirit.

Managed care's reckonings with human diversity also naturally follow particular American social proclivities. Diversity creates a kind of social uncertainty, the management of which has always been central to American majority concerns. The mutual adaptive processes between society and the diverse groups it is composed of have always been complex, particularly given that American society is bound by constitutional rather than tribal ties. The question for the culture becomes what are its essential characteristics and in what ways are they to be transmitted. It may be hard for members of the majority culture to imagine how this might occur differently, but if we consider, for example, integration as a *dialectical* relationship, then we are led to consider in what ways might two (or more) cultures adapt to each other. What may be most frightening about this to both cultures is the loss (however temporary) of a kind of cultural certitude, in addition to not knowing a priori what will be created. Isolationism or even genocide at least do not threaten majority cultures with the terror of change and transformation, which are ultimately the terror of self-examination. The question for psychotherapy becomes what constitutes change, what constitutes behavior, what constitutes happiness, what constitutes symptoms in a diverse culture. Managed care serves the fantasy that we can make a tidy fit of things through forms of therapeutic practice derived from particular scientific methods rather than through the nuanced understanding of the complex ways human beings express and accommodate to social and psychological struggle.

## The Effect of Managed Care on Psychotherapy

Therapists have responded to managed care in a variety of ways. Some have embraced it, particularly those whose forms of psychotherapeutic practice best matched the parameters of expectation, payment, and control delineated by the managed care companies. A majority of therapists have felt burdened by those very same expectations and controls.

A third group works outside the purview of managed care, either in organizations with no managed care oversight or in practices with no monetary reliance on managed care. But the most significant effect of managed care may not be on practitioners themselves but on the very ways in which mental health and, hence, psychotherapy are defined.

Thus far, the psychotherapies of symptoms and behaviors have done well by managed care, at least in terms of their acceptance and funding. These psychotherapies, of which cognitive-behavioral therapy is a paradigmatic example, provide a scientific rationale of generalizability within the model of the mainstream natural sciences. Their circumscription of psychological problems into operable units and their largely educative model of change fit well within the ex- pectations for manageable, replicable, short-term treatments (Kipnis 1994). And because the cognitive-behavioral treatment protocols are derived from samples of fairly homogeneous majority groups, these treatments also match the managed care companies' corporate in- terests to serve the majority culture in the manner most conducive to monitoring and oversight.

It is the psychotherapies of the human condition that seem least compatible with the managed care ethos. Certainly their derivation from more philosophical traditions of inquiry mitigates their adapt- ability to the methods of mainstream science. But their conflict with managed care expectations is even more profoundly tied up with their methods of inquiry. For example, in pyschoanalytic therapies, the management of "boundary" issues, such as the length of sessions, their regularity, frequency, and cost, as well as any issues concerning their payment, provides substantive data within the observational and in- terpretive matrix the therapist attempts to establish. With managed care, however, these boundaries or aspects of them are extruded from the treatment, taken over by managed care companies and their host of "treatment managers." Therapists attuned to the data of boundary management are left without a principal therapeutic tool and hence can only fulminate at their compromised position. To the extent that patients become involved in this conflict, the boundaries are further compromised and the therapy develops the quality of a sibling relationship, with therapist and patient joining as children might in complaining about how stingy their father is with their allowance.

It is this matter of allowance, of who pays the money, of how much and to whom, that may ultimately be where psychotherapy is most vulnerable to corruption. After World War II and the availability of large amounts of money for the mental rehabilitation of veterans, psychotherapy became a domain of intense competition between psychiatry and psychology, each over time developing more and more sophisticated justifications for their singularity (Sarason 1981). However, these struggles were largely fought in the arenas of medicine, in part because desires for legitimacy and desires for profit made medicine and psychotherapy enticing, if strange, bedfellows. The problem for psychotherapy, this applied arm of psychology, was that in trying to shore up its legitimacy through the medical establishment, it did not create an inherently meaningful foundation, a legitimacy grounded in its own considered purposes, interests, and scientific work. This left psychotherapy vulnerable to attacks on its value and efficacy. Perhaps even worse, however, is that it vitiated psychotherapy training by leaving it more attuned to monetary interests than to principled ones. For example, a recent (1996) draft of an American Psychological Association task force report on psychotherapy training strongly favors the development of training that will serve the needs of managed mental health care. Similarly, the Harvard Medical School training rotation in psychiatry is conducted, in part, in conjunction with a large managed care health system. However much doctors are revising their thinking about hospital stays and theoretically extraneous procedures, such an explicit adaptation to the marketplace would be inconceivable for, say, learning the techniques of surgery or obstetrics. By being so much in the thrall of market interests historically, and currently under managed care, psychotherapy has too often left unattended the self-reflection and self-scrutiny that might establish its genuine legitimacy (see also Sarason 1981).

## The Managed Care Conundrum

As we have tried to show in this chapter, managed care is as much, if not more, a cultural phenomenon as a financial one. As such, when we uncritically demonize it we risk demonizing ourselves. However imperfect, managed care is a significant attempt to bring some level of certainty and mastery to the confusing conditions under which our nation wrestles with the psychological frailties of its citizens. In a variety of ways it has its cultural appeal, linked both to mainstream science and to capitalist market forces. And in seeking, in a sense, to do away with the uncertainties of therapeutic dependency and the impenetrably chaotic nature of the human psyche, it is deeply responsive to our individual and collective wishes for management and control. Unfortunately, these wishes, to the extent that they are defensively driven, can lead to the creation of compromised solutions, ones that, as in the case of managed care, grapple with superficial trappings (e.g., the finances and certifications of mental health care) while leaving broader questions (e.g., what treatments are most effective for whom) unaddressed.

Addressing the broader questions as a society would be risky, as it would require a critical examination of some of our culture's foundational certainties. At the most basic level of mental health care, we would have to consider seriously what constitutes mental health for all our citizenry, whether its province is religion, philosophy, science, or some combination thereof, and whether its value is worth the price of providing it. Given the complexity of the human condition and the complications of diversity, we would have to wrestle with whether and how to privilege any particular method of addressing the human condition and its accompanying signs and symptoms. Fundamentally, we would have to recognize the defensive character of our attempts at mastery and control, and develop a sense of humility, even wonder, at the refractory complexity of our psychological needs. In the meantime, however, we appear to have created a quasi-scientific system for managing health care, which in reality remains as arbitrary as the previous system, but in a more socially acceptable garb. The essential problems of examining and treating our human condition, within the context of a stunningly complicated and diverse society, remain untouched.

## REFERENCES

American Psychological Association. (1996). Final report and recommendations of the American Psychological Association Working

Group on the impact of managed care and changes in the health services delivery system on the education and training and continuing education of professional psychologists. CMHS Contract: #95MF26942301D.

Barlow, D. H. (1996). Health care policy, psychotherapy research, and the future of psychotherapy. *American Psychologist* 51(10):1050–1058.

Becker, E. (1973). *The Denial of Death*. New York: Free Press.

Beres, D. (1980). Certainty: a failed quest. *Psychoanalytic Quarterly* 49: 1–25.

Emch, M. (1944). On "the need to know" as related to identification and acting out. *International Journal of Psycho-Analysis* 25: 13–19.

Fox, R. E. (1996). Charlatanism, scientism, and psychology's social contract. *American Psychologist* 51(8):777–784.

Fox Keller, E. (1985). *Reflections on Gender and Science*. New Haven, CT: Yale University Press.

Geertz, C. (1973). *The Interpretation of Cultures*. New York: Basic Books.

Gergen, K. J., Gulerce, A., Lock, A., and Misra, G. (1996). Psychological science in cultural context. *American Psychologist* 51(5): 496–503.

Gould, S. J. (1981). *The Mismeasure of Man*. New York: Norton.

Jacobson, N., and Christensen, L. (1996). Studying the effectiveness of psychotherapy: How well can clinical trials do the job? *American Psychologist* 51(10):1031–1039.

Kipnis, D. (1994). Accounting for the use of behavior technologies in social psychology. *American Psychologist* 49:165–172.

Latour, B., and Woolgar, S. (1982). *Laboratory Life*. New York: Basic Books.

Marecek, J. (1995). Gender, politics and psychology's ways of knowing. *American Psychologist* 50(3):162–163.

Miller, B., and Farber, L. (1996). Delivery of mental health services in the changing health care economy. *Professional Psychology: Research and Practice* 27(5):527–529.

Miller, I. J. (1996). Managed care is harmful to outpatient mental health services: a call for accountability. *Professional Psychology: Research and Practice* 27(4):349–363.

Riger, S. (1992). Epistemological debates, feminist voices: science, social values and the study of women. *American Psychologist* 47(6): 730–740.

Sarason, S. (1981). An asocial psychology and a misdirected clinical psychology. *American Psychologist* 36(8):827–836.

Seligman, M. E. P. (1995). The effectiveness of psychotherapy: the *Consumer Reports* study. *American Psychologist* 50(12):965–974.

# Index